BOYHOOD

The 1930s and the Second World War
Memories, Comments, and Views from the Other Side

By H. Peter Nennhaus

BOYHOOD
The 1930s and the Second World War
Memories, Comments, and Views from the Other Side

Copyright © 2002 by H. Peter Nennhaus

Boyhood
The 1930s and the Second World War
Memories, Comments, and Views from the Other Side

ISBN 1-886284-68-7
Library of Congress Card Number: 2001097380
First Edition
ABCDEFGHIJK

Published by
Chandler House Press, Inc.
A division of Tatnuck Bookseller
335 Chandler Street
Worcester, MA 01602
USA

President
Lawrence J. Abramoff

Director of Publishing
Claire Cousineau

Cover & Interior Design
Michele Italiano-Perla

Chandler House Press specializes in custom publishing for businesses, organizations and individuals. For more information on how to publish through our corporation, please contact Chandler House Press, 335 Chandler Street, Worcester, MA 01602. Call (800) 642-6657, fax (508) 756-9425, or find us on the World Wide Web at www.chandlerhousepress.com.

PREFACE

This book, the reader must know, violates a taboo. The evils of Germany's Third Reich left behind an unwritten, almost sacred, law, which states that no denial, mitigation, or other manipulation of the recognized guilt of the German government of those years, and no less that of the German people, can be condoned. Accordingly, seen against the background of the Holocaust, any attempt of lessening German disgrace and of doubting Germany's monopoly on the depravities of World War II has been seen as virtual blasphemy and as an insult to the dignity of her victims. With honest and deep conviction, founded on the abhorrence of the Hitler system, this law has been faithfully observed in politics, in publications, and in private conversations around the world and, not the least, in Germany itself.

I owe an explanation and an apology for having breached that taboo. Even though I had been aware of it all along, I still, while writing the chronicle of my childhood, did not realize how far I was venturing into this forbidden territory. When I first wrote down some of my wartime memories, it was meant for the benefit of my son and not for the bookstore. After all, my story was all too commonplace then, as millions of Europeans could have told similar or even more dramatic experiences. It was not until the 1990s that I was urged to consider its publication in the expectation that now, two generations after those events occurred, the story might be of interest for younger readers. There was no thought in my mind of it becoming a polemic or in any way a controversial text, as it was rather meant to be a suspenseful eyewitness account or an interesting sidelight of that war. The project, however, went through an unplanned evolution. The need for repeated explanatory chapters soon became obvious to me if people of today, unfamiliar with the issues raging in Central Europe in the 1930s and in the war, were to understand the unfolding crisis. This, in turn, required research of historical literature and that seems to be the stage where I was unwittingly lured into the forbidden territory mentioned above, for there were numerous texts written by notable British and North American scholars and also a Russian historian during the past two decades who had quietly begun to stretch the limitations of the taboo. They provided a more detailed look into people and events of that time and described facts, which challenged the black-and-white, parochial view of history. Quite innocently, as it seemed unthinkable to exclude the latest state of knowledge, some of these items became part of my account.

As a consequence, my chronicle in the end did not merely contain descriptions of the perceptions and feelings of the German man-in-the-street, which, the way I remembered them, might have been erroneous but certainly understandable and not at all malicious. It also contained aspects of warfare, misjudgment, hubris, and cold-blooded revenge on the side of the Allies that, I fear, are able to make some readers take umbrage.

Unperturbed by any thought of impropriety, I was fascinated by the analysis of the twisted psychology of war and the anger on both sides of the battle lines. Like a researcher, I considered its impartiality indispensable, no matter where the chips fell. And so it was not until the completion of the book that I discovered the impermissible, deep penetration of that protected area where the taboo ruled.

The late discovery was disconcerting, for it clearly meant that the book, even if a saint had authored it, should never have been written. I had ventured into the off-limits section where, so the world would say, the sensitivities of all decent people were being violated and where it was inappropriate to doubt the validity of the world's moral judgment against evil.

I would not, for anything, question the sincerity of such protest. Yet, in facing the choice of accepting or discarding my manuscript, I reached an audacious decision. I knew my writings, in spite of their degrees of irreverence, were written in good will and with utter honesty; and that their contents, to the extent of my ability, were true. It could also be expected that there were people out there who indeed, disregarding any injunctions, would want to know what in God's world transpired in the hearts and minds of the citizens of that ill-reputed country over half a century ago. And so I boldly decided to breach the weighty law.

Then again, after all of this has been said, there might not be any conflict at all. At times, we encounter disputes where both parties are right. In the days of the Third Reich, there existed two Germanys—on one hand, its government with its rabid ideology, its *Gestapo*, and its genocidal camps; and on the other, its common people. The world has been informed about the first mentioned for over fifty years. This book is a visit to the other Germany. I pray the reader will find the two opposing views of that fateful land, despite the taboo, to be quite compatible.

PART 1

AN AGE OF ANGER

THE BREATH OF HISTORY

IF YOU TRAVEL IN A NORTHERLY DIRECTION FROM BERLIN for about forty miles, you might come upon the farm, hidden among forests and wetlands, where my father was born. If you continue on your trip, the road may eventually lead you to the old seaport of Stralsund at the Baltic Coast. It is not a big town, but it is important to me nonetheless because it is my place of birth. Three magnificent gothic churches built in the Renaissance provide it with a pleasing skyline. Early in this century, the great bridge, which nowadays conducts cars and trains across the sound to the large offshore island of Rügen, did not exist. Instead, you had to traverse by ferry, which took you to a village whose name appropriately was Altefähr, Old Ferry.

The island measures about thirty miles in largest diameter as the crow flies and owes its idyllic appearance to the numerous peninsulas, spits, land bars, inlets, and bays. If you were to direct your trip to its western coast, you would find a small fish-ing village called Waase, but I am not going to take you there. I mention it only because that's where my mother was born. Instead, I want you to stop briefly at the town of Sassnitz, on the northeastern peninsula, because it derives its significance from the fact that it is the southern terminal of a ferry connection with Sweden.

From there, allow me to take you further along a narrow bar of land to the northernmost peninsula and to a village called Altenkirchen. Its name derives from a church, a very old church, which was built in 1168 A.D. by the Danes. It is also important to me because my grandfather preached there. In those days, you would reach Altenkirchen on a tiny narrow-gage train that sounded its warning bell across the fields of grain, potatoes, and turnips to announce its arrival. Not infrequently, it would stop in the middle of nowhere, maybe to let some cows cross, and Mother did not hesitate to get off with us to pick wild flowers during the wait. It was safe to do that because the little locomotive's starting speed allowed us to get back on easily.

Less than a mile from the village was our farm, or rather, the farm where our family used to live before I was born. From there, it required only a short bicycle ride through fields and a pine forest before you climbed over the dunes and down to the world's most beautiful, sandy beach. Life must have been tranquil up there among horses, cows, pigs, crowing roosters, storks nesting on the barn, larks and buzzards, and with the sounds of seagulls and the surf. Five miles to the north, you could see the lighthouse at Arkona—the northern outpost of Rügen. Beyond, there was ocean. At that location, in a way, one had reached the edge of the world.

But then, this was Europe. There was no location remote or secluded enough where the breath of its violent history could not reach. There was a photograph of my mother taken when she was nineteen years old, dallying with her sisters on the lawn. A date was written on it: March 1917. That was the time, if you add two or three weeks, when a very angry man arrived in Sassnitz, about fifteen miles from that lawn, and boarded a ship for Sweden. That angry man, on his fateful trip from Switzerland to Petrograd, was Vladimir Ilich Lenin.

La Belle Époque

THE DECADES BEFORE THE FIRST WORLD WAR were called La Belle Époque—the Beautiful Era. It was a time of lighthearted playfulness in bourgeois society. It was a world peacefully rising in prosperity, blossoming in magnificent culture, and progressing in science and technology. Yet, the auspicious term was a deception. In reality, it was a period of painful changes, dangers, and maladjustments that defied easy solutions.

Traditional sections of society were alienated by a changing world where cities grew to be large and ugly; huge industries disfigured the countryside and immense power accumulated in the hands of large money institutions and international financiers. Venerable pillars of society—the aristocracy, the churches, the Army, and the educated middle class, as well as all of the country folk, looked askance at the untraditional ideas of the liberals. They felt that universal suffrage and parliaments gave the Socialists a mouthpiece and undermined old-fashioned propriety, Christianity, and patriotism. Many an upright citizen viewed these developments as hostile and immoral and saw the working of the Jews both in political liberalism and in the citadels of money.

More important, yet, were the angry protests of social critics that denounced the unhealthy work environments, the sweatshops, and the cheap, crowded tenement buildings of industrial workers, as well as their economic exploitation by Capitalists.

From this, there grew the class struggle—the mounting confrontation between conventional society and the Socialists. The radicalism of the Paris Commune in 1871, and the brutality of its military suppression, had left a foretaste in the minds of people, both on the right and the left of the political spectrum, of the nature of potentially larger future repetitions. The Marxists proclaimed the need to eliminate money, capital, and personal property in order to achieve social justice; whereas the bourgeoisie, afraid of a violent revolution, looked to the Army as a last resort to quell a possible uprising of what was perceived as the menacing Red Mob.

In view of the vehement political disunity, governments resorted to the stimulation of patriotic pride as a device to reunite the nation. This, in turn, contributed to widespread rearmament, to the building of fleets, to foreign adventures such as the acquisition of colonies, and to waging far-away wars.

Imperialistic conquests, being carried out by European nations, Russia, the USA, and Japan were abundant in those decades prior to the First World War. Nationalism and irredentism were common; and captive nations were yearning for self-determination from Ireland to Palestine, and from Finland to the Balkans. Against a background of a frightening arms race, a system of defense treaties spanned the continent. It reflected mutual fear and the firm conviction that faithful adherence to these treaties was indispensable if disastrous defeat in case of war was to be prevented.

THE TRIP WIRE

For Germany, the military pact between France and Russia rendered such alliances inadequate. Its geographic interposition between the two major powers would force it into a two-front war, which entailed only slim chances for it to escape defeat. Russia, as Napoleon had shown, was unconquerable because of its size, climate, and inexhaustible population. To take on France, in addition, created an almost hopeless task. This predicament forced Germany to adopt a plan that was as logical as it was original: the Schlieffen

Plan. As a maneuver to circumvent disadvantageous geography, it utilized the element of time. Its foundation and distinguishing mark was the incredible initial speed of a campaign against France carried out during the temporary 105-day reprieve that Russia was thought to require for mobilization. A quick defeat of France was feasible if Belgium could be persuaded to allow the passage of German troops, which would thereupon be in a position to out-flank the French forces. Once France was defeated, Germany was in a position to turn around and oppose the dreaded Russian "steamroller" with all of its military resources. Success of the Schlieffen Plan was imperative. There was no other way known for Germany to escape defeat.

Its chances for success, however, were diminishing. By 1906, the period of Russian mobilization had been reduced to six weeks; and by 1912, with the help of France financing the con-struction of more Russian railroads, it was approaching eighteen days. The time factor, the basis of the Schlieffen Plan, was rapidly vanishing; and the need for the Germans to act with great initial speed, if they intended at all to adhere to the Plan, grew accord-ingly.

A fateful side effect arising out of this strategic imperative was that among the plans the European nations devised to fore-stall defeat, there was one that was in fact a trip wire. If pulled, an irrepressible force would cause a desperate Germany to launch into war against France in order to beat a fatal clock. That trip wire would be triggered by the simultaneous military mobilization of France and Russia. And that is exactly what happened.

This simplified description of the origin of that war is not intended to ignore the many additional forces that have been cor-rectly named as causative or as contributing factors. Nonetheless, the strategic predicament of Germany's geography and the aggres-sive military mandate, which was believed to result from it, is accepted here as central to the outbreak of that tragic conflict.

In 1914, there existed no European conflict that would jus-tify war. Austria's declaration of war on Serbia was impulsive and, with a bit of patience, a conference of major powers was expected to defuse the local crisis. But then Russia mobilized, which prompted France, being faithful to their treaty, to mobilize as well. Thus, the trip wire went off and Europe went up in flames. It was a disaster that erupted not for a valid reason but by mistake. Gen. Alfred von Schlieffen, in his attempt to defend his country, did not mean to plant a trip wire, nor did Russia and France know it was one when they pulled it.

In the East, the Russians invaded East Prussia indeed eighteen days after commencing mobilization, while in the West, an irate Belgium and a hesitant Britain joined the French. The Schlieffen Plan failed. It not only failed to protect Germany, but it unwittingly precipitated the very war that, on top of being unnecessary, Germany was bound to lose.

One of the many heart-breaking consequences of this most extensive and destructive war was the immediate development of an immense hatred. Its ugly shadows are still present today.

THE PITFALL OF RIGHTEOUS ANGER

Looking back at the time of the two world wars, and knowing they were waged among civilized nations led by educated and often God-fearing men, one cannot help but wonder about the existence of some kind of abnormal mechanism in the human mind that diverts us into insane violence and misleads even well meaning people into a world of savagery the way a train is derailed and turned into shambles. As the reader travels in this chronicle through the horrors the world experienced then, he or she may witness how human hatred, time and again, distorted and twisted reasoning into tragic misjudgment, and thus accounted for much of the political, social, genocidal, and military disasters that raised doubts about human civilization early in the last century.

Anger does not exist by itself. It is a reaction, a reflexive response to some form of trauma, fear, pain, insult, or indignation. This response is aggressive; it seeks retaliation. Before resorting to violence, men as well as animals often pass through an intermediary stage, that of posturing. Thus, one might visualize anger as the three-stage sequence of trauma-posturing-violence. It is a nature-made reflex; it is factory-installed; we all have it. There is a crosswise correlation of vehemence: small trauma leads to a small response, severe trauma to severe violence. Fig. 1 illustrates this mechanism, measuring the vehemence of anger on a scale of ten.

While there is little we can do about feeling angry, it is in the state of posturing where we have a choice as how to respond to it. In humans, posturing is mostly a hostile verbal process. We might fling a string of invectives at the supposed foe, accuse him of malevolence, or make threats of retaliation. It is at this stage of the unfolding reflex where I suspect several fatal flaws.

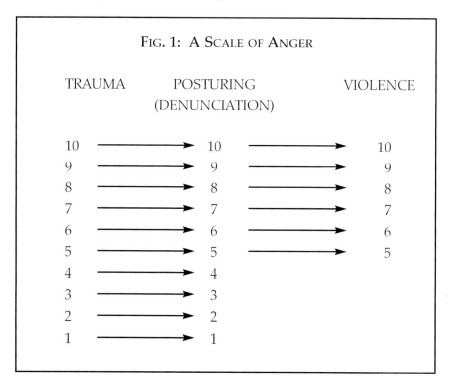

FIG. 1: A SCALE OF ANGER

An essential part of posturing consists of accusation. The perceived adversary is being held responsible for actions and damages. His intentions, character, morality, upbringing, and intelligence are being disparaged; and as we climb up the ladder of vehemence and reach levels of great fervor and deadly passion, we might then, rightly or wrongly, erupt into violence and execute a hostile plan of action, be it done with the fist, in court, or on the battlefield.

There are several potential malfunctions in this machinery of anger. One of them is the abominable way of reasoning likely to take place in the heat of fervor. Of course, we may be fortunate enough to keep a cool head, use common sense, and reach sound judgment. At the other extreme, however, we might carelessly draw conclusions from false, distorted, or exaggerated premises. That can be a project of massive proportions, since most fiery and belligerent ideologies have been forged in this manner. The process of thought may helplessly escape from the requirements of sound reason and logic by the indiscriminate introduction of unfounded insinuations, untrue myths, or popular misconceptions. In this extreme example, the hateful thought process is the antithesis to the disciplined and measured trial procedure in a court-of-law, as there is a lack of ascertaining the facts and the truth of the final judgment remains unquestioned and unverified. One might look at this in terms such as inappropriate, uncontrolled, disordered, twisted, or uncensored reasoning. Fateful and ominous, in addition, are denunciations that pervert the opponent into an archenemy and a demon, for that designation implies the need for mortal violence. As faulty as this process is, it is generally accepted wherever it falls on angry ears as evidence of the guilt and damnation of the adversary.

Another fateful flaw rests in the fact that such unquestioned judgments take on a life of their own. Their truth is accepted as final. Even worse, it is often enshrined within a magnificent armor of self-righteousness, a smug sense that is almost always present in anger and certainly in wars. In the mind of the irate person, it buttresses the devastating verdict and renders it unchallengeable.

A further flaw is the crowning of this accusative structure by the myth of divine sanction. In wars, God's partisanship has practically always been assumed on both sides. The illusion of God's blessing makes the disastrous outcome of hatred nearly foolproof. The greater our religious or patriotic fervor, the more compelling is the notion that God is not only closing his eyes forgivingly before our savagery, but that He is indeed our commander.

Add to this the very common, furtive substitution of what is deceptively labeled as "justice" for what really is malicious revenge and you have assembled, including the illusion of right-eousness and the myth of God's blessing, a perfect system of hoodwinking your conscience. Feeling righteous, serving justice, and carrying out God's mission, we are properly prepared to mow people down with a machinegun; to annihilate a city within a few hours; to stuff men, women, and children into gas chambers day after day; or to kill 100,000 enemies within one second with an atomic bomb. All of this can be done because our conscience has been turned off.

Righteous anger, or the wrath of the just, is commonly regarded as a proud and honorable response delivered by men of moral rectitude on perpetrators of evil. While that is indeed true in many cases, it is wise to tread on that territory with utmost cau-tion. That is so because it is also a dangerous, seductive, and treacherous moral minefield. It causes the disablement of the most basic moral taboos and, if not used conscientiously, has been the breeding ground of crusades, holy wars, final reckonings, and the Holocaust.

Few human crises are as likely to escalate hatred and to seduce us to enter the fields of aggression and violence with a pure conscience, as do wars. Being lifted into the orbit of holy fervor, millions of good people will feel convinced they are fighting a war sanctified by God; they will not rest until they suffer or inflict destruction and utter exhaustion, and even afterwards might never forget nor forgive their opponents. The First World War was such a conflict.

THE SIXTH DAY OF CREATION[1]

As had been feared, the Paris Commune had only been a forerun-ner, a preliminary temblor. The real socialist volcano erupted suddenly and with naked fury in 1917 in Petrograd, and it spread from there to the Black Sea and all the way to the Pacific. It is hard to believe that this socialist revolution was hijacked not only from the Russian people and not only from the Socialists, but also from its very Bolshevik wing by a single man. In defiance of widely popular political views, he turned the revolution into a nightmare of horror for a nation of nearly 150 million people.

Lenin was possessed by a mission to rescue not only Russia but also all of mankind from the evil of capitalism. In order to accomplish this, a fundamental upheaval of human civilization was necessary, he thought; and it was his monumental task to lead the masses, as it were, through the Red Sea; or, to use R. Pipes' phrase, to reenact the sixth day of creation. Ignorant mankind, however, was unwilling to undergo such transformation and, thus, it required a forceful leader, to wit himself, to compel people to do what history demanded, whether they understood it or not. The odds against him were unfavorable since most people vehemently opposed him. In Russia, he saw 90 percent of the population as "class enemies," namely the peasantry (80 percent) and the bourgeoisie (10 percent). Their progressive resistance enraged him. Thus, the Russian Revolution became an event of god-awful fury that the outside world watched in speechless fear.

Lenin destroyed the matrix of the state, the government, the bureaucracy, the police, the army, the laws, the courts, and the legal profession, so as to create them anew. People's Courts and Revolutionary Tribunals were installed in support of the revolution; their judges were required to possess no more education than the ability to read and write. The new Bolshevik security police—the Cheka—was given great liberty to dispose of saboteurs and counter-revolutionaries. The essence of the economy, that is to say the market and the principle of supply and demand, was liquidated, and a money-less economy was to be established. Inflation became astronomical. Armed bands from the cities, called Food Detachments, raided the country and confiscated the last bit of food from the peasants, including the seed grain for next year's crop. The Tsar and his family were murdered.

An assassination attempt on Lenin in 1918 prompted the unleashing of the "Red Terror," which raged until 1921. Like a vast collective brainwashing, this merciless subjugation of the people was to expel their last individual thought and willpower and transform them into trembling, obedient automatons. In order to achieve the most radical intimidation, the Cheka was instructed to kill not only the guilty, but also the innocent. Estimates of the death toll of the Red Terror range from 50,000 to 140,000.

Simultaneously, a Civil War raged from November 1917 to November 1920. Controlling most of the population, the Red Army was able to win victory. This war caused the death of one million combatants of the Red Army and 127,000 of the White Armies.

The prominent presence of Jews among the Bolsheviks, the Cheka, and the Food Detachments accentuated preexisting anti-Semitism and created the popular conviction that the Bolshevik "regime was Jewish and therefore so diabolical."[2] The resultant anti-Semitic pogroms were the worst since those of the so-called Cossack Rebellion in 1648. They ravaged from 1918 to 1920, with pilferage, rape, and the murder of between 50,000 and 100,000 Jews.

The war against the Church began in 1918 as well. Churches and monasteries were plundered; their sources of income were eliminated, and thousands of priests and bishops were lynched. By 1923, only a token Church survived. With the boot of the tyrant on its neck, it was forced to proclaim that the Bolshevik Revolution had been a "Christian Deed."[3] The Jewish faith suffered similar liquidation.[4]

As if the gods had cursed the land, a two-year drought compounded the tragedy. The destitute economy and agriculture had no reserves. It is estimated that Herbert Hoover's American Relief Administration saved nine million Russians from starvation. Nonetheless, more than five million perished from hunger.[5]

The toll of Lenin's revolution is represented by these figures: between one and a half and two million emigrated; two million were killed; two million died from epidemics; and whatever number of the five million famine victims that would have survived the drought had the self-proclaimed prophet in his obsession not already destroyed the economy.

The cry for Marxist Revolution was shouted all over Europe. The mutinous German sailors beat their officers and formed soviets. Immediately after the Armistice, a Bavarian Soviet Republic was proclaimed. There were numerous outbursts of revolution in the East and West and North and South. In March 1918, Bela Kun established a brutal Soviet Republic in Hungary. For all of them, Lenin served as schoolmaster and as a source of support.

The danger of Communist World Revolution persisted for decades. In Europe, country after country abandoned parliamentary democracy and sought refuge under authoritarian, conservative governments mainly as a protection against the revolutionaries in their streets and factories, and their intimidating Red Sponsor looming in the East.

Vae Victis

Before the war, mutual fear among European nations had been enormous. Since 1871, France knew it was too small to avoid defeat if engaged in war with the newly united Germany. It would have been in France's interest if Germany could be changed in a way that would deprive it of the ability to ever be a danger to France again.

There were feelings in Russia, similarly threatened by German strength and loose talk among Germans about possible economic ambitions, that peace would be preserved only if Germany were "crushed once for all and divided up again" into little states.[6]

The Germans, with their long history of being invaded by France and Russia, found themselves thrown on the horns of a fatal dilemma by the military treaties between those two countries. Thus, here too, there were voices demanding the imposition of changes upon Russia and France, which would permanently prevent them from imperiling Germany in the future.[7]

Britain, likewise, felt endangered by the "unmeasured aggrandizement of any power whatsoever."[8] It was this fear, upon which its decision to enter the First World War lastly rested, and it was even more powerful thirty years later when Churchill stated that Germany would have to be "dismembered."

In retrospect, there is little doubt that, as a consequence of the prevailing atmosphere of mutual threat and fear, whoever was going to win that war—the Central Powers or the Allies—would force upon the loser peace terms, which were designed to be territorially amputating, and economically and militarily disabling. As justified and rewarding as such terms seemed in the eyes of the victor, they were disastrous and intolerable for the vanquished. Defeat is dreadful.

The Germans, having agreed to the Armistice in the expectation that peace terms would be based on President Wilson's Fourteen Points, were appalled when confronted with a different reality. Britain's continued naval blockade after the Armistice resulted in one half to one million deaths from starvation. Overseas, Germany lost all of her colonies; and at home, 13.5 percent of her territory and 10 percent of her population. She had to surrender all of her navy and most of her merchant fleet. She was forced to pay economic indemnities in kind and money so huge and unrealistic as to produce a financial collapse where a U.S. dollar was worth one billion marks.

Major indignation originated from the War Guilt Clause, which claimed that Germany was solely responsible for the war and that she, therefore, deserved severe punishment. The emotional impact was cataclysmic: from being a proud and meritorious country, she was cast into the role of a despised pariah state.

In 1920, British economist John Maynard Keynes called the Treaty a "Carthaginian peace." That term referred to the conditions Rome imposed on Carthage at the end of the First Punic War in 241 B.C., which were so severe as to make a retaliatory war by Carthage predictable.

If Germany had won the war, there is little doubt the terms would have been similarly excessive. The force that overruled Wilson's wisdom was composed of the age-old combination of fear and hatred. "The name of a German stinks. The presence of a German is an outrage."[9] Woe to the vanquished.

THE OMINOUS HYPHEN

During those terrible years there was a phase, lasting perhaps from

1918 to 1921, when a fateful anxiety about the Jews swept many countries. Anti-Semitism, an old and universal phenomenon, had been focused chiefly on two major aspects during the last century: on one extreme, the Jews were resented as representing a power of money; and on the other, as a power of subversion. This reflected their prominence in banking, on Wall Street, and in Marxism. Marx was Jewish (although he was resentful of it), and practically all Socialist Parties in Europe had been founded by Jews. To the middle class and the rural population, both Big Money and leftist political agitation were repulsive. Prior to 1917, these were two major roots of nineteenth and early twentieth century anti-Semitism.

As seemingly obvious and understandable as that opinion was, it was tendentious just the same because it was based on partial evidence. After Europe had released the Jews from their ghettos, they had erupted with a storm of released energies and had gained prominence in practically every field of human endeavor—be that in art or literature, medicine or psychiatry, science or economics, or jurisprudence and politics; and they were about to win eight Nobel Prizes at this time. Their fervor and zeal had spread nearly across the full range of civilization, from human progress to human problems, and their prominence in capitalism here and socialist upheaval there was only part of the entire picture. But in the early post-war years, their function in this world was not seen that favorably.

However, beginning with the Russian Revolution and fed by the social upheaval at the end of the war, anti-Semitism grew in vehemence. Two Soviet Republics were proclaimed in Munich, one after the other, both by Jews. Rosa Luxemburg, in flaming oratory in Berlin, summoned the people to join the Proletarian World Revolution. There were armed communist uprisings in numerous German cities, and a well-armed Red Army held sway in the Ruhr, all or most of which were strong enough to require military force to subdue. Bela Kun, also a Jew-hating Jew, ruled in Budapest in 1919. The London Times referred to his government as "the Jewish Mafia",[10] there being twenty-five Jews among his thirty-two commissars. Trotsky, Kamenev, and Zinoviev were three Jewish aides to Lenin, and Jews were active at all levels of his October Revolution.

Eyewitness refugees from Russia reported about the role of the Jews in their dreadful experiences. From this, there grew the popular conviction that Bolshevism was the creation of the Jews, and "Jewish-Bolshevism" became a hyphenated word.

The Protocols of the Elders of Zion, a forgery originally concocted by the Tsarist secret police in the 1890s, surfaced once again and was widely published in the European and American press. It purported to document a Jewish conspiracy according to which, by exploiting democracy, the Jews would achieve world domination.[11] It provoked violent anti-Semitism on both sides of the Atlantic. In Germany, the Protocols contributed to paranoid fears that the country was being crushed by destructive powers coming from both the West and the East, and that they had already invaded the heart of the country through the Red Revolution, and that the impending disaster was the plan and work of a Jewish conspiracy.

In 1921, the London Times confirmed that the Protocols were a forgery. It appears that in subsequent years the fears subsided, and anti-Semitic hostility in Germany and elsewhere returned to the customary level two on our Scale of Anger. Only on the far right of the political spectrum was there a small group of angry patriots whose embittered minds never retreated from the memory of the Jewish part in the Red Revolution and from the myth of a malignant conspiracy. Their anti-Jewish abhorrence persisted at level ten, and had the compulsive power of an obsession.

THE BLACK SHEEP

Unbeknownst to the Germans, during the preceding half of a century a dark cloud had risen over Europe. When referring to it politely, the other countries called it "the German problem." It had begun to emerge in 1871. In that year, the sudden and unexpected unification of all the German kingdoms and principalities into a single country fundamentally altered Europe's political, economic, and military architecture. The new Germany had the largest population outside Russia. With rapid industrialization, its economic output soon outstripped everybody else's. She acquired colonies and built a sizable navy. Out of an impotent buffer zone in the middle of the continent, an empire materialized overnight that, on a one-to-one basis, was more than a match to any of the others.

To make things worse for Germany's competitors, this compilation of power occurred in the same century that witnessed a remarkable upsurge of her cultural creativity and in her achievements in philosophy, literature, music, science, technology, and medicine. She also became the first country to achieve 100 percent literacy. Thus, she emitted an image of dynamism that made her look intimidating and gave rise to fears that she might be seeking primacy and dominance in the world.

It is of interest to point to the parallelism between these events and the simultaneous soaring of the Jews' intellectual achievements and economic power. In a like manner, they generated much resentment including, once again, suspicions that the Jews were conspiring to achieve world domination.

Germany's ascension was particularly provocative because of her geographic location. Around the turn of the century, four empires were in dire straits: China, Russia, Austria-Hungary, and the Ottoman. Great Britain and France were still vibrant and powerful, but they were aging. There were, however, three major countries exhibiting the ebullience and youthful vigor of growth: Japan, the United States, and Germany. Among these three, Germany's strategic position was unique. Japan and the United States had no creditable rivals. Japan devoured Korea, and America pounced upon the Spanish colonies, neither action causing an international ripple. Germany's vigor, by contrast, was bound to elicit instantaneous protest. Europe was packed too tightly for anyone to spread his wings, and any unusual or tactless activity of the Strong Man in the center would make him an objectionable bedfellow. Its location, its size, its advanced development, and its youthful dynamism combined to such a state of superiority that, if it so chose, it could gain dominance over Europe and establish a Pax Germanica over it. Even without trying, its very presence represented an existential challenge to everyone around.

To Britain, both a Napoleonic Europe and a large continental fleet were unacceptable. It was equally impossible for France to even think of not regaining its cultural and military primacy and glory. It was not any different in Russia, where nationalism and imperialism were second to no one else's. Nor would any of the smaller countries have looked favorably on being incorporated into someone else's designs.

It appears that after Bismarck, who was fully aware of Germany's precarious station, few German politicians ever knew the problem existed. Until 1914, Germany was a resented and feared country. Germany was no exception in a world that was full of blustery imperialism, of nationalistic hubris, and of military pomp. But because of Europe's overcrowded geography, Germany should have been different from the rest. She did not have America's luxury to afford a swashbuckling president like Theodore Roosevelt. Rather, history demanded that her Kaiser be gentle, tactful, and pliant in order to instill a mood of reassurance among the neighbors. But history did not inform anybody. There was no worse way to goad Europe into uniting in a camp of anti-German fear than Kaiser Wilhelm's naïve and arrogant manners of saber rattling.

Instead there came the war. G. F. Kennan has aptly called it the great seminal catastrophe of the century.[12] Without it, there would have been no Lenin, Bolshevism, or Stalin. Without it, there would have been no Hitler, Nazism, or World War II. Without it, anti-Semitism would have traveled along at a moderate pace that never came near a Holocaust. And without it, the anti-German resentment would have continued, but without sentiments of dread or thoughts of waging war against her. But because of the war, Germany presented a different image. She was seen as cruel and reckless, as jingoistic and militaristic, and as immensely powerful. It had required four empires to wrestle her to the ground. The world was holding its breath in fear that she might again restore her strength. This fear was so enormous that in the 1920s and 1930s, at least in the English-speaking world, it obscured the dreadful and menacing events simultaneously transpiring in the Soviet Union.

The hostile psychology generated by the "German

Problem" explains a number of events otherwise mysterious. They include the irate reaction of Belgium to engage in a predictably unsuccessful and self-destructive war at the German request for peaceful passage, the head-over-heels decision of Great Britain to enter the war in spite of being totally unprepared for it, and the American decision to provide support and join in battle for the Allies. Indeed, this psychology of the "German Problem" is indispensable for understanding several most astounding attitudes and decisions that were yet to come.

IN THOSE DAYS, EUROPE WAS A HOTBED OF PASSIONS. These were some of the currents influencing her mind and heart when my generation was born.

PART 2

THE PHOENIX

ON THE ISLAND

IT APPEARS THAT THE DANES, in those days eight hundred years ago, were unfamiliar with church steeples. Grandfather's church was a single-nave stone edifice, but the belfry, built like an afterthought, was a separate wooden structure erected some thirty yards away from it. The sexton went in there and pulled on a long cord to toll the bells. He wasn't much for children, the way I remember, but he constructed a beautiful bow and arrow for me once as I watched. The bow was as tall as I was when it was stood upright. I promptly shot the arrow into the top of the lilac bushes to where I couldn't retrieve it; nor could Gisela, my sister. We were always together.

They said Ernst Moritz Arndt had slept in the attic bedroom on the southeast corner of the parsonage. That was during the Napoleonic wars. He was a famous patriotic poet who exhorted the people to shake off the French yoke and to fight for the freedom of their country. But at that stage, I knew neither Ernst

Moritz Arndt nor Napoleon. I believe I was four.

The gabled side of the parsonage was covered with the abundant growth of Wisteria. I will never forget the blooming splendor of hundreds of its flowering clusters cascading down, crowding the windows, and spilling over onto the veranda. Not far from the veranda, there was a young copper beech tree in the center of the lawn. I liked to sit inside the foliage, which came all the way down, and ride on its lower-most branch with my feet touching the ground. I imagined it was my motorcycle.

We never visited our old farm while spending a week or two with the grandparents since it belonged to someone else now. That was because our family had left it soon after I was born. Years later, I learned how it had all happened.

My grandfather, the village pastor, had been successful to obtain the lease on a nearby farm for his oldest son, Siegfried. However, by the time the lease was to commence, Siegfried was still away fighting in the trenches of World War I. As a consequence, an estate manager was hired for the interim. The arrival of that young gentleman created an unintended complication, for not only did he take over the duties of farming; but he also, promptly and fortunately for me, began to stalk the pastor's youngest daughter who, to judge by photographs, was a lovely young woman. Having a Doctorate in economics, he was considered a good catch in that rural and insular community, and so Grandfather surrendered not only his daughter but also the leasehold to him, thus furthering Nature to take its course.

In 1920, nine months after they had married, my oldest brother Friedrich was born. My second brother Dieter followed him two years later. It is easy to calculate that they were born precisely at the right time to serve their fatherland in the next terrible war. But ignorant of any such foreboding, the family spent ten happy years on that farm. There were farm hands and live-in maids, as was the custom then, and all those who lived and worked on the farm were united in a somewhat patriarchal but harmonious little society according to a long tradition from previous, more class-conscious times. The well-to-do farmer was somewhat of a country gentleman while, of course, he never equaled the social esteem of the landowning aristocracy. This venerable social structure had as yet not been disturbed by the inflammatory slogans of the Socialists. Although the 1920s were in large part an economically difficult time for Germany, and in one phase even a disastrous one, life on the farms seems to have been spared from some of the turmoil created by the Great War and the Treaty of Versailles. At any rate, the years our family spent in that rustic scene were not only enjoyable for young and old, but they were also a time for our relatives to take happy refuge there while visiting during school vacations. The cousins joined to roam the fields, the stables, and the large garden, and to adopt them as their playground. The house was large enough to accommodate many guests. Even late in the century, some of my older cousins were still mentioning how the good times and the hospitality they had enjoyed on our farm had remained a lifelong memory for them.

Then came the year 1929. The lease came up for renewal (the farm was the property of the city of Stralsund) and my father lost out to a competitor who, as I heard mentioned repeatedly, had connections in the mayor's office. That was in the same year of the 1929 stock market crash on Wall Street and of the beginning of the Great Depression and it initiated several difficult years for our family. However, that was also the year of my birth and, for better or worse, the loss of our farm was the reason why I grew up in the city and not on a Baltic island.

My arrival that year was a blessing for my sister, Gisela, who was four and a half years old. "Gila," as I called her, was less fortunate than the rest of us right from the beginning. She was cross-eyed and battled with a bad case of stammering for years. She did not intrigue her two older brothers at all, and so she took to me. We were playmates and comrades-in-arms, and grew up together.

First Steps

The very first memory of my life relates to my brother Dieter, notwithstanding my sister. He appears in it as the vague outline of a blond figure shrouded in mist. The event is a blurred mental image, and sometimes I have wondered whether memories, indeed, could go back that far in one's life.

I wanted that cookie. It was right in front of my face. I opened my mouth and tried to bite it, but it moved away. My hands were holding onto the rail. There were people watching me, friendly people, but they were silent. Dieter, holding the cookie, smiled and said something like, "Come on, *Süsser*, come on, you can get it." I followed the cookie. Every time I tried to bite it, it moved away. I followed it but was disappointed time and again. I did not give up though. Finally, I reached the corner. Then, all of a sudden, the room erupted in laughter and joyful applause. Just before the mist closes in, I seem to remember a split second of surprise and the thought: they tricked me. I am certain I got the cookie and was lifted out of the playpen to be hugged, but that is lost in the mist.

Helper in the Night

One night, I had a nightmare of sorts. I was wondering about what they had told me regarding the life hereafter. It had sounded alright initially, and I had seen the pictures in the book. After you die, you go to heaven. There, you are an angel and are near the Good Lord for the remainder of time, and you play with other angels, unless you are busy helping Santa Claus make toys. The pictures had shown a most idyllic landscape that rested on fluffy clouds and was populated with happy angels. What bothered me, in the darkness of the children's bedroom, was the phrase, "for the remainder of time." It meant forever—a time period without end. I began to feel oppressed by the awesome concept of Eternity. There was no end, no outlet. I felt trapped and began to cry. Within a second, Dieter was out of his bed and by my side.

"What's the matter, little one?" he asked soothingly and leaned down to stroke me. I sobbingly explained the reason for my tears. He maintained that it was nice to be an angel, but I cried that that wasn't the point. There was no end! Always and ever, and after that still forever!

Now that he understood the very nature of my problem he quickly dispersed it. He said that wasn't true, and that angels didn't stay there forever. "After a while they come back down to earth, maybe as people, or as bunny rabbits, or as kittens."

"Oh," I said relieved, thinking of the kittens on my uncle's farm as they played with a ball. That was all right. I thanked Dieter and I remember I felt a bit sheepish about having disturbed his sleep all over a little misunderstanding.

THE SAD NEWS

We were vacationing at the seaside. There weren't many people on the wide beach. Every thirty yards or so a family had settled down in their wicker beach "baskets". They were benches enclosed on three sides with wickerwork and a roof to provide shelter against wind and sun. They are commonly seen on German beaches still today. Many had erected masts in the sand, held up with stays, from which pennants fluttered in the salty breeze. I was sitting in our beach basket and was drawing pictures of houses. I always

drew pictures of houses. Suddenly distant, excited shouting interrupted the peaceful calm. Dieter came scrambling across the
dunes. He was returning from the small store, a few hundred yards
away, where he had been permitted to buy something.

"Dad! Mom!" he shouted, coming down to the beach.
"Hindenburg has died!"

The news quickly spread down the beach. We had lost our
president—even I knew who he was. People brought their little
flags down to half-mast. There was a new word for my expanding
vocabulary:"Halbmast". I was five years old. The day was August 2,
1934.

An Acrobatic Easter Bunny

We all liked our new apartment, which was just a block away from
the Berlin-Potsdam thoroughfare. Our street was small, cobble-
stoned, and shaded by large chestnut trees. Our apartment
building was surrounded on three sides by a narrow strip of land
no more than thirty feet wide, and it was separated from the neighboring properties by tall fences. This was called"the garden," even
though nothing grew there except for some phlox, marguerites,
and shrubs left over from days past. Despite its auspicious designation, the"garden"was no more than a children's playground.

One day around Easter time, a most extraordinary event
happened there. Dieter showed up and proposed that we play
hide-and-seek. The request was unprecedented, to say the least,
but I eagerly agreed to it. I was inside the back door counting to ten
while he was supposed to be hiding somewhere, when, instead, he
shouted my name and called me to come quickly.

"Just now,"he said,"the Easter Bunny came jumping across
this fence."The fence was a seven-foot solid wooden wall separat-
ing our grounds from the large park, which belonged to the Jewish

Home for the Blind behind our lot. "He zipped down the length of the garden and dashed out on the street!"

Wouldn't you know it? I had wanted to meet the Easter Bunny so badly, and here it would have to be my turn to stand inside the house counting, just when he came through.

I looked at Dieter dejectedly and said, "Shucks. Why didn't you call me?" He replied, "I did! But he went through so fast, it was all over in a few seconds." Well, Dieter suggested, maybe we should look if he had laid any eggs.

"Forget it," I said. Easter Bunny or not, nobody could dash down here in a few seconds and lay eggs at the same time. Dieter insisted that we could at least look, and as he smiled down at me with his friendly blue eyes, it would have been rude to turn him down, and so I obliged.

What I discovered was downright incredible. The sheer mechanics of the Easter Bunny's feat puzzled me for a long time to come. The northern boundary of the garden consisted of a wire fence mounted on a two-foot high brick wall. The nest was precariously perched on the narrow upper ledge of the brickwork, half leaning against the wire. How any Easter Bunny could lay eggs on that two-inch wide ledge, so high up in the air, and right after that gigantic leap over the other fence, was beyond me. I could easily visualize the trajectory of anybody catapulting over that fence and, surely, that bloody brick wall was no place to land on. And if you did land on it, you wouldn't likely lay eggs there that same instant, I thought, let alone arrange them neatly in a little green nest, even if you were an Easter Bunny in a hurry.

A WONDERFUL WORLD

It was a good time to grow up. Gradually, as the perimeter of my world expanded beyond the confines of my family, where I felt secure and warm and where we all belonged together, I sensed how wonderful a world it was to be part of. There was a spirit of excitement in the air, the excitement of success and of relief that after a long bad spell things were going for us again, at last.

There had been a time, so I heard, when a lot of daddies had no work and the children were cold and hungry; when it wasn't safe to walk down Schützenstrasse because the Communists were shooting down the street—yes, actually shooting, as they do in wars. Taking a walk at night in some of the darker streets hadn't been safe either because teenage punks were there in groups loitering, smoking cigarettes, and bothering people. Now that was all different, thank God. The Hitler Youth was good for these kids, I heard grown-ups say. They were disciplined and respectful again, as children should be. They had decent haircuts, too, and you didn't see them smoking any more either.

There was much more, though. I could see it with my own eyes. The whole world was gathering in my hometown for what they called the Olympiad. They had respect for us again, the other countries. There had been a time when they didn't; when they marched right in and took what they wanted, or told us what we were permitted to do. That was because we had lost the war and were helpless. There had been too many enemy countries, my parents explained; we were in the middle and they were all around us.

Well, anyway, it was different now. We won more than our share of gold medals, too. That was showing them. We were proud of our great leader and grateful, grateful for what he was doing for the country. That's what Miss Östereich had said in school. When he gave a speech, we were all gathered around the radio, the whole family. It was terribly suspenseful, and I was fully aware of the awesome importance of the event. Every time, it was as though I was witnessing a turning point of history.

Then again, I apparently didn't see the whole picture the

way adults did. Somehow, there must have been a downside too, to judge by the way they sometimes reacted as if to spoil the fun. You might be sailing along at full-speed with the wind of enthusiasm, and then, out of the blue, get hit with a damper.

There was, I remember, the new greeting in school: at the beginning of the day, when Miss Östereich entered the classroom and we all rose, we no longer wished her a "good morning," but rather, we now proudly greeted her with "Heil Hitler!" It made me feel so grown-up and, of course, I happily told Mother about it. I don't think she actually said anything, but it was obvious from her expression that something, whatever it was, had soured her mood.

There was a similar episode at the time when Mussolini paid a state visit to our capital. I had heard about the preparations the government was making for it. When his name was mentioned at dinnertime, I asked who in the world this Mussolini was. There was that peculiar discrepancy again, this time between what obviously was some kind of national celebration and Daddy's disdainful hand motion and unceremonious reply. He murmured: *"Ach, noch so einer wie der Hitler*—another one like that Hitler." I dropped it right there. You could never be sure where you stood with grown-ups. I had spoken out of turn anyway.

REDEMPTION

WILLIAM SHIRER WROTE, "Germans, despite their dislike of much in Nazism, are behind Hitler and believe in him." That was a correct observation. Hitler, indeed, led Germans to successes and triumphs and rapid recoveries of economic vitality, of social peace, and of national self-esteem. The accomplishments of his regime were striking. They resembled almost a god-sent redemption after a decade and a half of anguish and affliction, that it was not difficult to tolerate the disagreeable aspects of the new administration. This was particularly true after the overbearing and abusive Storm Troops (the "SA") had been reined in during the summer of 1934. Had the new chancellor done no more than turn around the depression and reduce the suffocating unemployment, he would have received wide acclaim. When he came to power, 30 percent of employable people were out of work. In 1934, this number was down to 13.5 percent and in 1936, 7.4 percent.[1]

Where there had been street battles with hundreds of dead and wounded, and where Berlin had been in a state of semi-siege, peace had returned to the tortured land. People gave up their antagonism, largely by trust and hope rather than by compulsion, and followed the man who was rapidly acquiring enormous popular appeal. People of all walks of life, from Communists to the bourgeoisie, and from the officer corps to the clergy, began to support him, and a spirit of unity descended over the nation. Like F. D. Roosevelt, he instituted new benefits for low-income groups. In different ways, he attacked the social evil of the hateful confrontation between the classes, and worked to reduce class barriers and reconcile social distinctions. People knew that the magnificent network of four-lane divided highways being built across the country—the *Autobahnen*—had no parallel in the world and saw in them a glorious vision of the "New Time" he was promising. His government received credit for Ferdinand Porsche's newly built Volkswagen, an economy car that was affordable by average people. This, too, gave the impression of the marvelous progress he was providing to their country. Foreign visitors reported, "The criminal courts have never had so little to do and the prisons have never had so few occupants."[2] Genuine patriotic gratification grew out of the exit from the League of Nations, which had nurtured Germany's outcast status since the day it was created, from the return of the Saar territory from French custody after its pro-German plebiscite, and from the entry of German troops into the demilitarized zone of the Rhineland. There was not a soul in the country that did not share in the deep gratitude at these events, including the clergy of both Churches. The Olympic Games in Berlin in 1936, where Germans won the most medals by far, and which appeared to be well-received by the world, was a gratifying celebration of their country's regained pride and international recognition. In contrast to almost all other countries, the yoke of the Great Depression was being lifted from the people while the intolerable disgrace of the Treaty of Versailles was being wiped away.

In those early years of the Third Reich, voices of approval—some moderate and some eager—were heard from German and international notorieties alike. Pope Pius XI expressed his pleasure at Hitler's anti-Communist stand and had his bishops support the regime. Others included authors Gerhart Hauptmann and Oswald Spengler, philosopher Heidegger, Cardinal Faulhaber, composer Richard Strauss, Swedish explorer Sven Hedin, former British Prime Minister and co-author of the Versailles Treaty, David Lloyd George, historian Arnold Toynbee, and playwright George Bernard Shaw. American writer Gertrude Stein, who was of German-Jewish origin, voiced her opinion that Hitler deserved the Nobel Peace Prize.[3]

Nonetheless, in spite of such acclaim, Shirer was correct in noting the people's "dislike of much in Nazism." The undeniable achievements outbalanced but never eliminated subdued suspicions and whispered objections. Particularly after the first four years had elapsed, concern and opposition grew in various centers, despite general enthusiasm and success.

Among these groups, the Churches were the first to react because they were, after the voiceless and defenseless Jews, the first to suffer. Pope Pius XI soon discovered that the regime, in defiance of the 1933 Concordat, did indeed interfere with the work of the Catholic Church. The ensuing confrontation was punctuated by protests, silent resistance, and massive attendance at two Catholic Synods held in 1937 in Aachen and Bamberg. Also in 1937, the Pope issued his Papal Encyclica "Mit brennender Sorge" (in severe concern), in which he decried abuses of the Concordat, of human rights, and of Christian values.[4]

The Protestant Church, likewise, had to face attempts to be brought under the control of a government-appointed bishop, to evict non-Aryan churchmen, and to abolish the Old Testament as a "Jewish script" and other strong-arm infringements. Pastor Martin Niemöller, a First World War U-boat captain, founded the Pastors' Emergency League (*Pfarrer-Notbund*) that was quickly joined by seven thousand other churchmen. Out of this grew the movement known as "the Confessing Church," so named because it pledged to adhere to the confessions of their faith. It attempted to protect the rights of the Church within the state, and it objected to state anti-Semitism, to illegal actions of the Security Service and the Gestapo, and to poorly disguised efforts to deify Hitler. In 1935, over seven hundred pastors were arrested. In the same year, Niemöller was imprisoned and, a year later, he was placed permanently into a concentration camp.[5]

The bifid trends in people's hearts and minds persisted until the end. The fact, however, that the loyal side never lost its preeminence was, besides other reasons, largely due to the inexhaustible credit that he had garnered from his uninterrupted string of Napoleonic successes and victories during his first nine years in power. Only toward the end was this faith fading. Loyalty persisted nonetheless because popular trust was replaced by that defiant siege mentality that one finds among defenders of a doomed fortress.

THE FOUR HORSEMEN

ONLY ONCE DID WE ATTEND AN EVENT during the Berlin Olympics in 1936. It was a handball game between Germany and Hungary, played the European way on a soccer field. It left few memories and I don't even remember who was the winner. But the magnificent stadium and the huge sports complex surrounding it overwhelmed me.

A year later we visited the Olympia Stadium again in order to watch a performance celebrating the seven hundredth anniversary of the city of Berlin. I will never forget those four horses. All of a sudden, from the entrance-portal there emerged a horseman on a splendidly decorated white horse. While they chased at an incredibly fast speed around the arena as if the devil were after them, a penetrating scream pierced the silence shouting only the two words "*Der Krieg*" (war). This repeated itself with a second rider, the terrifying cry this time saying "*Die Pest*" (the plague). It was downright bone chilling and gave me goose pimples all over. Another horseman came forth and raced around the track, and then a fourth one; one for "hunger" and one for "death." If I remember correctly, the horse representing death was raven-black. They were the Four Apocalyptic Horsemen. I had never heard of an apocalypse before, nor did I know what it had to do with four horses and, in fact, I have never seen them again since. But Daddy explained that it was written in the Bible and was meant to describe the worst disasters befalling man and that during its history, Berlin had been struck by all four of them.

To be more precise, the Apocalyptic Horsemen were, of course, not meant to describe the past but rather the future, to be a foreboding of approaching peril and doom. But among the thousands of Berliners in the Stadium, there were probably few who knew the difference or worried about it.

THE GOOD-NATURED THINKER

There was more to Father than what met the eye. Everybody knew him as a congenial neighbor, a happy husband, a content family man who regularly went on an evening stroll hand-in-hand with his wife, and as the good-natured man who generously gave of himself to those he loved. They probably did not notice that he stayed home when his family went to church. They did not know that there was quite a section dealing with religion in his library, and that he had once started to write a book explaining why in this scientific age, painful or not, the notion of God and religion had become untenable. I never realized he was an atheist until I was seventeen years old. That was so because he never interfered with Mother's raising us in a Christian way. Mother, the pastor's daughter, said Grace before and after meals—breakfast, lunch, and dinner—meals we all shared as a family, and he never gave an indication of not being part of the pious moment.

He was, by nature, a thinker and dreamer who endeavored to identify the principle behind the phenomenon, to diagnose the disease rather than lament the symptoms, and who would have felt dissatisfied had his work served no deeper purpose than to provide personal income or prestige.

During the 1920s, an economic decline had developed in the rural eastern part of the country due to the progressively bankrupt state of the farmers—large and small. Being a farmer himself in those days, he was no stranger to this problem. But it was the economist in him that diagnosed it as a national calamity that would have to be corrected on a national level. He conceived of a government-sponsored program that would restore agriculture to a viable sector of the national economy by some form of reallocation of debts. In a somebody-must-make-a-start type of attitude, back in the twenties, he had tried to promote it through publications and by joining a conservative party favored among farmers in those days; but, having no political talents, let alone instincts, he got nowhere.

When, in 1933, the National Socialists formed the government, Dad was seized by the wave of hope that uplifted the country. This was the nation's chance at last, he felt like so many other good citizens, and we all had to pitch in and help the man. Then again, the political landscape changed very quickly and his party, as if by sleight of hand, was absorbed into that of the National Socialists.

As he told me years later, it took him only one year—to wit, until the "Night of the Long Knives" in connection with the Röhm affair in June of 1934—to regret his membership. "They were a bunch of rogues," he said. By that time, however, the intimidating atmosphere of the police state had made it dangerous for anyone to declare his exit from the Party, nor was it entirely clear that so risky a step was justified at that early stage. After all, the new government, only one year old, was spectacularly successful in various ways. With time, one could expect it would mature and purify its ranks.

Out of the political changes of 1933, however, grew a bonus. The new government, along with its other vigorous programs to revive the economy, attacked the East German agricultural dilemma much along the lines that Father had proposed; and so he ended up in the Ministry of Agriculture, helping to implement the program that was dear to his heart.

THE LANDOWNER'S SECRET

On occasions, Father had to go and inspect farms or estates that were being processed. From such visits evolved several friendships with landowners whom he had helped out of their plight.

One of them was a Mr. Volkmann, who invited us to spend a vacation on his large, beautiful estate on the island of Rügen, which was not far from Grandfather's old village church.

In the train on the way back to Berlin, against her usual custom, Mother told me something, foolishly, I suppose, for children are not known for keeping secrets. She said Mr. Volkmann had been in a concentration camp. Just three months, she said. I had heard about them. They were a special type of penitentiary and somewhat mysterious. I wanted to know what they were like. Mother explained that Mr. Volkmann did not speak about it; not only that, he had vowed he never would. I was incredulous. There was not a thing I would not at least tell my parents about. Mother stated that they had told him he would be right back if he ever said a word to anyone. I asked, "Not even to his mother?" She nodded.

That is what made it sink into my mind as something terrifying. Not something evil or illegal, mind you, since crime and punishment naturally went together in an orderly society, and it was upon the authorities to uphold the law. I probably had never given it any thought before; but, from this day on, I knew I would never ever want to tangle with the law of the land.

"What had he done?" I inquired.

But Mother must have thought the conversation had gone far enough. "Just said something," she said.

A Paranoid Obsession

OF THE 500,000 JEWS LIVING IN GERMANY IN 1933, 400,000 were native Germans.[6] The feeling of their German identity was sincere and deep and often outweighed their sense of Jewishness. In the post-war decade, about one third of them intermarried with gentiles.[7] Typically, they lived in the cities and were in business and the professional occupations. The members of the majority cast their votes for the political center. They were anti-Zionists because

they belonged to a moderate wing of Judaism and had no intention of leaving their homeland.[8] The remaining 100,000 Jews were
immigrants from Eastern Europe, and only they were adherents of
Zionism; that is to say, they promoted the establishment of a religious Jewish state in Palestine.

Upon Hitler's taking power, 37,000 Jews left the country,
many going back to their Eastern European countries of origin. But
only one year later many of them returned, being convinced that
the violent subjugation of the Storm Troops under Ernst Röhm's
command, in 1934, had restored legality in the country. Jews, however, had been evicted from employment in the civil service, and
when the regime was only two months old restrictions were placed
on those engaged in the professions. Then, in September of 1935,
the enactment of the Nuremberg Laws further demoted them to
second-class citizens by disenfranchisement, by outlawing intermarriage, and by forbidding them to fly the German flag.

There were, at this stage, no clear goals of the government's anti-Jewish program other than that of inducing them to
emigrate. By 1936, their thriving and economically productive
community had been reduced to progressive hardship through the
loss of jobs and businesses. Almost 100,000 had fled from the
country and 83,000 were in sufficient need to receive aid from the
Jewish Relief Organization.[9]

Attempts to emigrate, the obvious solution to their
predicament, frequently failed to succeed for a variety of reasons.
European countries and the United States issued only a limited
number of visas to German Jews. Quite possibly, it was the worldwide economic depression that had accentuated anti-Semitism in
their own countries, and they did not dare to further aggravate it.
Immigration to Palestine, on the other hand, was severely restricted by the British, in deference to the rising Palestinian opposition.
In addition, the Zionists already living there rejected the admission
of anti-Zionist Jews. For many Jews, their advanced age, lack of
funds, and absent religious life in prospective countries of refuge
further interfered with their efforts to escape.

Initial hopes that the government might be short-lived
faded as the years passed. Progressive impoverishment, a new

strangulating outburst of arrests, expropriations of businesses, the prohibition of four thousand doctors and seventeen hundred lawyers to practice their professions, and the exclusion of all Jewish children from school attendance in 1938 deprived Jews of whatever illusions they had left.

Idols and Idealism

At school, when it came to a little game of one-upmanship, I could always mention my oldest brother Friedrich. None of my classmates had a brother as old or as important. He was very popular in the Hitler Youth, where he had been promoted to chieftain over a cohort of fifty boys. Besides, he was very good looking with his manly face, wavy brown hair, and dark blue eyes. Outwardly he was very resolute, but underneath this sturdy hide he was concealing a softhearted and bashful core. His pensive, purposeful, and methodical ways contrasted with Dieter's dashing and mischievous nature. There were occasions when he would smile helplessly at Dieter, who had caught him off guard and disarmed him of his big brother status.

Rarely, he would sit down and play the "Merry Peasant" on the piano. But he had given up taking piano lessons, and, instead, he would retire to his room and accompany himself on the guitar singing.

Dieter got tired of his advance into the world of études, sonatas, and preludes too. But unlike Friedrich, he did not abandon the piano altogether; he rather switched to playing popular hits and songs, which were more in keeping with his vivacious and fun-loving personality.

If Dieter was the more joyous of the two, then Friedrich was clearly the more impressive one to me. He was so mature and grown-up. When we had company, he would help the visitors out of their coats, see to their comfort, and make courteous conversation. He was developing the spit and polish of a mannerly and well-bred young gentleman. I would try to be just like him when I grew up.

That is not to say that Father was not an idol or a gentleman. He was. But his seniority allowed him the luxury of relaxing the strict rules of social propriety by being his natural self: roly-poly, slightly balding, and cigar smoking, he was a jovial sort of character who would delight the ladies with his good-humored wisecracks.

What Father and his two oldest boys had in common was an abiding sense of idealism. You stood up for what was right. You did so whole-heartedly and without having to be coaxed or prodded. Mother was a little more pragmatic about that. She thought that before you plunge yourself headlong into some honorable deed you should make sure it doesn't backfire first.

THE BALL, THE FENCE, AND THE MOLLY

There was the recurring problem of the ball flying over the fence. We had a choice. We could walk around to the Jewish Home's entrance in the neighboring street. There, the receptionist would summon the gardener, not without lecturing us first on the dangers of the ball striking one of the blind. Then, under the watchful eye of the displeased gardener, we would locate the blasted ball under some shrubbery, would ceremoniously be escorted back through the sparkling and somewhat sweet smelling mansion and, after several respectful "thank you's," we would eventually emerge giggling on the street. That would require about twenty minutes.

Or, we could do what the Easter Bunny had done. Clearly, this is what we preferred. Conveniently, there stood a carpet-beating rail close to the wooden fence, which facilitated the athletics required to get over the top of it. On the way back, there was the gardener's compost pile to help us scale the barrier. This route was much more dangerous, though, because if he saw us he would come after us with some gardening implement, and we were not always sure of being able to make it over the fence in time. He was such a surly fellow, I thought, and probably didn't like children. Of course, sometimes we did throw a pebble or two at the blind as they were unsuspectingly sitting on a shaded bench reading in Braille to one another.

Molly was a great one for that, Molly Lohmann that is. She was a tomboy, three years older than I, and her real name was Gerda. Walter and Carla, her siblings, called their younger sister "the Molly" and used the pronoun "he" rather than "she" to refer to her. He was a mischievous girl, the Molly was. She taught me the word "jazz," which we pronounced "yuts," and she had a whole album full of Shirley Temple pictures.

Molly had to go to Mass on Sundays along with Carla and Mrs. Lohmann. They were Catholic. Walter didn't. He and his father were Lutheran. The latter two never went to church. Dr. Lohmann was a tall and imposing figure with a well-trimmed beard and obvious self-assurance. He had a position in the Ministry of Agriculture, like my father, but his was of a much higher rank. Because of us children, a warm friendship was developing between our parents, even though I once heard Dad remark to Mother that he felt Dr. Lohmann should not make fun of his wife's religion.

Whispered Stories

The Köpkes, on the second floor across from the Lohmanns, kept more to themselves. Maybe that was because they were Catholic, but they were nice people too. Mrs. Köpke always had red eyes from crying when they returned from Sunday Mass. They would stop on the sidewalk and greet me by saying, "Good morning, Peter." I would run to shake hands with them through the wrought iron fence, a handshake that was always accompanied, for boys, by that quick bow of the head. She would smile at me so kindly every blessed Sunday, but always with red eyes.

Mr. Köpke used to repair our watches for us. He operated a watch store downtown. Once, he told my parents that his store was visited by Göring, the number two man in the political hierarchy, along with a retinue of security men. Göring had thrown his weight around, shouting, "*Wo ist denn der Besitzer von diesem Mistladen?* Where is the owner of this dung-joint?"

The story, the way I remember it, was told with a subdued voice, and the grown-ups shook their heads. I had heard that some of our leaders weren't very refined. Some were said to have been dockworkers in their earlier days, and I understood that was low on the social scale.

The Köpkes had two children. Maria was my age. Jochen was Dieter's age, and while very much a normal boy, he was unusual in two ways to me. For one, whenever he was climbing the stairs to their apartment, he was given to announcing his presence to all the tenants of the building with a noisy proclamation reverberating in the stairwell. It was meant to imitate a street crier, I suppose. It began with nonsensical word salad and it culminated into an offer to sell potting soil. My parents benignly attributed this performance to a transient aberration of adolescent mentality, and so I, too, accepted the recurrent potting-soil act as a fact of life.

The other remarkable aspect of Jochen Köpke was that he had never been enrolled in the Hitler Youth. Now that was strange indeed. Everybody else was.

Two Visions

IN THE 1930s, the conflicts between conservative society and the Marxists continued. A bloody riot occurred in 1934 in front of the French Chamber of Deputies. From that time until 1937 France repeatedly lingered on the verge of revolution. Also in 1934, the Austrian Chancellor Dollfuss, after using the military against the Socialists, assumed dictatorial powers. Much of the same confrontation led Gen. Metaxas, in 1936, to establish a dictatorship in Greece. Also in that year, Gen. Franco initiated the Spanish Civil War by revolting against steps of the decaying Republican Government to enter into a communist or anarchist revolution. The most terrifying events, however, transpired once again in the Soviet Union, surpassing even the nightmare of Lenin's October Revolution.[10]

These events began in 1930 when the Central Committee resolved to carry out mass collectivization of agriculture. The peasants' violent resistance and the government's subsequent forcible confiscation of all of their grain led to a catastrophic famine. Between 1930 and 1933 roughly ten million peasants in the Ukraine and adjoining areas perished.

Magnifying this calamity even more, a Purge Commission was established in 1933 to dispose of members of the right wing of the Party. Thus began the period of the "Great *Chistka*"—the Great Purges. It officially lasted until 1939, but its terror never abated until Stalin's death in 1953. At that time, the population of the

Gulag, the vast system of Soviet concentration camps, reached its peak with twelve million inmates.

The technique employed in this purge followed three steps: (1) the accused was arrested; (2) he was then tortured until he confessed to the accusations; and (3) he was then sentenced either to the camps, which had an annual mortality rate of 10 to 20 percent, or to death. Commonly, the execution was carried out on the same or next day. The spouse and other relatives frequently ended up in the camps as well. As the persecution-wave gained more speed and vigor, it became customary for the victim to be forced to reveal, in addition to his own confession, the names of "accomplices", often a requested number of them. The accomplices would then, in turn, be arrested and processed through the same mechanism.

While it appears that Stalin's wrath initially was aimed at people in the upper echelon of power, even as early as 1935, thirty to forty thousand conspirators were deported from Leningrad to camps in Siberia and the Arctic. The death penalty was also imposed for citizens trying to flee the country. If family members knew about such an attempt they were punishable with ten years in the camps, and if they didn't know, with five years. Not even old Bolsheviks and long-time comrades of Stalin would be certain to escape the henchmen. All of the ten contemporary Politburo members died, as did the ten previous Politburo members, almost certainly as Stalin's victims between 1934 and 1940.

In 1936, with Nikolai Yezhov becoming chief of the NKVD, the Political Police, the campaign became massive and exceeded conventional concepts of brutality by far. All the different sections of the administration and the society were subjected to merciless persecution: the apparatus of the Party, the bureaucracy, the economy, the police, the arts and sciences, common workers and peasants, men and women, the Armed Forces, and foreign communists residing in the Soviet Union. Even the NKVD itself was decimated, and Soviet agents on foreign assignment and generals serving in the Spanish Civil War were summoned back and shot.

The conditions in the Gulag camps were indescribable. They were sites of unspeakable horrors and of a mortality rate that turned many of them into death camps. One cluster of camps was located in the Pechora region, at the Arctic Circle, at the northern end of the Ural mountain range. Here, in numerous camps in the frozen tundra, around one million prisoners were held at any given time."Few would be alive after a year or two." There are reports of barge loads of unwanted prisoners having been sunk in the Arctic Sea.

The most deadly Gulag region was probably the gold field near the Kolyma River in the Far East, north of the Sea of Okhotsk, where the temperature sinks to negative seventy degrees Celsius. It has been calculated that two million prisoners died there during the entire Stalin era.

In addition to the millions dying from the incredible abuse in the camps, there was a program of outright mass executions. In August 1936, Stalin ordered five thousand"oppositionists", then in the camps, to be executed. In 1937, he ordered the appointments of Troikas of three NKVD and of Party officials in every part of the land, whose task it was to issue the death sentences for large numbers of "enemies of the people". There were forty thousand executions in Uzbekistan, ten thousand in Kirgisia, fifteen thousand in Sverdlovsk, thirty thousand in the Ukraine, nine thousand in Vinnitsa, forty thousand near Leningrad, fifty thousand north of Vladivostok, fifty thousand in Kuropaty near Minsk, and many more in numerous other centers. Most of the victims were ordinary workers and peasants. The executions were carried out by a shot in the neck—a method not always fatal—and many of them required a second and a third shot. They had to lie down in the mass grave, on top of previous victims, to receive their shot. After the row was full, sand was thrown on them to prepare for the next layer. There were reports that sometimes, afterwards, the sand was still moving for a while.

For the convictions of upper-rank officials and their wives, the approval was signed in the Kremlin by Stalin, Molotov, Kaganovich, and Malenkov themselves—hundreds or even thousands at a time. It is estimated that the total number signed by them, personally, amounted to 230,000 executions. Once Yezhov assumed direction of the NKVD in 1936, the team of his predecessor fell out of favor. Twenty thousand of them are said to have been either executed for showing insufficient Stalinism or to have committed suicide.

The military did not escape the cleansing wave. Marshall Tukhachevsky and seven commanders of the Red Army were tried for treason and executed the same day. This was followed by the arrest of nine hundred eighty members of the officer corps including numerous generals, in addition to twenty thousand political commissars, and then, in turn, of those who had just been promoted to fill the vacancies. Of nine Fleet Admirals, only one survived, albeit only to die later in prison.

According to R. Conquest, the camp population was thirty thousand in 1928; over six hundred thousand in 1930; two million in 1931 and 1932, and four or five million at any given time from 1933 to 1937. The last number he provides is seven to eight million at the end of 1938. The number of deaths is estimated as ten million from the famine in 1930-33; and, in the Yezhov period 1936-38, one million by Troika executions and two million in the camps. Thus, by 1938, Stalinism had created approximately thirteen million wrongful deaths. (His ultimate death toll, until 1953, is currently estimated at no less than twenty million.)

* * *

The attitude toward Stalinist Russia on the part of Germany was fundamentally different from that entertained by western nations. This difference played through much of the war that was soon to start.

There had been German fears of "Asiatic hordes" emerging from Russia and descending upon Central Europe long before World War I. The violent eruption of Lenin's October Revolution and his proclaimed intention to spread it over the whole world contributed to the German vision of the horror prevailing in this eastern neighbor of theirs and to the dread of expecting a barbaric invasion in the not too distant future. S. Fritz states:[11]

> Any reasonably diligent newspaper reader in Germany in
> the 1920s and early 1930s would have been well

informed—certainly more so than one in London or New
York—of the various atrocities, especially those of Stalin,
visited on the unfortunate population of the Soviet Union
by the Bolsheviks.

Even though only parts of Stalin's terror after 1930 became
known, the evolving vision of him among Germans and, quite likely, among most other Central and Eastern Europeans, was not far
from that of another Genghis Khan, who was only waiting for his
time to strike. An evil Moloch, so they thought, was rising in the
East.

By contrast, the vision of Stalin prevailing in the western
countries was one of idealism and benevolence. The "Socialist
State" was in high repute and was believed to be a proud effort to
build a better world out of the ruins of Russia's past. Its revolution
was seen as an extension of the French and American Revolutions,
its anti-imperialism implied pacifism, and its communism meant
humanism and progressive Christianity. Journalists and intellectu-
als who visited the Moscow show trials in 1937 failed to see their
obvious mendacity and absurdity. They returned home idolizing
Stalin and ascertaining the legal correctness of the proceedings.

The benign and admiring vision of Stalin and his empire
persisted through the war and into the 1950s, and even to the student rebellions of the late 1960s. Reporters of leading newspapers,
scholars, celebrated literary and scientific luminaries, and Nobel
Prize winners are among Stalin's advocates, such as Romain
Rolland, Thomas Mann, George Bernard Shaw, Lion
Feuchtwanger, Albert Einstein, the Archbishop of Canterbury,[12]
Arnold Zweig, and Jean-Paul Sartre.[13] Numerous reports and
books, on the other hand, describing the true, unmerciful disaster
in the Soviet Union, contradicted their laudations. But they were
ineffective in their attempt to correct the pro-Soviet view. In recent
years, since the fall of Communism, Russians have voiced the
reproachful question of how the free western world could have
misjudged their plight so utterly and failed to pillory Stalin's
crimes.

The reason for this misconception can be understood from

this statement of W. Laqueur:[14]

> What attracted Western fellow travelers to the Soviet Union? Above all, the apparent decline of the West, as manifested in the Great Depression, and the seeming inability of the Western governments to cope with it. Later it was the threat of fascism, and still later the alliance with the Soviet Union in World War II...The impact of Hitler was even greater. Between Hitler and Stalin, the choice was a foregone conclusion.

Similarly, R. Conquest writes:[15]

> But on the whole, in the atmosphere of the late 1930s, fascism was the enemy and a partial logic repressed or rejected any criticism of its supposed main enemy, the USSR.

This was before the war and years before the Holocaust. Hitler had about ten thousand concentration camp inmates and had executed eighty-four[16] (or was it between one hundred and two hundred[17]?) men in the 1934 Röhm affair, whereas Stalin had seven million Gulag inmates and thirteen million dead victims. In German eyes, it would have been incomprehensible to believe that in the judgment of the West there was no doubt, that it "was a foregone conclusion," that Germany was malignant and the Soviet Union was benign.

The underlying cause for this astounding vision was hidden in that entity referred to as the "German Problem." In comparison with the Soviet Union, the danger emanating from Germany was perceived as much more intense and acute. The scale of comparison was pre-weighted in disfavor of Germany. In World War I, it had almost defeated three of the greatest empires of the world and now, after having been disabled so profoundly, it seemed to be rising like the Phoenix from its ashes, right next to the victorious nations, which continued to struggle in the depth of the Great Depression. It seemed to display a frightening degree of irrepressible vitality. From within the fears of the "German Problem," German vitality was indistinguishable from German virulence.

In their hearts, the worried Germans felt the dire need to be prepared for a possible assault from the East. The monstrous and godless empire of the most evil tyrant known in the world, Joseph Stalin, was mobilizing his innumerable masses in the terrifying Red Army and made no secret of his and Lenin's ideology that demanded the spread of eastern tyranny and communism across Europe and the whole world. In the western democracies, anxious people had identical fears with regard to the Germans, whom they looked at as if they were the Huns reincarnated. It was as if all Europeans were fearfully gazing east—the Germans at the Soviet Union, and the Atlantic countries at Germany. They both had good reason and were ready to demonize the source of their fears. Their fears were akin, but their visions differed.

In the war that followed, the fear of Stalin and his tyrannical system grew into an all-consuming dread for the Germans, as well as for people in other continental countries. The existence of that fear has, however, been deleted from the record, or it has, at the most, been called "mythical".[18] It was an erroneous subtraction from the psychological equation of that war for if there was a groundswell of sentiment that united people in different Central and Eastern European countries, it was the apprehension generated by the Red Empire. It grew into deadly terror as the victorious Red Army was advancing toward Germany, causing the exodus of millions of desperate refugees from eastern countries toward the West. This vision among the Germans, whether it is judged justified or not today, was as real as was the other one that fearfully stirred a feeling of dread toward the Germans in the hearts of the people of the western countries.

The Trickeries of Joe Louis

MOTHER AND I LISTENED ATTENTIVELY as Dieter explained through what unfortunate circumstances Max Schmeling had lost that fight. We naturally deferred to Dieter's judgment in matters such as this. The news of Joe Louis' victory over our national hero, and so early in the fight to boot, had thrown everybody into a state of shock, and it seemed Mother was just as anxious to find out what had gone wrong as was everyone else.

At the time of that famous fight we were spending the summer vacation on the country estate of the Wallersbrunns, in the charming province of Mecklenburg. Everything about it reflected old wealth as judged from the well-kept park surrounding the manor, as well as from the decor and furniture inside it. It was of a kind that I had never seen in the apartments of Berlin, such as the magnificent brass stallion on a carved wooden pedestal in the drawing room or that huge oil painting of a princess-like lady that adorned the wall by the red-carpeted stairway.

There was an elderly couple living there—I have forgotten their name—who were probably the real owners. We were all joined around the dining room table for meals, but I remember little else about them. I had heard that Mrs. von Wallersbrunn, a young lady of considerable charm, was their adopted daughter, inasmuch as they had remained childless. This farm, too, had been restored to solvency through Father's good services, and I suppose it was he who opined that Mr. von Wallersbrunn, a handsome and athletic young aristocrat, would have never been able to acquire a country estate of this size or charm otherwise. Surely for him to marry into this family had been an unusual stroke of fortune.

Well then, here we were standing in their ornate living room as Dieter demonstrated Joe Louis' boxing technique. He bowed his head forward—I can still see it today—and held his arms over the top of his head with his fists clenched, resembling a stag with its antlers lowered for attack. Then, he moved forward and let his fists swing out, causing Mother to move out of the way. The demonstration convinced me that no European boxer, not even Max Schmeling, would have been prepared for so unconventional a boxing posture.

To top it off, according to Dieter's explanation, Joe Louis had employed another unfair trick. He had used a *Nierenschlag*, Dieter said. *Nierenschlag*, or kidney punch, so he explained with a resigned shrug of his shoulders, was illegal in Germany, but not in America, where this bout had taken place. Thus for me, Max Schmeling was fully exonerated, and Mother clearly felt similarly reassured.

It was good to have a big brother who seemed to have all the inside dope on matters that parents didn't know the first thing about.

Festive Times

Yes, it was a great and beautiful life. As I look back, it is as if everything was bathed in sunshine. Life seemed to be cheerful and resembled one of those Sundays when our parents took us to the Botanic Gardens where we fed the swans and Gila and I, all dressed up in our Sunday's best, played hide-and-seek around the artificial hills covered with rock gardens. I remember the time as if it had been a continuous holiday.

Grade school was fun and I had two good friends, Erhard and Peter, and we were all near the top of the class. I was well liked and never had to hesitate to bring home my report cards.

My walk home from school took twenty minutes and was not without interesting sights. I walked past the tennis courts, where we ice-skated in the winter. Around the next street-corner was Peter's apartment on a street where we often, as I grew older, rode our bikes to the Grunewald forest. Then I walked along a tree-shaded street with beautiful mansions hidden under old trees and behind high brick walls. Just where I had to turn left, was the house of an American diplomat. His car was parked in front. It had a most unusual long luggage trunk, almost as long as the hood, giving it a configuration I had never seen before. Near his house was the Home for the Blind, where residents made wickerwork furniture so artfully that one found it hard to believe they could not see. Then, of course, there was the other Home for the Blind, the Jewish one, around the corner from our apartment building. It was a stately mansion with that well-tended park-like garden in the rear. Our piano teacher lived in the apartment building across the street from it. And if, before turning the last corner, I turned left, there stood, behind some gardens, our marvelous, perhaps fifty-year old church. From the inside it was magnificent to behold its Gothic arches, and I had never heard more joyous and moving music as when its huge organ played. For me, that church and its organ were indispensable parts in the miracle of Christmas Eve.

One day, we all rushed out on the wide Berlin-Potsdam thoroughfare in order to admire a zeppelin that was poised there. It was low over the roofs of the city, all silvery and glistening in the sun. Hand-in-hand with Daddy, I listened to him explain everything to me.

On another occasion, perhaps two or three years later, I was given permission to watch one of the many parades downtown. There were flags and banners everywhere and a large excited crowd, as the military band was blasting away and tanks rolled by, followed by blocks of troops goose-stepping past us with inimitable precision. Then the excitement heightened as the black Mercedes-Benz, with its top down, approached. And there he was, standing up with his arm stretched out. He was a little far away from where I was standing, but there was no doubt it was him, with his hair partly covering his forehead and his trademark mustache. People cheered and many youngsters perched in the trees waved paper flags.

Oh, and then came the day when Friedrich returned from school beaming, and with obvious relief announcing, "I passed." He had completed eight years of high school and had now mastered the final hurdle, the Abitur examination. And if that wasn't enough for me to brag about, he had decided to enter a military career. Until recently, in many European countries the officer corps had always been provided by the nobility, and even now his chosen profession had a highly respected and almost aristocratic glamour about it.

And then, at about the same time, there came the event that made everyone erupt into an outburst of enthusiasm from the coast in the north to the Alps in the south. I had never witnessed such a universal celebration of pride and delirious joy as on that day when, unexpectedly, German-Austria and Germany were at last united in one state. It felt like the heart-warming reunification of a long torn-apart family.

TEARS OF JOY

ONE OF THE REASONS WHY AUSTRIA did not participate in the German unification in the nineteenth century was the presence of its multi-national empire. The desire to do so, however, was strong among its German-speaking people and once their empire was dissolved in 1918, as a result of the lost war, and all of her non-German constituents obtained independence, they voiced their desire to unite with Germany. In the peace treaty, however, the victorious Allies proscribed such a union and even forbade them to call their country

German-Austria.

Sharing the sufferings of many other countries, Austria was in deep economic difficulties as a result of the Great Depression, as well as from the violent and armed confrontations between its Communists and Nazis. Since 1931, it had been ruled under a mild dictatorship that had outlawed the Communists and restricted the Nazis.

In February of 1938, Hitler subjected the Austrian Chancellor, E. Schuschnigg, to a harangue of accusations and created a crisis that was accentuated by German troop concentrations near the border. His intention apparently was to impose a National-Socialist government on Austria and then to force it into some form of coalition with Germany, perhaps similar to the one that had existed between the old Austria and Hungary.[19]   Schuschnigg, in self-defense, ordered a plebiscite in the expectation that the Austrians would declare, before the world, their desire to remain independent. Schuschnigg's hope was Hitler's fear. He, too, thought the Austrians would vote for continued independence, and in order to prevent that from happening, he threatened with invasion. The plebiscite was indeed canceled, and the Austrian government fell. But on March 12, 1938, Hitler invaded the country anyway. Both he and Schuschnigg were in for a monumental surprise.

There was no need to impose anything upon the Austrians. Jubilant crowds received the German troops, with flowers thrown by ecstatic women and children, and with kisses and tears of joy.[20] Upon Hitler's arrival in the town of Linz, a throng of 100,000 was awaiting him in a state of excitement beyond belief. When Gen. Guderian's troops reached Vienna after midnight, an Austrian military band was there to greet them and guide them into the city center. There the people, in a frenzy of joy, lifted the general on their shoulders and carried him to his quarters.[21]

Thus, Austria became a belated member of the German Reich and was incorporated the way all the other German-speaking kingdoms and principalities were seventy years before.

Never in anybody's memory had the population on either side of the border been in such a seizure of joy. A month later, a plebiscite asked for approval of the union, or *Anschluss*. The Austrian prelates recommended that their faithful vote "yes".

Nobody knows whether the approval by over 99 percent of Austrians and Germans alike was genuine or a manufactured figure by the Party, but there is no doubt that it was overwhelming.

Mussolini cursed, "That damned German!", but he mailed a congratulatory telegram after all.[22] Chamberlain, on March 13, declared in the House of Commons that no action would be taken. "The hard fact is that nothing could have arrested what had already happened—unless this country and other countries had been prepared to use force."[23]

One might ask, if a nation is enraptured by an event of great fortune, why would, in a normal world, other countries even think of using force to prevent it? But, of course, this was not a normal world. This was Europe. This was Europe between two world wars. Without question, Hitler's military invasion was outside international standards of behavior and brazenly illegal. There is no doubt it was a clumsy method to achieve a shotgun marriage. But such legalistic protest was not the true cause for the world's alarm. There was fear. There was the "German Problem." For the other countries, German happiness was not the issue. The issue was that the larger the country grew, rightly so or not, the greater in their eyes was her virulence. Once again, the visions differed.

While the sentiment of belonging together was genuine and lasting among Germans and Austrians, Austrian enthusiasm is said to have soon sobered. Austrians are a pleasant and laidback breed. They were not fond of the Nazi Party either.

DOLPHY

HAPPINESS CONTINUED. That summer of 1938 we spent our vacation in the Black Forest. I had never seen the mountains before. We took daylong hikes—Mother, Gila, and I. We saw incredible vistas from the summit of the Black Forest's highest mountain, we stood in amazement at the bottom of a thundering waterfall, and I drew a pretty good pencil sketch of one of those picturesque Black Forest farmhouses.

Among the guests in our farmhouse lodging was a kind couple who owned a car. Once or twice, they treated us to sight-seeing tours in areas out of reach on foot. We reciprocated with two bowls of blueberries that we had picked in the forests. At sup-pertime, with all the guests joined around the long table, stories were exchanged about the experiences of the day.

One day, this couple had taken a trip into nearby Switzerland, and they reported on it to the rest of us at night. The Swiss, they said, recognizing the German license plates, had waved at them good-naturedly and inquired, "*Was macht's Dölfle? - How is Dolphy doing?*"

We all erupted in laughter. How irreverent, and how quaint of the Swiss, to call him "Dolphy"!

Many an evening the three of us sat at the forest's edge on the hillside overlooking the peaceful valley and harmonized to those beautiful old folk songs as the sun was setting behind the distant, purple mountains. One of them, a favorite of mine, was "*Kein schöner Land zu dieser Zeit*" (No land more beautiful at this hour). It was capable of touching the softest part of your heart, when Nature was preparing to go to sleep at dusk.

I could almost feel the warmth of the blessings God was bestowing upon us, our family as much as our country.

And there was more to come.

Germans in the East[24]

GERMAN RELIGIOUSLY INSPIRED crusades-of-conquest in the East lasted from 1140 to 1180 A.D. in the territories east of the Elbe River, and approximately from 1200 to 1300 A.D. in the Baltic countries, and in what was later called East Prussia. After 1300, the influx of Germans into Eastern Europe was one of peaceful colonization and invariably occurred upon the invitation by noblemen, kings, and tsars.

In the time during and right after the great European crusades into the Holy Land, this German migration was in part driven by religious zeal as well. Much more important, though, was an irresistible and mutual economic benefit. There is a remarkable similarity between those events and today's policies of rulers of developing countries who attract Western investments, experts, and know-how so as to develop the resources of their lands more rapidly and to modernize their economy. In the early Renaissance, the Slavic and Hungarian nobility invited Westerners—mostly Germans, Dutch, Flemings, Luxemburgers, Alsacians and French—to develop and enrich their domains, to build towns, and to promote manufacture and trade. Not only were they enticed by the new upsurge of Mediterranean culture, the Renaissance, but this was also the time when western agriculture was employing such down-to-earth innovations as the wheeled plow, shoed horses, farming by three-field rotation, the cultivation of vegetables, animal husbandry, and improved water and windmills. In addition, it appears that the Germans had acquired a reputation for the building of towns that might be populated with busy merchants and artisans, and that they also performed most of Europe's mining of iron, lead, copper, and tin. Western Europeans had learned the technology of clearing forests for the expansion of land under cultivation, and Cistercian monks from France were just as efficient in draining swamps, as were the Flemings.

Furthermore, this was a troublesome period for the German homeland, which was suffering from never-ending political fragmentation, robber barons, near anarchy, and a powerless emperor. Thus, they eagerly followed the call of Eastern rulers to supply their skill and labor. They were assigned land in the Czech and Slovak countries, Poland, Hungary, and Rumania. This colonization wave lasted two to three hundred years. Around 1700, a new wave was initiated by the arrival of expelled Huguenots from France. Large government-sponsored programs under Peter the Great and Catherine the Great of Russia and the Habsburg Throne in Vienna created German settlements from the Balkans to the Volga River, and even to lands south of the Caucasus Mountains.

In the lands of the Czechs, that is to say, in their two provinces Bohemia and Moravia, as much as in the other recipient countries, a remarkable memorial of this German influence is the great number of towns the Germans founded in the fourteenth century. As intended, they became centers of economic activity and were populated for a long time by German-speakers with their own administration, marvelous Gothic churches, schools, and guilds. For a long time the citizenry was divided into German townspeople and Czech country folk. This changed in the age of industrialization, which caused a growing number of Czechs to move into the cities so that, as a consequence, they ultimately predominated. Nonetheless, in 1857, German speakers still accounted for 50 percent of Prague's population, and as late as 1918, for 60 percent in their second largest city Brno (Brünn).

The land of the Czechs shared with Germany the immersion into the Renaissance, and the political and cultural fate of the German-speaking world. That was so not only because of the presence of Germans in their towns and the western orientation and marriages of their nobility. It was also because the country was surrounded on three sides by German land, and because it had also been, since their king became German Emperor Charles IV in 1347, actually a permanent part of the Holy Roman Empire and later of that of the Habsburgs.

German contributions to their history and achievements include the ancient beer breweries in Pilsen and Budweis, some of the architectural and cultural splendor of Prague, the mining industry (including that of gold and silver), the famous Joachimsthaler mint (giving rise to the word dollar), and the names of the geneticist Gregor Mendel, the author Franz Kafka, and the designer of the Volkswagen, F. Porsche.

But, for special reasons, it was never an altogether happy land. This was manifested as early as around the year 1400 when Jan Hus, a remarkable teacher, religious reformer, and patriot initiated a militant movement against both the Roman Church and the Germans living in his lands. The Hussite Wars lasted from 1420 to 1434 and included an outburst of massacre and arson on most German settlements in the interior. These hostilities caused the Germans to leave for the safety of the mountains surrounding the Bohemian basin, an area which was unpopulated and where, therefore, their presence did not interfere with an indigenous population. There they cleared the forests to build new villages, and engaged in agriculture and such crafts as weaving and glass blowing. One part of the horseshoe-shaped mountain range bore the name of Sudeten, a term more recently used to designate the Germans living in the entire area.

The division between the two groups was further accentuated a hundred years later when many of the Sudeten-Germans turned Lutherans, while the Czechs had reverted to Catholicism.

The Hussite expulsion characterized an enmity that never abated. It might have been foreseeable. Here were two ethnic people, living in the same land, speaking different languages, adhering to different religions; one more prosperous than the other and more favored by the authorities, and the two of them never blending. These differences were indeed a prescription for perennial and intractable antagonism in which it is not so much the people per se as rather the setting of their relationship that causes them, even though they may both be decent and peaceful, to be each riled by the presence of the other. This phenomenon, with different variations, has also prevailed in the other German settlement areas in Eastern Europe and is well known in diaspora-like areas such as the British living in Ireland, the Turks mingling with the Greeks, the Chinese living in Indonesia and other south-east Asian countries, and the intermingling people in the Balkans and in India, and above all, of course, in anti-Semitism.

The creation of the new state of Czechoslovakia in the Peace Treaty of St. Germain in 1919 was tainted with a tinge of idealism inasmuch as it was to be a land as internally harmonious as Switzerland. Alas, in view of the fervor of nationalism in the twentieth century, this was an unrealistic experiment for it blatantly violated the accepted principles of self-determination. That principle had called for the dismantling of the Austro-Hungarian Empire, and here now, in the newly created Czechoslovakia, there was an identical multinational state all over again, with its constituents, the Czechs, Germans, Slovakians, Hungarians, Poles, and Ruthenians having little tolerance for each other. Furthermore, the new country was surrounded by neighbors who were each aggrieved about the amputations the Treaty had inflicted upon their own soil. Dr. Benes, the creator of Czechoslovakia, was a great patriot and was worthy of the admiration of his people, but it is unlikely, even if he had possessed the gifts of a genius, that he could have provided his new republic a promise of permanence.

Peaceful Agreement

Yes, life was good, but it was also breathtaking. Right on the heels of that enormously gratifying unification of the two German sister states, a terrible friction arose between our country and Czechoslovakia. A sense of crisis was in the air, and it was the first time that I heard adults speak of the specter of war. The crisis developed from a conflict between the German population of that country and the Czech government in Prague. There were demonstrations and police crackdowns in the German-populated towns. Germans reportedly had been killed, and according to newscasts, their blood was running in the streets.

These events touched raw nerves on both sides, nerves left

acutely exposed by the Treaty of St. Germain-en-Laye, but which, in fact, had been raw for many centuries.

I was, of course, unfamiliar with the historic details of the Germans in Bohemia and Moravia, and I still wonder how much other people knew about them. But everybody knew that here was a land that both Germans and Czechs called their homeland, and where they shared a long and productive history. The perception was, further, that the spirit of President Woodrow Wilson's Fourteen Points and the principle of self-determination had been promptly violated by the victors of the war when they created Czechoslovakia. The inclusion of the German Sudetenland in the Czech-dominated state was viewed as deliberately vengeful and, thus, there was a powerful, popular groundswell of righteous indignation at the violent developments in the Sudetenland.

One might say that the described perception reflected a one-sided view of a complex situation. The cession of the Sudetenland surely would trigger identical demands from Poland and Hungary on Czechoslovakia, and its remaining rump state would have been economically disabled and militarily deprived of its geographic line of defense. In other words, ceding the Sudetenland could easily lead to Czechoslovakia's disintegration and thus endanger the European balance of powers, which was so vital to Britain and France. It is also true that the iniquities exacted upon the German minority by the Czech government had been greatly overstated by propaganda. They had not been "oppressive" or "terroristic," but merely marked by "tactlessness" and "discrimination,"[25] and could have been corrected by gentler therapies. But then, in this imperfect world of unabashed nationalism, the road of modern history has often been paved with acts of righteous fervor based on one-sided views.

Consequently, at the time of this crisis, for a German worth his salt to support the Sudeten-German right to self-determination and to brand the Czechs as oppressors was almost inescapable. As for myself, unburdened by much factual knowledge but fully seized by the general horror at the news stories of violence and the wave of injured patriotism, I watched the unfolding events with bated breath.

The way the crisis built to a climax and then resolved by peaceful agreement in Munich would have brought fame to a Hollywood producer creating a combination of thriller and epic drama. As a tense world was looking on, the chief actor was performing his act at the edge of disaster; and so it appeared to us, through his uncanny negotiating skill he brought the other gentlemen around to seeing things in the Sudeten-Germans' way and to affix their signatures to an agreement that righted a wrong and restored international harmony.

It was the second time in six months that this star performer had exhilarated the nation with triumphs so miraculous that nobody would have dared to dream of them before. These two victories clearly dwarfed his considerable accomplishments of the previous five years. In the eyes of the nation, their leader had proved himself magnificently as a hero in international contest, as a healer of the wounds of our humiliation at Versailles, as a peacemaker in the face of frightening crises, and as a man of reason. Not a few began to rank him as a giant on a par with Bismarck and Frederick the Great. A nation of eighty million people felt uplifted in a manner unparalleled in anyone's memory.

The ones most overjoyed, as I verified in personal conversation decades later, were the Sudeten-Germans themselves. They felt delivered and liberated and, in their gratitude, saw him as their savior and as a man without an equal in the world.

His popularity among the citizens, by this time unmatched by any contemporary world leader, was overwhelming; and the faith his grateful and trusting people had in him was boundless.

He had strictly adhered, so they felt, to what was just and righteous. His critics, if there were any remaining, had to know it.
Overnight, their chances to succeed in stopping him or removing
him from power had been washed away by the flood of patriotic
euphoria. In the fall of 1938, challengers confronting him would
have resembled David facing Goliath. People would have laughed
them right out of the arena.

Lost Chance

AT THIS TIME, A GROUP OF MEN existed that, behind all the brilliant
victories, recognized that the country's leader was a loose can-
non—a reckless gambler steering the world headlong into another
world war. They all agreed that the time had come to remove him
from power. The precipitating cause was his preparations to declare
war on Czechoslovakia. They correctly saw that a coup d'état
against a man so popular among the people and the younger officer corps was guarantied to fail, unless it could be shown that the
step was mandatory to prevent war. The linking of his arrest to the
imminent outbreak of war was pivotal, if a civil war was to be
avoided. The coup would have to be precipitated by Hitler's order
to implement Case Green—the invasion of Czechoslovakia—and
not a minute before.

The Resistance Network combined leading representatives
of the *Abwehrdienst* (military intelligence and counter espionage),
the Foreign Office, the Army, and the Berlin Police, as well as the-
ologians, the conservative opposition, and the civilian nobility.
Their leaders were Gen. Ludwig Beck who had just resigned from
the post of Chief of the Army General Staff, Dr. Wilhelm Gördeler,
a one-time mayor of Leipzig, Adm. Wilhelm Canaris, the head of

the *Abwehr*, and his right hand man, Gen. Hans Oster. The president of the Berlin police, Count von Helldorf, and his deputy, Count von der Schulenburg, were to prevent the police from interfering in the coup. Gen. von Witzleben, commanding the troops around Berlin, and Gen. von Brockdorf-Ahlefeld, commanding those in Potsdam, were going to isolate Berlin, while special forces were to enter the Chancellery and seize Hitler. The legal preparations to put him on trial were made by von Dohnanyi, a son of the composer and a lawyer working with Gen. Oster, who possessed a large dossier of unlawful Nazi acts, and Dr. Karl Bonhoeffer, head of a family of several famous and tragic conspirators, who assembled psychiatric material to declare the dictator insane. At this early stage, only Gen. Oster was realistic enough to judge that nothing short of the dictator's death would suffice, and he gave orders to his men to accidentally kill Hitler during the melee with the body guards.

Adm. Canaris sent a secret messenger to London who spoke with Sir Robert Vansittart, adviser to Foreign Secretary Lord Halifax. The messenger informed him that there was only one extremist in Germany, namely Hitler; that even Himmler and Goebbels could not be so described, and that all the generals were dead against war but lacked the power to stop him unless there was help from the British. Without Britain taking a firm stand on entering into war, in case Czechoslovakia was attacked, the German Resistance could not act.[26] The British ambassador, Sir Nevile Henderson, also reported that he found Goebbels and Göring non-militant while, by contrast, expressing the impression that the Führer was on the borderline of madness and could go over the edge.

At the Conference of Munich on September 29, 1938, British Prime Minister Chamberlain and French Premier Daladier yielded to Hitler's demands. He had won another splendid victory—the transfer of the Sudetenland to Germany. Not a single person, not even the conspirators, doubted the principle justness of it, and he had done so in a peaceful manner. The agreement of Munich rendered the high-minded German conspirators and their plans irrelevant. For them, the outcome was a bitter defeat and for some, in fact, a source of abashment. Surely, Churchill was not far from the truth when he said:[27]

> All these generals were patriotic men... They therefore felt smitten in their hearts at having been found so much below the level of the event, and in many cases their dislike and their distrust of Hitler were overpowered by admiration for his commanding gifts and miraculous luck. Surely here was a star to follow, surely here was a guide to obey.

This was the first of eleven attempts by the Resistance to either remove Hitler by coup d'état or to assassinate him. (There were four additional attempts at assassination by individuals acting on their own and not connected with the Resistance.) All of them failed. In some of them, his escape was so utterly surprising that, if it were not superstitious, one could almost suspect some mysterious, unnatural force was protecting him.

Broken Glass

IT WAS NOVEMBER OF 1938. Out of the blue, so it seemed, interrupting a continuous string of happiness and successes, a brief spell of ill temper and violence erupted. It began with an assassination in Paris. A Jew had shot and killed a young German embassy official. There followed a great uproar, and then, in the morning, people on their way to work had found an awful lot of shattered storefront windows. The dairy shop of the two Jewish spinster ladies, where we bought our milk, looked pitiful. Splintered glass was strewn all over the sidewalk. I had never seen anything like it. The newscaster spoke of spontaneous outbursts of anger among the population, and of synagogues that had been set on fire by enraged patriots. Daddy explained to me that a synagogue was a Jewish house of worship.

I don't recall any comments of my parents on these events except that I was instructed to "stay away from there". My memory seems to suggest the same silence prevailed in general, as if people were keeping their thoughts to themselves. There is one exception, however. In my memory, there is the image of two women talking about it in the street, two housewives carrying their shopping nets, and my overhearing one of them say: "*Von wegen, spontan!* - Spontaneous? Come on, now!"

Whatever the source of my opinion, in my youthful mind it was common knowledge that this had been the work of special squads acting under government orders. Because of the abundance of splintered glass in the streets, the incident was dubbed the "crystal night".

NO GOODBYE

It must have been at the same time when my friend Peter no longer came to school, and when I learned that the Rosenbergs had moved away. I felt a little hurt and surprised as there had been no warning, and he hadn't even said goodbye.

He, Erhard, and I were classmates and had been a trio of friends for some time. Erhard lived near our elementary school in a small apartment with his mother and elderly father. I remember, his father was sixty already, and they lived on the meager pension of a retired army captain.

Peter lived in a more spacious apartment on the fifth floor right under the roof, in a building that I passed every day on the way to school. I could see the geraniums way up there in their balcony flower boxes. We had played in each other's homes and gardens, had invited each other to celebrate our birthdays, and had enjoyed a good friendship. Now, only Erhard and I were left.

Mother, in search of an explanation for Peter's sudden disappearance, suggested that it might have to do with their being Jewish.

"Jewish?" I asked her. "Are the Rosenbergs Jewish?"

It was a deeply astounded inquiry. In the narrow sphere of my life, that question had never before been raised. It belonged in the world of public affairs—the newspapers and broadcasts and motion pictures—where Jews were being mentioned quite regularly, it seemed. But it had never before touched my own private world.

Did I grow up without prejudice? No, my world did have categories. For me, the Germans and all other Northern Europeans were considered "us;" the Mediterranean peoples were "them". The Lutherans were "us" and the Catholics were "them". The Jews, too, were "them". The designation "us" implied something that was familiar, "them" was something that was strange or foreign. I am not certain whether I thought it also meant a lower ranking in some form of universal value system. If it did, that aspect was not very relevant. Maria and Molly were Catholic, Peter was Jewish, Erhard was Lutheran, and all of them were my friends.

Of course, I had heard that message being proclaimed loudly across the nation that blamed the Jews for much misfortune and depicted them as public enemies. I was not disrespectful enough to doubt the truth of what the authorities were saying, but somehow that truth was more important in their world than in mine.

Mother gave me an affirmative answer: yes, they were. As I remember her face, she said it with a mixture of pensiveness and gravity.

Two Tracks

IN WORLD POLITICS, there are times when unpopular steps need to be embarked upon for the welfare of the nation. A statesman, confronting such a necessity, must then find a way to make his people pursue those steps, even against their will. That was a particular challenge for both Lenin and Hitler because their plans were so big. Lenin had reached his goal only after he had caused millions of his countrymen to either die or emigrate. Hitler was much more civilized.

He believed to be confronted by an emergency of epochal dimensions. He estimated that by the early 1940s the farmers of his crowded country would no longer produce enough food to feed its people. That was not as exotic a notion as it sounds today, since in those days hunger and want were widespread in the world. For her survival, he thought, Germany had to conquer additional tracts of land and she would have to look for them where they were available; that is to say, in Russia. In today's world, such proposition would provoke insurmountable moral objections, but in those days that was not entirely so since some of the principles of the nineteenth century had not been completely overcome. Conquering lands that belonged to someone else and exploiting them for your own purposes was a popular enterprise in the colonialist world, and it caused no moral qualms because, as it was seen then, obviously the indigenous people in the colonies had racially, the way God had made them, a lower rank; and furthermore—this was a popular opinion then—if you were scientifically inclined, political Darwinism taught that to be the way of Nature. Even if one were to forgive that way of thinking on the basis of a prevalent and historical misconception, it was still unbelievable what dimensions Hitler was thinking of. In order to annex part of the Ukraine, Germany had to first expand eastward in order to get near it, and that meant Czechoslovakia and Poland had to be disposed of on the way.

In his mind, impending famine was not the only reason for the urgency of the matter. Another reason was that he estimated the military balance in the world would shift in Germany's disfavor by the year 1943; this prediction was not far off the mark. Hence, if this is a correct interpretation of his unbridled thoughts, in 1933 he had only a ten-year period available during which to seize power, revive the moribund economy, rearm the country, eliminate Czechoslovakia and Poland, defeat the Soviet Union, and, if France objected, defeat her as well.

There was more, however. Germany's necessary strength to achieve those conquests, he believed, was diminished by an infestation of parasites that were sucking its blood. By intermarriage, he said, they undermined the glory of patriotism and the mentality of bold, racial self-preservation, and they preached such poisonous notions as internationalism, democracy, and pacifism. They were the Jews, a people he called "masters of international poisoning and race corruption".[28] He never doubted they were in control of Bolshevism and that in much of the world they were considered an affliction and a plague.

The logical conclusion in his tortured and passionate mind was, accordingly, that the future of his beloved fatherland depended on the conquest of the Soviet Union. It would accomplish three necessities in one blow, namely to eliminate Bolshevism, to exorcise the Jewish parasite that was particularly prevalent there, and to provide the extra land needed by his country to feed its millions.

He, naturally, didn't talk this way; but, unbelievably, he had actually written some of this in his 1923 book so that the world should have known. Very few, however, had managed to struggle through that book, and those who did ended up confused and did not take him seriously.

Lenin, as described earlier, encountered great difficulties in compelling his Russians to become obedient. He saw himself forced to unleash a bloody deluge of coercion before his trembling nation followed his leadership. As far as Hitler's methods are concerned to make his people do his bidding, it is uncertain to what degree it was designed and how much came naturally. But in the way it actually transpired, there was very little coercion required. The introductory phase, lasting six years, was peaceful and consisted of a continuous sequence of successes, which conveniently diverted the public eye away from the ignoble aspects of his regime. One might almost call it a golden age, which crescendoed into a breathtaking magnificence. At the end of that phase, the majority of the population was seized by a spirit of gratitude, admiration, and enthusiasm. The outbreak of the war, for which in his schedule it was then high time, could be made to look as an attack from the outside with little difficulty. After that, popular support was as good as guaranteed because wars, as they have always done, will foment patriotism and gather the people around their leader. At that point at last—and that was indeed his devised plan—he could embark on the execution of the criminal work which, he felt, was of life-saving importance for all civilized humanity, but which no conventional leader would venture to carry out. The method to be employed was to wage a two-track war: one, a conventional, i.e. honorable and chivalrous war, that was meant for everyone to see; but parallel with it, hidden behind the turmoil and smoke screen of that war, he would send in his ideologically fanaticized, private army to carry out the ethnic cleansing and mass killings so as to create a new reality in accordance with the mission, which, he believed, Providence had assigned to him.

The use of war as a tactical camouflage of unlawful killings was clearly on Hitler's mind, as demonstrated by Dawidowicz. She writes:[29]

> In 1935 he (Hitler) referred to war as a cover for planned murder, when he told Gerhard Wagner, the NSDAP's top medial officer, 'that if war came, he would pick up and carry out this question of euthanasia,' for then 'such program could be put into effect more smoothly and readily' and in the general upheaval public opposition would be less likely.

She further established the diagnosis of his strategy, which nobody familiar with the subject will dispute:[30]

> War and annihilation of the Jews were interdependent. The disorder of war would provide Hitler with the cover for the

unchecked commission of murder. He needed an arena for this operation where the restraints of common codes of morality and accepted rules of warfare would not extend. He had set into motion a two-fold war—one that was traditional in its striving for resources and empire and that would be fought in traditional military style, and one that was unconventional inasmuch as its primary political objective was to attain National-Socialist ideology and that would be conducted in an innovated style of mass murder.

Thus it came to pass that the German nation, while in horror of another war, nonetheless entered into it naively, thinking it was chiefly launched and precipitated by the enemy, and that it was about no more than Polish atrocities and the city of Danzig. It fought for nearly six years in good faith, and never in doubt before God and the world about the righteousness of its cause. The exhilarating, golden overture of six years of his peaceful triumphs, a little deception at the outbreak of the war, and the clandestine and unknown nature of his private, second track of war: such were the three methods, by means of which he successfully fooled his nation.

Hitler and Lenin were not the only statesmen successful in moving their people into events, which they did not want. Franklin Roosevelt, while of course being a totally different and sane person, was quite artful himself in manipulating his reluctant nation to enter the war. But among the three, Hitler was supreme in his way to make his unwilling people do what they were opposed to. In comparison with Lenin, he was incomparably more elegant.

WHAT A WORLD TO LIVE IN

Winter came and passed. Friedrich had spent Christmas at home on furlough wearing the uniform of a private of the 25th Infantry Regiment that was garrisoned in the Pomeranian country town of Stargard. I had never been prouder of my big brother.

I was fascinated by the reports about the exploits of our expeditionary air force squadron, called *Legion Condor*, that was assisting Generalissimo Franco in the Spanish Civil War. They employed the newest fighter plane there, named Me-109 (Me stood for Messerschmitt, the name of the designer). It was said to be far superior technically to those of the enemy, which, I thought, one would expect. I knew Germany was among the leaders in the world of technology and science. Sometimes I daydreamed of becoming a fighter pilot in a Me-109 and flying like an eagle high through Spain's warm skies. Franco's victory over the communists was at that time not far away.

There was other excitement, too. I don't mean my birthday or Dieter's, or even Gila's impending confirmation. Rather, having reached the age of ten, I was not only to enter high school soon, but also to enroll in the Hitler Youth. To wear that uniform, with a military belt buckle and a shoulder strap and a black neckerchief, seemed like a marvelous step in the direction of becoming a victorious air force pilot.

Right in the middle of all of this, there transpired another remarkable political event: the Czech government, unable to handle mounting internal strife, had requested that their country be protected and administered by Germany. I didn't understand from what kind of strife or disruption they suffered for them to undertake such an unusual step, but it reinforced my pride in my country, and it was so pleasant to look at the new map. To have

Czechoslovakia stick into Germany's belly like a dagger—one that France some day might employ in hostile fashion—had always seemed unnatural to me, and so it was reassuring now to have that dagger disappear and also, I thought, to watch how every few months Germany's territory was growing at such a mighty rate.

Yes, life looked good. They had developed a new car, a car for ordinary people.   Friedrich, when home on furlough, had brought a prospectus of it. It was called Peoples' Car. It had a price tag of 990 marks and everybody knew its gasoline consumption of seven-liters per one hundred kilometers was as low as it came. People were amazed about its engine being lodged in the back instead of the front, and that it did not need any water because it was air-cooled. Friends of ours had an Opel Kadett that sold for fourteen hundred marks. Of course, they were very wealthy; they had a house of their own, a townhouse with a back yard ringed with forsythias. But now, at a price of less than one thousand marks, even people like us could perhaps own one of these unconventional looking Volkswagens, some day maybe. Friedrich must have thought of saving for one, the way he had studied the prospectus.

He had left it on the balcony table. The afternoon sun managed to send a few rays through the chestnut trees onto the flowered tablecloth. I had helped Mother bring the plates back to the kitchen. Flies were busily working on the leftover crumbs of coffee cake. I felt fascinated leafing through the illustrated pages. I had never seen a new-car prospectus before.

A car for common people! What an age to live in!

President Hacha's Request

AFTER THE SUDETENLAND had become part of Germany last autumn, the Poles and Hungarians also seized their parts from Czechoslovakia, and it took no more than four months before the Slovakians made moves to separate from the Czechs as well. It required no more than a little intrigue, and some push here and pull there from Hitler, to let it happen at a desired point in his schedule, and to ascertain that the proceeds of the transaction fell into the right lap. At a meeting on March 13, 1939, with Monsignor Josef Tiso, the prospective Slovakian President, he nudged the Slovakians to declare their independence, which they promptly did the next day. This prompted Dr. Emil Hacha, the President of Czechoslovakia, to request a meeting with Hitler. It took place after midnight on March 15, in the Reich Chancellery, and was a disgraceful scene of merciless verbal assaults on him, and threats to bomb Prague and to annihilate the country, and of chasing the frail, elderly gentleman around the table in pursuit of his signature. At 3:55 A.M., after receiving repeated vitamin injections from Hitler's doctor, he signed a declaration stating that he confidently placed the fate of his country into the hands of the Führer.[31] About 50 percent or perhaps even 75 percent of the causes for Czechoslovakia's collapse arose from its own internal misalliance and from its population's divergent nationalisms; but surely, the remainder was supplied by Hitler's expert role as a catalyst.

An opinion poll probably would have shown that the average German man-in-the-street was under the impression that the Czech state was indeed disintegrating under its own power, and that for so small and so land-locked a nation the request for a custodial union with Germany was understandable and would prove to be beneficial. He had no knowledge of any threats, violence, or verbal assaults, let alone vitamin injections; and, as the poll would have further shown, he believed the origins of the crisis lay in the Czechs' own country. In addition, Germany's willingness to accept their request to assume custodial oversight seemed not altogether unnatural, inasmuch as Bohemia and Moravia had been part of a

German Empire for six centuries. Such an arrangement would have seemed, in his eyes, not much different from Russia's overlordship over the Ukraine or Britain's over Ireland. Above all, the opinion poll would have reflected his gladness that, in this manner, at least one European focus of hostility had been amiably eliminated.

At the first anniversary of these events, on March 15, 1940, William Shirer, who was hardly more fond of the Germans than he was of the Nazis, noted in his Berlin Diaries: "Strange how few Germans know *yet* of what took place that night."

A New Crisis

S PRING HAD ARRIVED. In the Botanic Gardens there were hosts of blooming tulips, daffodils, and crocuses. As she did every year, Mother was planting geraniums in the balcony flower boxes. We had a nice celebration for Gila's confirmation. I started out studying English as my first foreign language in high school. Dieter played popular tunes on the piano, which lingered in my memory for decades. One was "Taboo," a haunting melody in the minor key, of a lovesick man yearning for a lady who had made herself unapproachable. There was the wistful song about "A little white house by the great blue sea." Then, of course, there was "*Nachtgespenst -* The Night Monster," which was fast and a little frivolous. With his right foot working the pedal, he would in true-fashion beat the rhythm with his left foot on the floor, as he played away, and he had a way with his seat muscles to make his whole body rock along. Sometimes Mother would open the door with her elbow, her hands wet from chopping carrots, and ask smilingly,

"Does it have to be so loud, *mein Junging?*"

We had to be considerate of the Lohmann family upstairs. Well, Dieter wasn't worried; Walter Lohmann, his peer, sometimes practiced playing his trumpet with the window open.

In spite of these happy and normal events, it was a tense spring and summer. Czechoslovakia's disintegration had barely taken place when a new crisis emerged. The newscasts reported about the persecutions of ethnic Germans by the Poles, while, at the same time, there were maps in the papers illustrating the encircling policies of France and Great Britain who had signed treaties with Poland, Rumania, Greece, and Turkey and who were also negotiating with the Soviet Union. The maps and reports conjured up potential military confrontations east and west, and the dreadful threat of another two-front war.

Western Poland was a tinderbox of conflicting nationalisms much the way the Sudetenland had been. Again, Germans had lived here together with the Poles for up to seven hundred years. At the First (1773) and Second (1793) Partition of Poland, Prussia had annexed Danzig and those territories with partly German population, namely West Prussia and the Posen province while Russia and Austria took the remainder. The peace treaty of 1919 had recreated the Polish State and restored these areas to it. German resentment was similar to that of the French after they had lost Alsace-Lorraine in 1871. In particular, the separation of Danzig, whose population was 95 percent German, from Germany and its transformation into an independent city-state, which was economically dependent upon Poland, was seen with much grief. How could Great Britain own Hong Kong at the other end of the world, but deny the Danzigers the right to be part of Germany? Even more difficult to accept was the separation of East Prussia from the German mainland by the so-called Polish Corridor.

The Germans saw the territorial and minority dispute as a

genuine one that had to be addressed sooner or later anyway, in search of a more equitable solution. Now, however, it had acquired great urgency, because of the outrages allegedly being committed by the Poles.

FRUITS OF HISTORY

HITLER DID NOT HAVE TO CREATE THE CRISIS. The foundations for it existed long before he came to power. The tinder, ready to be ignited, was assembled not only by the First World War, but more importantly by a history that had composed an area with two poorly mixing ethnicities, by the hot wave of nationalism that was raising tempers all over Europe that was no less fervent among the Germans than among the Poles, and, finally, by the bitterness left behind by the Treaty of Versailles.

There exists an old-fashioned policy, applied by rulers to unwelcome minorities, that one might call ethnic encroachment. The Spanish Inquisition used it with the Jews by confronting them with the choice of either converting to Christianity or emigrating. In the nineteenth century, the Tsar, wishing to Russianize the Baltic countries, encouraged the strong German element there to speak Russian or otherwise to leave. In 1886, identically, trying to Germanize the Polish minority, Bismarck forbade all teaching of Polish in schools of Posen.[32] About the same time, the London government enacted much the same rule to suppress the Welsh language in Wales. The Hungarians did it to the Slovaks in the nineteenth century, and the Slovaks to the Hungarians in the twentieth century. Mussolini moved to Italianize the Austrians in South Tyrol after World War I, and Communist Bulgaria, decades later, imposed this policy upon its Turks. The bitterness of the

Sudeten Germans grew from similar ethnic imposition, but the Czechs' measures were mild in comparison with the severe policies employed by the Poles toward their numerous minorities.

When the state of Poland was reborn in 1918, it was not given a good hand of cards. Poland was created in a world disrupted by anger and passion. Circumstances allowed her to draw her borders far beyond linguistic boundaries resulting in 30 percent minorities living among 70 percent Poles.[33] The poison of recurrent ethnic conflict was placed into her cradle, for the Poles and the minorities were mutually divided by ethnic pride and incompatible nationalisms. Poland belonged to the most underdeveloped European countries. Her material means were pitiful, and she had to protect herself against two large, embittered neighbors who were each in inner turmoil and were enraged about large territories they had lost to Poland. A light of hope lit up in 1922 when the land elected a moderate, friendly, and non-nationalist professor for President. But he was promptly assassinated, and after that, the country had either impotent governments or military rulers, Marshal Pilsudski being the most important one. He must have been a great patriot, but he also was a man of his violent times.

In order to secure the newly acquired eastern territories, false elections in Vilna (Vilnius) were engineered to legitimize this Lithuanian area's incorporation into Poland. The White Russians were violently suppressed and seven thousand White Russian prisoners were executed so as to eliminate their social elite. A violent pogrom was conducted against the Jews in Lvov in 1918. Of 2,612 Ukrainian elementary schools previously maintained by the Austrians, only five hundred were still open in 1931. An uprising by the Ukrainians in 1930 was suppressed "with atrocious cruelty".[34]

Repression of the German minority in western Poland was not as physical but just as determined.[35] It was the intention, from the start, to drastically reduce the number "of the foreign element" (over two million Germans living there in 1914). Hundreds of thousands were forcibly expelled. Discriminatory legislation allowed the Poles to confiscate German farms and to evict their owners. This resulted in reduction of German-owned land by over one third. Innumerable complaints, filed with the League of

Nations and reviewed by the Court of Justice in The Hague, attested to systematic violation of the Minority Rights Treaty of the League of Nations. Interference and restrictions were severe in the towns and cities. Hence, most of the massive exodus involved urban dwellers. Increasing interference with the function of societies, clubs, churches, and interest groups are listed in the reports, in addition to termination of lease contracts and concessions, of state and communal employment, and the withdrawal of teachers' licenses. Many schools and newspaper publishing houses were closed, and there were frequent calls to boycott German merchants and tradesmen. The German population felt rejected, intimidated, and locked-out, and a mood prevailed of being defenselessly delivered up to the powers of a foreign state. Many turned into victims of panic, and fearfully sold their properties and left their homeland. It is difficult to see a difference between this hostile and expulsive campaign against the German minority in Poland, and the ethnic encroachment imposed by Hitler upon the Jews before the war. Just as hundreds of thousands of Jews fled Germany, so by the early 1930s the German minority in Poland had shrunk to somewhere around 1.3 million.

No, Hitler did not have to create the crisis. It is even difficult to blame it on the Poles, for their lack of wisdom was no greater than that of other countries who embarked on the same kind of policies before and since then.

After Hitler's successes in Austria and the Sudetenland, the confrontation worsened acutely. Hopes were planted in the hearts of the Polish-Germans that their own liberation was next on the list, while the Poles, conversely, saw the same possibility with abrupt fear and anger. Thus, during the summer of 1939, the German minority was subjected to a wave of closing schools, newspapers, trade unions, clubs, shops, and manufactures, and of firings and expulsions from the land. It was not until this stage that physical assaults occurred and that people were arrested and sentenced to draconian penalties for trivial trespasses. An understandable fear and hatred took hold of the Poles who suspected the Germans to be spies, traitors, and a Fifth Column. Quite possibly, also, it was only now that the ethnic Germans, tired of being cast into the role of unwelcome intruders by this program of Polonization in a land where their roots were centuries old, lost their loyalty to the state and developed a spirit of resistance and hope for assistance from their brothers across the border.[36] At this point, the embers of interethnic conflict would have been glowing dangerously in western Poland, even if Hitler had not blown into it.

But, of course, Hitler did stir the cauldron and fanned the flames so as to create a war that could be blamed on Poland. Nonetheless, up to this point, there were naked hostility and isolated instances of shedding blood all right, but there were no massacres. What did happen, instead, was that once the German military onslaught commenced, the country was enraged against the Germans much in the way the Americans were against Japanese-Americans after the attack on Pearl Harbor. It was at that time that fear, anger, and hysteria combined to make them lash out against their Germans. It was a gruesome eruption of violence characterized by beatings, stabbings, and shootings, and where eyewitnesses related horror stories of smashed-in facial bones, gouged-out eyes, and disemboweling stab wounds. Some fifteen thousand were forcibly marched eastward for hundreds of kilometers without food or water, and a veritable blood bath occurred on September 3 in the town of Bromberg. Because of the rapid advance of the German troops, such violence was limited only to the first few days of the war, but nonetheless, over five thousand German civilians were said to have been slain.[37]

Whereas this unrestrained outburst clearly was triggered by the German assault, and whereas the Germans might have acknowledged their own aggression as its cause, that is not the way it impressed them. Rather, the cruelty displayed by the Poles during those first days of the war seemed to confirm what Goebbels' propaganda-mill had put before them all summer long. Much like a self-fulfilling prophecy, in the German mind, there was a logical line of progression from the Poles' suppressing the ethnic Germans for the preceding twenty years, to their violence in 1939 as reported by Dr. Goebbels, and then to their atrocities in early September. To many of them, it was evidence of the Poles'

belligerence and it fully explained why it had to come to this undesired war.

FEAR AND HOPE

IN THE SUMMER OF 1939, fear of another war was profound. The
adults would not have agreed to engage in war over the question
of Danzig or the Polish Corridor, but the disturbing reports of
Polish atrocities upon the German minority presented a powerful
and persistent challenge to such restraint. There was, of course, the
question of what amount of violence actually did take place and to
what degree it was maliciously exaggerated in the news media. I
thought that my parents, although deeply impressed by the atroc-
ity stories, were suspicious of Dr. Goebbels forcefully stirring the
drum of an inflammatory propaganda campaign so as to seed dis-
cord in the disputed land.

Nevertheless, propaganda or not, most people believed that
enough of the statements describing violence were true, and that
the confrontation had reached a point where it demanded an
urgent resolution. Yet, they also believed the Poles to be only partially responsible. In popular opinion, much of the crisis originated
in Paris and London. It was these governments that were creating
Germany's encirclement by forging treaties with countries surrounding her. They were the ones who had composed the injustices
of the Versailles Treaty. They were the ones who had thrown
Germany in an outcast status. They were the ones who had
devoured Germany's colonies. And now, so it was thought, they

harbored cold-hearted jealousy of Germany's remarkable recovery and successes. As a ruthless merchant might attempt to eliminate a strong upstart competitor in the rivalry of the marketplace, so now Britain and France had supposedly grown combative at the sight of Germany's vitality, and had conspired to use Poland to initiate hostilities in the east, so as to trap Germany between the pincers of a two-front war.

If in today's view that reasoning sounds far-fetched, it was not then in the mind of a country where the government controlled the media and therefore directed public opinion, and where, in addition, people felt their country had been on the defensive against incomprehensible hatred and contempt by its neighbors for a quarter of a century.

Hence, for average Germans, their country was once again the target of foreign hostility. For them, all the moving forces of the new conflict came from abroad: the irredentist problems endorsed at Versailles, the reported Polish atrocities, the political and military encirclement, and the supposed spirit of combative hatred. Suffering terrible fear at the thought of another war, they fixed their hope on another exercise of what had seemed such miraculous diplomacy in Munich, to once again lead to a just and peaceful solution.

DANZIG WAS IRRELEVANT

On May 23, 1939, Hitler assembled his senior military officers so as to inform them of the future course Germany had to take in order to ascertain its survival. He explained that the question of justice and injustice had to yield to the necessity of safeguarding the lives of eighty million people. Much in the way of the American expansionist concept of "manifest destiny" of the nineteenth century, he enlightened them about Germany's need to conquer *Lebensraum* to secure food supplies, and, for this reason, Poland had to be destroyed. He said, "Danzig is not the subject of the dispute at all."[38] On his far-reaching schedule, the great hour to launch the campaign for huge eastern conquests was about to strike. The generals were perplexed and did not believe that he meant what he said.

One might look at that day—May 23, 1939—as the first manifestation of a major diversion between Hitler's goals and those of his people. While they traveled on the same road with him into the war, average citizens thought the issue was the legitimate right of over a million ethnic Germans and their protection against hostility. Not even at the end of the war, six years later, did they realize that for Hitler, Danzig and the Germans in the Polish Corridor had been no more than a pretext. In their opinion, Danzig and the Germans in Poland were a limited and obviously just issue, generated by the terror exerted upon them, and Germany had no choice but to deal with it. As in the case of the Austrian *Anschluss* and the Sudetenland, they saw this as dealing with Germans on German land rather than a foreign conquest. The meeting of May 23, 1939 spells out the fact that Hitler's course and that of his people were an eternity apart.

More important yet was the date of September 3, 1939. It was the day, which introduced a third objective into the field of contest and, thereby, rendered the opinion of the German people even more irrelevant. That day, when Great Britain and France declared war on Germany, brought forth the purposes of the war as seen by the Allies and, surely, their visions of what this war was about were different yet. In Paris and in London, too, the leaders judged that Danzig was not the issue. For them the conflict was about the desperate need of stopping Germany for good, because, in their own fearful interpretation, Germany was determined to conquer the whole world.

Thus, there now existed three objectives of waging war: the German people meant to protect and repatriate Danzig and the

Germans in Poland; Hitler meant to extirpate the cancer of "Jewish-Bolshevism;" and the Allies meant to extirpate the cancer of the German Reich. The war was only three days old when history disqualified the ideas of the German people and eliminated their motives from the playing field, just barely late enough to allow them, naïvely and in good faith, to enter into the war. After Britain and France had declared war on them, they had no choice but to fight back and defend themselves, no matter how remote such a war in the west was from their own ideas. Their ideas, however, were no longer needed. From that day forward, it was merely a contest between Hitler's goals and those of the Allies. From that day forward, the people were merely pieces on the chessboard. It was one of the several episodes in twentieth century, where a great nation was fatefully deceived by his powerful leaders, and railroaded into peril by the merciless concatenation of international conflict.

STALIN'S SIGNAL

DURING THE LAST TEN DAYS OF AUGUST the tension became unbearable. The news stories reported many German farms being on fire, Germans fleeing from their homes, and that Poland was mobilizing its Armed Forces. There was chaos in Upper Silesia, three civilian German planes had been shot at, and the stories recorded the latest number of Germans killed. People believed these reports and were terribly enraged and depressed. It was a "how-dare-they" type of indignation, one that questioned what this hateful world had come to. My parents, though in many ways so critical of the propaganda minister's methods, believed it, too.

"The Poles," Mother said, "can be very cruel." As will be seen, the Lohmanns were equally affected. But the mounting indignation collided with the abysmal fear of entering another war. The nightmare of the last war had ceased only twenty-one years before.

The way Britain and France were committing themselves, and in view of their encirclement policies, it certainly looked like another major military conflict involving large parts of Europe, including the renewed danger of the vise-like squeeze of a two-front war.

Then, on August 23, 1939, came the news of the non-aggression pact between the Soviet Union and Germany. It was a bombshell. Germany and the USSR had been archenemies. France and Britain had been trying to enroll Stalin in the anti-German alignment. But now, Stalin was on our side. While that sounded advantageous, everybody, just the same, understood its real meaning. It was Stalin's pledge to Hitler that a war against Poland would be safe to undertake. If Britain and France entered into it, Stalin's neutrality would save Germany from a two-front war. In my parents' opinion, Stalin wanted to promote a devastating war to break out among the capitalist countries so that, once they were exhausted, he could step in and reap the harvest. In fact, even today, historical texts do not doubt that the pact was indeed Stalin's go-ahead signal for Hitler to proceed.

LAST OFFER

The days passed. I must have been fully seized by patriotic fervor. I trusted the truthfulness of the disconcerting newscasts and watched my parents' grave concern. They were concerned, if war came, that Friedrich would go into battle, of course. What bothered me was my suspicion that they were doubtful about our government's peaceful intentions. They did not say so, but did not look convinced when listening to the newscasts. It would have been painful for me to differ from them in such an ardent, patriotic matter. I was hopeful they would soon see it my way.

I did not have to wait long. On August 31, there came what in my mind was the decisive news that would convince not only them but also the whole world of our country's good will. It was indeed of far-reaching importance because for a surprisingly large number of people it locked in place the conviction that the guilt for the imminent war was, so God knew, not ours, but that of our hateful enemies.

It was broadcast as a *Sondermeldung* in the evening, a special message interrupting regular radio programming. Our government had proposed a plan of peacefully resolving the conflict, the concept of which was so simple and fair that even I could have designed it. What was the use of all the violence if one could simply conduct a plebiscite and then redraw the boundaries as reasonably as possible along ethnic lines? Let the will of the people living there determine where the chips would fall. If the outcome was pro-Polish and the Polish Corridor was to persist, our proposal had stated that a railway and Autobahn line would be built to traverse it so as to connect East Prussia with the German mainland. If, conversely, the vote was pro-German and Poland lost access to the sea, then Poland would retain its seaport of Gdynia and receive a railroad-Autobahn line to connect it to Poland.

If the alternative was war, I could not see how anyone, in God's world, would not at least agree to start negotiations on that basis. In fact, it was hard to see why this obvious solution had not been offered months ago, before much of the violence had developed. The radio message, however, unfortunately went on to the statement that the Poles, incredibly, had not sent a plenipotentiary to negotiate and had given no explanation why they didn't. Instead, we learned that their troops were shooting across the border. In my opinion, quite obviously there was nothing else we could do. They had most certainly reached the limit of our tolerance. On the next day, September 1, 1939, the leader of our nation, the victor and savior of Munich, announced in bitter resignation: "Since 4:45 this morning, our troops are shooting back."

THE FIG LEAF

ON SUNDAY, AUGUST 27, 1939, Birger Dahlerus, a Swedish businessman, flew from Berlin to London and later back to Berlin. He was an acquaintance of Göring, the second most powerful man in the Nazi hierarchy and commander of the Luftwaffe, who employed him as a semi-private intermediary in an attempt to reach a peaceful solution. At the same time, official negotiations naturally went through Sir Nevile Henderson, the British ambassador in Berlin, who also made flights between Berlin and London. No direct German-Polish negotiations were held, even though Poland was the subject of the dispute. Hitler tolerated Göring's private initiative and met with Dahlerus as well as with Henderson. Göring's proposal, so transmitted to London, suggested that Danzig and the Corridor return to Germany and that Poland retain the port of Gdynia with a connecting railway-highway line. Mr. Dahlerus returned with the British answer the same evening and presented it to Hitler at 1:30 A.M. on Monday, August 28. London insisted on an international guarantee of Polish borders to which Hitler agreed. That same Monday Henderson returned from London with an official version of the current state of discussion. He saw Hitler that day and again on the next. The previous preliminary agreements led nowhere, and both meetings were argumentative. At the second meeting on Tuesday, August 29,

Hitler requested a Polish plenipotentiary to come to Berlin, no later than the next day. Henderson, and later Prime Minister Chamberlain, rejected the request as an ultimatum. Göring, however, persisted in his own efforts. He told Dahlerus on that same Tuesday of an offer Hitler was preparing for the Poles that was so magnanimous they could hardly turn it down. Dahlerus willingly delivered the message to Chamberlain on Wednesday, August 30, but encountered little faith. That midnight, Henderson, in Berlin, saw Foreign Minister Ribbentrop again. At this much-mentioned meeting, Ribbentrop read Hitler's sixteen-point offer to him in German and at a fast speed. It included an internationally controlled plebiscite in the Corridor. It was, from start to finish, a document that was praised by non-German observers as extremely liberal, reasonable, and magnanimous. However, Henderson's ability in the German language, though adequate, was insufficient to grasp more than the rough outline because of the gnarled and rapid presentation, and when he requested to see the written text, Ribbentrop incredibly withheld it from him. He claimed that it was not necessary since the offer had expired anyway, in view of the fact that no Polish negotiator had arrived on August 30. On August 31, the Polish ambassador, Mr. Josef Lipski, called at the Foreign Office, but Ribbentrop refused to accept the diplomatic note that he presented.

That evening, at 9:00 P.M., twenty-one hours after the expiration of the ultimatum and eight hours before the outbreak of hostilities, the German radio announced the sixteen-point offer as a *Sondermeldung* with the conclusion that Poland had not responded to it. At 11:00 P.M., the Polish radio responded negatively, calling the Germans the "new Huns" and the proposal "impudent".[39]

There is no question that the "magnanimous offer," the "*grosszügiges Angebot,*" was meant for no more than internal propagandistic purposes. There is also little doubt that it achieved the desired effect of a sense of righteousness among many of the citizens. When, shortly after World War II, the secret details of this affair became public, everyone clearly remembered the event and the revelation was perceived as an eye-opener. Hitler was determined to wage this war so as to destroy Poland. The schedule of his grand design called for it at this time. Somehow the world, and his own people, had to be fooled to believe the war to be unavoidable and that he had acted as a responsible statesman. He needed a cover to conceal his machinations and his evil plan. This was his fig leaf. Granted it was small but it served its purpose.

Nonetheless, even if this ploy had not been used and if the people had been truthfully told that the Germans fired the first shot and not the Poles, the difference on public opinion might still have been only moderate. The prevailing paranoia was great, and the conviction that the ugly Polish crisis, from start to finish, arose from never-ending foreign hostility, old and new, was deeply rooted. In fact, that conviction was not altogether incorrect. The moving forces—the Versailles Treaty, the hostility in Poland, the encirclement, the combative jealousy—they were all there. They were all foreign. They were indeed hostile, and much of the hostility was decades old. What the Germans did not know, however, was that the most avid moving force was residing in the Reich Chancellery in Berlin.

PART 3

A WAR UNWANTED

Stolen Initiative

IN THE COURSE OF THE NEXT TWENTY-ONE MONTHS, Hitler overpow-
ered nine countries between the Arctic and the Mediterranean.
There would have been no one in the world denying that he, after
first having started the war, kept the initiative in his hands and
directed the course of events. Yet, that is far from the truth.

It was the British and the French who stole the initiative
from him on September 3, 1939. That day, psychologically speaking, changed everything regarding both Hitler and the German
population. All of his subsequent campaigns were merely desperate attempts to regain the initiative and to rid himself from the
Western Powers' interference by either persuading them to make
peace or, if they were unwilling, by defeating them, so that he, at
last, was free to return to his original master plan. These attempts
were indeed desperate for him because his eastern conquests had
to be completed before the rapidly approaching end of his military
superiority, as he thought, in 1942 or 1943. It was not until two
years later, in 1941, that he finally proceeded with his eastern campaign, but by then it was too late. The Soviet Union had grown in

strength; more importantly, the economic and military behemoth of the United States was entering the stage.

It was chiefly the British who, although suffering from a long series of military humiliations, stubbornly kept withholding the initiative from him. They did so by refusing to make peace, by luring him into undesired campaigns in such out-of-the-way places as Norway and Greece that had not been a part of his strategy and held no gain for Germany, by invoking the backup of the world's largest power, and by threatening to annihilate him and his country. Against his expectations, he was suddenly facing an inexorable opponent in Britain. She was an opponent whom he did not hate, and with whom he wanted no war. But, instigated into maximal hatred by the sudden explosion of the "German Problem," she was declaring the confrontation to be nothing less than a struggle over life and death.

While politically moderate and conservative elements of the European continent were convinced that the real menace was rising in the East, an insane and mortal war emerged with the West that in the end helped Stalin gain his terrifying victory. In the minds of the Germans, this underlying non-hostility toward the English, indeed admiration and their sense of kinship, created a two-tiered attitude. Hostility evoking hostility, they did indeed cheer when a royal battle cruiser was sunk, or when the British were defeated on Crete, or when Gen. Rommel conquered Tobruk. But at a deeper level, it was viewed more like a chivalrous contest than a war, and if Britain had changed her mind and had agreed to make peace and friendship, the German cheers would have been deafening.

For the outsider, the different and changing mental vectors in the beginning of that war are not easy to understand. The French, British, and American people wanted peace for anything in the world, but their leaders, compelled by Hitler's militaristic and expansionist policies, saw an irresistible necessity of stopping and annihilating him. Hitler, conversely, did indeed want war but only in the East so as to acquire *Lebensraum*. For that purpose, his plan necessarily demanded peace and cooperation in the West. The German people, finally, wanted peace more than everyone else, but

Britain and France's declaration of war tossed them into a conflagration from which they could not escape.

In his *Berlin Diaries*, W. Shirer describes this wistful German sentiment, so it seems, at every occasion. Quite unmistakably, he was not fond of the Germans or their country, and yet, from the time of the Sudeten Crisis in September 1938 until after the fall of France in July of 1940, he mentions their desire for peace and their incredulous disappointment every time their peace offers were rejected, not five times and not ten times, but rather on twenty-seven separate occasions.

The third of September, however, rendered the gaping dichotomy between Hitler's ideas and those of the people, as they applied to the need for fighting an essentially meaningless war. Their opposing hopes and purposes - his violent and theirs pacific - were forced upon the same road by the inescapable necessity to defend themselves in this new, western war, which they equally detested, although for different reasons.

The German propaganda ministry coined the term "*Der uns aufgezwungene Krieg*" and used it as if it were a single word: "The-war-that-has-been-forced-upon-us". It never entered common vernacular and remained limited to the news media. Yet, in the minds of average people it was at least 90 percent truthful.

VICTORIES BUT NO PEACE

VICTORY GENERATES SELF-PROPELLING MOMENTUM. The tension had grown to be so intolerable that the outbreak of war was, in a way, a relief, and the rapid advance of our troops was greeted with enthusiasm. Wars were terrible, my parents said, and this was confirmed by the news reports, which gave a devastating image of how much destruction modern war technology was wreaking. I can still hear the howl and scream of the dive-bombers, the *Stukas*, displayed in the newsreels, the way they plunged down unmercifully upon Polish targets and caused devastation.

Our reaction at the sight of all the misery brought down upon the Poles, shamefully to say, was remarkably detached. I suppose it was identical to public opinion in the Allied countries when they witnessed the assault of their air forces upon German cities, where homes, kindergartens, schools, churches, and all the other sites of civilian life were annihilated from the air. The British and the Americans probably felt they had good reasons to shrug off blame, and so did the Germans in the Polish campaign. "Well, yes," we might have said, "but you see, the Poles were the ones who committed the atrocities; they have started the war. As everyone knows, they have brought this upon themselves. They should not have let the French and British goad them into this conflict."

Also, people now began to say that the British had the habit of abandoning their conscience when it was a matter of protecting their worldwide Empire where the sun never set. They compared Danzig to Hong Kong and wondered why the British thought Danzig was a reason to fight a war over. Dad quoted their lapidary maxim, "Right or wrong, my country." He quoted it in English. My parents were very somber. One could hear the embittered opinion that while the British liked to have other countries fight their wars for them, they should watch out; modern warfare might disclaim the safe refuge islands used to offer in the past.

Old wounds, well on their way to healing since 1918, opened up again. Old scores demanded to be settled. "They robbed us of our colonies. They tried to starve us with their naval blockade after the last war." They believed that now they had to show the western powers how dangerous it was for them to start another war. I remember the proud feeling that we were strong and brave.

A glorious wave of patriotism swept the country. In church, Rev. Garten had us pray for victory. "Early," he said, "early victory." The Lord was on our side, how could He not be.

Poland was subdued in only twenty-eight days. There was a new word: *blitzkrieg*, lightning war. Stalin's Red Army had occupied its eastern half. There was nothing the British and French could do to alter it. Our government launched a peace offensive. Surely they had no choice but to agree to it. It said we had absolutely no demands other than the return of the colonies. We had even offered general disarmament, but in public opinion our proposals, which had sounded so reasonable and conciliatory, did not cut any ice and were ignored in Paris and London.

It was dark now at night in the city. The streetlights were no longer lit. The lights of the cars and buses had to be completely covered except for a small slit, barely big enough to show their presence. All the windows of the apartments and homes had to be covered to not allow the slightest beam of light to show in the night. Ration cards for food, soap, and clothing had been issued. A very cold winter was on its way, and supplies of heating coal were insufficient.

War actions were limited to the air and the sea. British bombers ventured across the North Sea to bomb German port cities. Then suddenly, there was news of a striking victory: a U-boat commanded by Capt. Günther Prien had penetrated the defenses of the British naval base at Scapa Flow and had sunk the battleship "Royal Oak". To top it off, he had escaped detection and had managed to get away.

Capt. Prien was awarded the Knights' Cross. It filled me with awe. That decoration, the Iron Cross worn from the neck just like the order of *Pour-le-mérite* in the last war, very quickly became for me the symbol of the highest possible honor that a brave man could achieve, one capable to be won only by a few among the elite.

Then there followed, shortly before Christmas, another naval transaction, this time in the South Atlantic, between the German pocket battleship *"Graf Spee"* and three British cruisers. Whereas both sides suffered severe damage, in the end the German captain had to scuttle his proud vessel not far from Montevideo.

Meanwhile, another war had broken out. The Soviet Union had attacked Finland. There apparently had been no provocation or recognizable reason for the conflict. Because of our pact with Stalin, we were not supposed to voice our opinion, but everybody was greatly delighted about the embarrassing inability of that huge bully-of-an-empire to make any progress against the plucky Finns. Along with the other Scandinavians, the Finns were held in high respect. My parents had traveled to Finland on their honeymoon and still spoke with great warmth of it. There were speculations as to what Stalin's motives might have been for the uncalled-for invasion. According to one opinion, the Red Army's poor performance was merely theater. Stalin wanted to encourage us to continue with the war by demonstrating that the Soviet Union represented no danger in our back, pretending that it was barely strong enough to defeat Finland.

Special Duty Groups

WITHIN THE VAST SECURITY SYSTEM THAT ENCOMPASSED the ordinary police, the political police (Gestapo), the autonomous paramilitary force of the SS, and now growing from it its elite combat forces named the Waffen-SS there emerged a subset detachment called *Einsatzgruppen*. The term can be translated as "task forces" or as "special duty groups". As a paramilitary police force, it was given the assignment of entering an occupied country on the heels of the invading army, in order to ascertain security against possible political opponents. They stood under the command of Reinhard Heydrich, an ideological and racist fanatic who wielded almost as much power as his superior, the chief of the SS, Heinrich Himmler. *Einsatzgruppen* were initially used in Austria and Czechoslovakia, but their true terror manifested itself in the occupation of Poland.

A program of ethnic cleansing was initiated to rapidly achieve Germanization of those mixed-population territories that were reincorporated into Germany. Large numbers of ethnic Germans were invited to leave their homes in the Baltic countries and territories held by the Soviets, and they were to be resettled in the recaptured lands. Given the appearance of a legitimate population-transfer, resembling that of the Greeks and the Turks in 1923, it was in fact a ruthless and brutal action in which 1.2 million Poles were expelled from their ancestral homes and turned into refugees in one of Europe's coldest winters.[1] Simultaneously, an order by Heydrich instructed the *Einsatzgruppen* to carry out cleansing missions against the Jewry, the Polish intelligentsia, the clergy, and the nobility.[2] Before the advent of winter, 3,500 members of the Polish intelligentsia had already been "liquidated".[3]

In the German-occupied part of Poland there lived two million Jews. Directions were issued to forcibly remove them from those provinces, which had been returned to Germany, and to gather them in occupied Poland east of it. The *Einsatzgruppen* arrived a day after the Army passed through. In the words of L. Dawidowicz:[4]

> All over Poland the synagogues went up in flames. Everywhere the Germans organized pogroms, rounding up the non-Jewish population to witness and learn how to mock, abuse, injure, and murder Jews.

There was "unbridled killing and senseless violence." Citing the action in a township named Aleksandrow, she writes:

> After three months of terror, arrests, shootings, expropriations, impressments into forced labor, the Jews were expelled on December 27, 1939. In the depth of the Polish winter, they were marched out on the highway.

To the extent that these incidents became known to the regular Army they generated shock and hostility.[5] There existed no command structure available to impede them, because the SS units were autonomous from the regular armed forces, and official protests were censored and suppressed. In face of this impotence imposed by the icy seclusion of the dictator, the responses varied from the one of the general who said "draw the curtains,"[6] to those who kept a detailed record of the atrocities,[7] and to those who transmitted the information to the Resistance.[8]

The Polish Jews were relocated into major cities to be isolated and controlled in ghettos. Internal memoranda of the SS leadership now brought up the question of the "final aim" of these policies. At this time, and for another year, the scenario of a "Jewish Reservation" was under avid discussion. They could, perhaps, be relocated into inhospitable regions, such as the American Indians were forced to do; one thought it perhaps beneficial to assign them to the island of Madagascar or an asylum of similar isolation where they could, in Hitler's 1935 words, "disport themselves according to their nature."

HALLOWED EVE

FRIEDRICH, HAVING RETURNED SAFE and sound from the Polish campaign, came home for Christmas. As we always had on Christmas Eve, we went to church at 5:00 P.M. while Father and

Friedrich put up the tree, decorated it, and set up the gift tables throughout the two living rooms, with one for each of us. It was then not customary to place the presents, all decorously wrapped, around the bottom of the tree. Instead, they were placed unwrapped on several cloth-covered tables, and Mother always decorated them with boughs of spruce.

As was done every year at the church service, the story of the Nativity was recited from St. Luke's Gospel, and I was attempting to listen to it patiently. The recitation was presented in sections, separated by the clear voices of the choir singing gospels and hymns. The Rev. Garten was a good pastor, and, I'm sure he rendered a moving sermon and led us in prayer for forgiveness and peace, but I was too excited to pay much attention to it. The most impressive part of the Christmas Eve service for me was always when the colossal organ accompanied us as we sang "Silent Night, Holy Night." The glorious experience of that mighty carol created a sensation as if my whole inside was trembling under the touch of holiness.

Gila and I always enjoyed "walking through the woods" on our short way home. At the street corner, there was a large lawn where Christmas trees were for sale, and on Christmas Eve there were always many remaining that stood there all covered with snow. We would walk among them and say, "Look, Mom, it's like a winter forest."

At home my impatience was stretched to the limits, as we were required to wait a few more minutes outside the closed living room door, while the parents put on the final touches and lit the candles. Finally, Mom and Dad opened the door, all smiles, and we rushed in, but then, overwhelmed by the sight, stood suddenly still. The lights were off, and there were only the twenty or thirty candles flickering on the tree. Every year, especially for us children, this beautiful sight always created a deep and silencing effect. We would stand there for a moment to look at the beautiful tree and the glitter of the tinsel, and to smell the spruce and melting wax of the candles, and would say "Awe!" in a whisper.

I knew where my gift table was. It always stood closest to the tree next to the gun cabinet. There, then, followed the usual shouts of "Ahs" and "Ohs" and "Thank you, Mom" and "Who is this from?" Toys were tried out, and new clothes were put on, and we'd visit each other's tables to share the excitement. Nobody would have thought to have a radio play on these occasions, and, of course, there was no television then. It was just us, our whole family.

After half an hour or so, there came the next act of the show. In today's world, it might seem too saintly or too melodramatic; but in those days, it was an essential feature of Christmas, and we all, young and old, needed and loved it. We sang. We settled down on the sofa and easy chairs—for many years I sat on somebody's lap—and, looking sentimentally at the tree, we sang all the carols we knew so well.

Although the caroling was easy and spontaneous, it must have been quite a performance, as I look at it now. My sister had one of the most beautiful voices I have ever known. We used to say that hers was a fountain of pure gold. All of us being quite musical, we harmonized; Mother and Gila's bright voices contrasted harmoniously with Friedrich and Dieter coming in deep and full. Only Dad never sang, but he loved every moment of it. I can still see him as he sat there quietly, his right index finger slowly circling the button of his jacket as the many flickering candles were reflected on his glasses. Once or twice, he would bring up his hand to clear his throat.

Upstairs, meanwhile, the Lohmanns had gone through much the same routine except they did not sing. At this point, Molly would shout, "They are singing already!" in the cheerful anticipation that, as soon as we were finished, they could come down and visit. Then, there would follow the inevitable moment when we heard a thundering racket from the staircase as the four young Lohmanns came scrambling down, unnecessarily ringing our doorbell, before we had a chance to let them in. They were followed, at a more measured pace, by their smiling parents. Later on, we returned the visit, again notifying all tenants of the event by causing the same ruckus on the way up. Thus, our two families always celebrated this wonderful holiday eve together.

In many ways, after 1939, Christmas has never been quite the same.

SWEDISH STEEL

I eagerly studied the pictures of the large illustrated book entitled "Ten Hours Earlier." The cover depicted naval vessels plying through the stormy sea. The title implied that our country's last minute reaction had prevented Great Britain from gaining a strategic advantage by their attempt to occupy Norway. The illustrations showed German naval vessels in the fjords and alpine troops taking possession of Norwegian harbors. The bitter six-week battle over the northern port of Narvik, against vastly superior British forces, caused everyone to hold his breath. Even more exciting than this book was the footage of the maneuvers of magnificent naval vessels in the newsreels. This military campaign had been entirely unforeseen—Denmark was also occupied, but peacefully so, to safeguard access to Norway—since we were at war with France and certainly not with Scandinavia.

It was only later that I learned why both Britain and Germany so precipitously grasped for this neutral and respected country. Britain intended to arrest the flow of steel to Germany that was being mined in northern Sweden and shipped south via the ice-free Norwegian port of Narvik. While clearly a flagrant violation of Norway's neutrality, it was for the British an irresistible temptation to quickly cut Germany's umbilical cord, if you will, to her ability of waging war by interrupting the supply of steel. Irresistible for the British, it was equally vital for Germany to prevent them from succeeding. Not only would the lack of steel have been disastrous, but it also would have bottled up the German Navy in the Baltic Sea and prevented it from operating in the North Sea and the Atlantic Ocean. The Royal Navy commenced mining the Norwegian coastal waterways on April 8, and the Germans landed on April 9. The British had to withdraw from their attempted landings at Narvik, Namsoe, Trondheim, Andalsnes, Bergen, and Stavanger.[9]

I appreciated as much as everybody else how unexpected our victory was. This was a naval engagement. Every child knew that Britain ruled the seas. After all, she was a sea power, and Germany was no match for her. We were only in the early stages of rebuilding a new navy. The news reports convinced me that overcoming our naval inferiority was the result of our greater competence and valor, and to me, there could have been no better explanation.

DEFENSELESS HEART

Dieter had chosen to follow his brother's example and had volunteered for a professional career in the Army, at least for now. But he did so with much less exclusive dedication. For him, there was too much else in life to live for. His clean, good looks, his impish smile, his dashing ways and roguish pranks, his quick wit, and his plain, open-hearted charm made him welcome among friends and successful with the girls. He loved to dance and as far as I knew, it was he who introduced the revolutionary "swing" into German dancing.

From skiing and playing ice-hockey in the winter, to swimming and playing tennis in the summer, let alone partying during any season, he had a busy time during his last year in school sampling the many joys of life.

In fact, his schedule became so crowded, I am sorry to confess, that he was forced to skip school repeatedly, one day here, a couple of days there, in favor of various pool-side and tennis club engagements. It was an arrangement, which would have been unthinkable if Father had known about it, and if Mother had not collaborated. Smiling his way into her defenseless heart, he got her to write the necessary letters to the school, in which she blamed his absence on recurrent attacks of ill health. She once quietly said to me, "You know, he'll soon be in the Army and in the war. But I don't think Dad would look at it this way." I kept the secret.

Even so, however, it was not all that easy. The teacher had begun to show suspicion, perhaps because Dieter's suntan was improving too rapidly, and he needed a little extra help from Mother. She was equal to the challenge. I was present when she called the teacher on the telephone and gave a magnificent performance of the distraught mother who was concerned not only about her son's failing health, but also, and even more so, because of the associated scholastic setback. No sooner did she put the receiver down, than Dieter picked her up and, swirling her around in the air, shouted, "*Mutti*, you're wonderful! You're wonderful, wonderful, wonderful!"

THE PRINCIPAL'S VICTORY SPEECH

Dr. Vanselow, the principal of Paulsen High School, had us all assemble in the large hall. The triumph of victory was in the air, victory over France. What had eluded our fathers during four years of bloody and dehumanizing trench war, our brothers had accomplished in six short weeks.

Dr. Vanselow gave a speech. I quickly sensed this to be different from other victory speeches I had heard. We cheered our gallant troops, he proclaimed, and we were grateful for God's assistance in bringing this war to an early end. There was no reference to our enemies' guilt or cowardice, none about the military genius of our leader, no word of retaliation for the inequities of the Treaty of Versailles, and no patriotic breast-beating. There seemed to be a little restlessness stirring in the crowd of boys. A smart-aleck behind me whispered, "It was Hitler who conquered France, not God." The principal went on to plead that it was upon us, the victors, to show magnanimity and mercy toward the conquered and to make not only peace but a good peace, one that would bury hatred and build friendship, a peace inspired by the Ten Commandments.

He was a mild-mannered person, imposing neither in stature nor demeanor, more of a fatherly chap, but, on this day, he spoke with unaccustomed determination and without a smile, looking over our heads as though he was facing somebody on the back wall and saying his piece straight to his face.

Even the conclusion of this patriotic observance was unusual. Instead of intoning the national anthem, and instead of having us raise our right arms in the Party's salute, he had us sing the hymn *Now thank ye all God*.

About Mice, Storks, and Bulls

Uncle Siegfried, on whose farm we spent many an enjoyable summer vacation, was very fond of Friedrich.

As usual, cousin Karl-Hermann had picked us up at the small rural railway station, and the twenty-minute ride in the horse-drawn carriage back to the farm always had been a special treat for us. We would drive around the circular flower bed in front of the entrance, where Aunt Dora was already waiting, while the barking dog was fiercely pulling on his chain, and there was a special skill the way Karl-Hermann made the horses stop smartly, right smack in front of the doorstep.

Usually, Uncle Siegfried would be busy in the fields or, perhaps, emerge from the barn or cowhouse and cross the quadrangular farmyard to greet us. But this time he was already standing next to Aunt Dora. It was a special occasion—we brought good news from Friedrich after weeks of anxiously waiting.

He pulled me on his lap and listened intently to what Mother reported: Friedrich was alive, though wounded, had been released from a prisoner-of-war camp near Marseilles and would soon be returning to Germany.

Once Mother had completed her report and this matter had been discussed at length, it was Uncle Siegfried's turn to report. It became apparent that he was not that fond of Dieter, at least not just now. Dieter had arrived at the farm a week earlier, and there had been some unfortunate incidents.

The way I look at it now, Karl-Hermann and Dieter should have never been allowed to spend their time together. Individually quite manageable, they meant peril when in combination and left to their own devices. Years ago had had a stunt where they would catch a field mouse, tie one end of string to its leg, the other to the belt of their pants, and tuck the mouse into their pocket. Thus prepared, they would enter the large kitchen to let the mouse go, which would send the women-folk screaming. Then they would pull the mouse back in by the string and depart contentedly. Now, this time, it was not just a mouse; it was sacred fowl and big game.

For years, there had been no stork family nesting on the high, thatched barn roof. To the Pomeranian farmer, the stork on the barn is a must. They arrive in spring and raise a family. The young ones grow to become magnificent birds that learn to clatter with their beaks, and they leave in fall for warmer climates. When the storks didn't nest, it seemed as though there was something amiss with the farm, as though God was withholding his blessings. This was the first time after many years that the wagon-wheel-sized nest on Uncle Siegried's barn was occupied, and he was so happy that had he been a religious man, he would have uttered prayers of gratitude.

Karl-Hermann and Dieter, however, had discovered a stork problem and were overcome with the urge to solve it. They had noticed that one of the fledgling birds lacked the courage to depart from the nest. They felt a little encouragement would be helpful and decided to bring it about by throwing missiles at him. When it was all finished, the nest was no longer habitable for the accumulation of dried mud balls in it, the poor stork had been shot down, and the rest of the family had understandably left and was never seen again.

This accomplished, the two, armed with slingshots and suitable rocks, roamed about the farm in search of further targets. In the cowbarn, they came upon the bull. Now, this was no ordinary bull. He was a prize bull and had the size, the massive strength, the meanness, the prowess, and the ferocity that prize bulls are known for. In their malicious curiosity as to "what would happen," they elected to fire a rock at his testicles.

At this point of the narration, Uncle Siegfried was breathing heavily and his fists were clenched as he unforgivingly looked at my mother and informed her that this act had thrown the beast into such a murderous rage that nobody, not even the dairyman, had been able to enter the stable for the remainder of the day.

Turning Point of History?

AFTER THE END OF THE FRENCH CAMPAIGN, under circumstances few people were aware of or remember today, Europe came agonizingly close to an about-face at the edge of disaster, an opportunity that would never return.

A victory parade of German troops was to take place in Paris on July 27, 1940. There were men who thought this presented a tempting opportunity. Dr. Eugen Gerstenmaier was a theologian who, after serving as foreign affairs officer for the Evangelical Church, became an informations officer in the Foreign Office. In that capacity he joined the Resistance. Count von der Schulenburg, who as vice-president of the Berlin Police Department was involved in the aborted coup d'état of 1938, joined the Army in 1940. Together, Gerstenmaier and Schulenburg prepared for Hitler's assassination, or his arrest, at the Paris parade. At the same time, D. F. Stevenson, Director of Home Operations in the British Air Ministry, designed a plan to kill Hitler by bombing the parade.

At that time, the old Marshal Pétain headed the new French government, which resided in the spa town of Vichy. Having in mind a variety of pragmatic and quite progressive reasons, it desired to promote the conclusion of the war and therefore offered to the Germans its friendship and assistance in building a European cooperative system that would include other nations, if in return France were given the status of an equal and respected partner.[10] There were enthusiastic supporters of this French idea among high-ranking Germans, and there was indeed a realistic chance that the French proposal could have become a reality. If it had, the disaster of the next five years of war, and probably much of the Cold War during the subsequent forty-five years, would have been averted. What separated Europe and the world from that opportunity was one small item: a bullet.

Hitler's exit from the scene that summer or autumn would have changed everything. There would have been hardly anybody in the hierarchy of his party who was able to carry on the war or to sustain his so-called ideology.[11] His party friends were all fellow travelers; not one was highly respected by the people. The political Resistance, on the other hand, was chiefly based on the Army, against which Himmler's police, Gestapo, and Waffen-SS were no match. In 1940, the Army counted 4.37 million men, while the Waffen-SS had merely 125,000.[12] After Hitler's death, a military government would have been almost mandatory because of the on-going war. Such a government would have been recruited from the conservative members of the General Staff, most of whom were either active in the Resistance or in silent agreement with it. Thus, it would have largely reflected the Resistance's conservative and Christian values and philosophy. It would have led to a subsequent civilian government that was composed of members of the intellectual, social, and religious elite of the country, which had been kept in abeyance for so long. Such a government would have desired a quick and wise peace with France, one that was "inspired by the Ten Commandments", to use my high school principal's words, and would have found Pétain's offer one that was made to order. Britain, even under the belligerent Mr. Churchill, would have found little support at home or in the United States to continue a war against a de-Nazified Germany. A compromise peace with Britain would certainly have included restoration of Poland and of the Czech Republic. The Holocaust would not have occurred. The war would have lasted no longer than one year. The idea of a European Common Market would have emerged then instead of in the 1950s, and other countries would have been anxious to join. In the absence of an exhausting European war, Japan would have had little encouragement to tackle the United States in the Pacific. Unless the Soviet Union started a war, Europe and the world likely would have enjoyed a peaceful period for decades.

The flow of history's violent forces passed through a temporary stage in 1940, where the throwing of a switch determined whether it steered into disaster or away from it. It is astonishing to realize that, here as in other pivotal historical road-crossings, the throwing of that switch meant no more than the presence or absence of one single person. Few are the men who, through their charisma, demagogic radiance, intellectual authority, and willpower, have the ability to master the minds of millions and, thereby, direct the course of history onto the road of madness and disaster. Far beyond being leaders, they are magic prophets of fervor and fanaticism, who gain control of the media and deploy their private army of obedient disciples to herd the masses. We know several of them: Lenin, Stalin, Mao Zedong, and Pol Pot. After they have left, some of their ideas may linger, but most of their magic power is gone. They are like an anesthetic; when it is turned off, the patient wakes up. Regardless of their far-flung organizations and fan clubs, they are one-man shows. Hitler was a perfect example. There was nobody in his political movement to inspire the masses or to carry on his game. He, too, was a one-man show.

Mr. Stevenson's proposal to kill Hitler from the air was not approved because of the anticipated strength of German aerial defenses. The German victory parade, on the other hand, was canceled for fear of air raids and other reasons. The assassination did not take place. History failed to turn.

Look at That Sword!

FRIEDRICH HAD PRACTICALLY RECOVERED from the bullet wound penetrating his right shoulder by the time he returned from France. He had happily bounced through the door, and with a big, indulgent smile he had allowed Mother to embrace him. The many nights of anguish and fear that she had spent during the weeks when he was missing-in-action were reflected in the way she held on to him, not letting go of him for a long time. And when he then sat down at the piano, proudly playing the simple tune of the "Merry Peasant" as though it was a march of triumph in his own honor, we all felt a bit choked, and Gila's eyes were flooded.

Now a second lieutenant, he was the proudest sight I had ever laid eyes on. I can still see myself standing in my diminutive chamber, which he was now using when home on furlough, and admiring his uniform. It was suspended on a hanger from the top of my toy cabinet: top grade fabric, a smooth gray-green, custom-tailored, a neat row of silvery buttons down the front, the officer's shoulder straps, and the Iron Cross 2nd Class and other medals. And there was his short, ornate, silvery sword, about fifteen inches long that would dangle horizontally by his left hip when he wore it, sword knot and all.

On the floor were his jackboots. I had polished them for him. I always did when he came home, every day. Ten Pfennigs a shine.

Very soon now, Dieter, having graduated from high school, was due to leave our home as well in order to commence basic training in Stargard.

He was so fortunate, I thought enviously. He was old enough.

Tit for Tat

In August of 1940, the air war with Britain accelerated. There were two kinds of air raids. The term "terror raids" referred to Royal Air Force attacks on German cities, whereas air raids carried out by the *Luftwaffe* upon Britain were named "retaliation raids." The British visited the city of Berlin every night now. By the same token, we bombed their cities and fought tremendous air battles with their fighter planes over their island and the English Channel.

The boys in school eagerly followed the exciting events. There was no one who did not know all the different types of planes. There was a contest in diagnosing the make of the plane by the sound of its engines long before one could see it, and we were up to date on the latest score of enemy planes downed by our fighter pilots. Our English teacher cleverly used our latest fad for his own purposes. He had us write a composition about the air battles in English, phrased as if it was a newspaper report. My paper was three pages long and was illustrated with photographs of Stukas and Messerschmitt-109s. "Our brave fighter pilots are shooting down many Spitfires and Hurricanes," I wrote. It turned out to be an admirable masterpiece of an account written with all the enthusiasm of an eleven-year-old patriot.

As the weeks passed by, the optimistic spirit, at least of my parents, seemed to change into one tinged with worry and bitterness. Initially, there was general hope that Mr. Churchill's recalcitrance would be swayed by his witnessing of the heavy damage inflicted from the air. A little more bombing, and surely he would make peace. As that hope faded, the next chance seemed to be the invasion of their island and to enforce our desire to make peace. With the new blitzkrieg method that would hopefully be accomplished before winter, and our soldiers could be home for Christmas. But then, the fear that the few ships of our young Navy would not suffice for such a major operation proved to be true. The more important failure of the *Luftwaffe* to gain the upper hand against the Royal Air Force was not known to us then. No invasion was attempted, and the dream of peace escaped into the mist of an uncertain future.

October passed. In November, the *Luftwaffe* inflicted more grievous damage on Coventry than any city had suffered so far. To all appearances, such an attack upon an industrial English city was no more than a tit-for-tat for the British attacks on the cities of the German Ruhr basin. But I also suspect such escalation of the bombing war on large population centers to express a vexing frustration and to have been a desperate attempt to force Britain to the negotiating table, so as to end the war that was serving neither side.

Then again, there was *Reichsmarschall* Göring, whose *Luftwaffe* carried the load of waging war that autumn. My parents did not think the prominent role of this presumptuous man to be auspicious for peace. In a table pounding speech, and in a snide tone of voice, he had announced, *"Wir werden ihre Städte ausradieren* - We shall erase their cities."

Mother looked angrily at the radio. *"Ausradieren,"* she hissed, *"ja, ja, ausradieren*! Erase! That's him for you! That's all he can ever think of!"

The British and a Silent Request

The British usually showed up around 1:00 A.M. But the number of attacking bombers was small and so, even though the night was filled with the deafening din of flak fire, it was all bark and no bite. Soon we went outside, instead of in the air raid shelter that was located under our dining room. At least Dieter and I, if not joined by others, were standing in the darkness near the trash cans and the multi-purpose carpet rail, peaking past the walnut tree in the hopes of seeing one of the many search lights lock on to a Blenheim bomber or some other kind of excitement—perhaps one of them being blasted out of the sky, or something.

We never did. In fact, it became such a boring nuisance every night that before long most of us stayed in bed. The din and ruckus of the anti-aircraft guns would permit only fitful sleep, to be sure, and after all had turned quiet there would come, once again, the bone-piercing siren sounding the all-clear, but these disturbances were clearly preferable to getting up and sitting in the cellar.

The siren was close enough, having been mounted on the roof of the Jewish Home for the Blind.

One night, I had what one might call a religious experience. It was the only one of the kind I ever had and, hate as I may to admit it, full credit for it had to be given to our English cousins. I was lying awake in my chamber listening to the gunfire subside and as it gave way to only a distant rumble, I could hear one residual, steady, droning sound way up in the sky. Then, suddenly, something whistled through the silence and crescendoed into an unexpectedly loud explosion. It scared the devil out of me. I quickly folded my hands in prayer and said, being very brief and to the point because of the urgency of the matter, "Dear Lord, please let him drop his other bombs elsewhere. Amen."

I had never really quite comprehended before what the pastor meant when he said that if you delivered yourself unto the Almighty God, you would experience an incomparable inner peace. But this, I felt, must undoubtedly have been what he meant. My prayer was followed by an instantaneous sense of relief, peace, and shelteredness. I rolled over—to the left, I remember, facing the wall—and soon fell asleep.

THE PROS AND CONS OF AIR RAIDS

The significance of air raids is relative; it depends on circumstances and viewpoints. From my viewpoint, air raids were useful and desirable and, on certain days, virtually indispensable.

For one thing, there was the shrapnel contest. We all carried in our bookcases a cigar box that served as receptacles for the shrapnels that we gathered from the streets and sidewalks on the way to and from school. In the classrooms, in the hallways, and on the school yard one would see the boys holding their open cigar boxes, bragging about having the most or the biggest, or laying them out in blocks or rows to verify the latest count. There was an unbelievable variety of shapes and sizes, and I remember it as such a captivating, even addictive sport that if there were another war, it is quite possible I would start a new shrapnel collection. Actually, however, this has also been one of my more painful memories because I trailed so far behind. Several boys had well over two hundred each while I, last I recall, had no more than forty-seven.

The indispensable nature of air raids arose from the strictness of German schools and our heavy load of homework. It soon became evident that assignments requested for the first two periods did not have to be completed because the 8:00 to 10:00 A.M. classes were routinely canceled after air raids. The British were, however, not totally reliable and took a holiday now and then. As a consequence, without any doubt, there were school children in Berlin who prayed to heaven for the British to come and others who went to school on some mornings, angrily scolding them for their failure to show up.

Early in the war, most of us youngsters enjoyed the air war as if it was an exciting adventure.

THE DECISION

LATE IN SUMMER IN THE YEAR 1940, a most astonishing decision was made. It raised the stakes of the war a hundredfold. The regional war, started by Germany over the Polish Corridor, which was instantly turned into a European war by the entry of Britain and France, was advanced by this decision into a full-fledged world war.

The military hostilities had reached a stalemate. Germany lacked the naval and air power to invade Britain, and Britain, in turn, was even less able to defeat Germany. Neither Hitler nor the

German people—though for different reasons—had any interest in continuing it. Hitler advanced an "appeal to reason". He asked Great Britain to make peace. It was to be an easy peace. Except for the return of the German colonies (which would have turned out to be a regrettable development), there was no intention to diminish the British Empire. Britain's only loss was to be the recognition that Hitler had achieved preeminence on the continent and that he needed a "free hand" in the East.

To reject the peace offer would maneuver Britain into a perilous position. Hers had been a declining empire since before the First World War.[13] In order to sustain and defend herself she needed imports of both food and weapons. Her treasury was approaching the point of bankruptcy. Her colonies and dominions were beset by their own problems and were too far away to provide help. The only available source of the necessary amount of assistance was North America, and even if that source could be tapped, she still lacked the funds to pay for it. The merciless naval blockade by German U-boats rendered the successful transfer of substantial quantities of goods across the Atlantic Ocean unlikely. The idea of a supply program based on what must have looked like a delirious assumption, namely that America would produce transport ships and cargo faster than the U-boats were able to sink, meant to accept an insane loss of human lives and material. It would have been extraordinarily optimistic to expect the American people to agree to it. Besides, they were isolationists and determined to stay out of the war.

Furthermore, the support required would be enormous. It would include the mobilization and transfer of a huge American army that, together with the smaller British forces, could venture to face the German Wehrmacht, which, at that time, was believed to be nearly invincible. None of this could even be conceived unless three fundamental tasks were accomplished first. It was necessary to infuriate the pacifistic American mind, to retool America's huge peacetime industrial complex for the production of massive quantities of arms, ships, and planes, and to train, equip, and deploy immense military forces for offensive warfare on the land, on the seas, and in the air.

Adding to the stunning magnitude of such tasks was yet another prohibitive prospect, namely the prolongation of the war by many years and the corresponding escalation of losses in lives and property. It would take an immense amount of time for all of these preparations to be achieved and, after that, to fight a victorious war. The United States would have to start from scratch. She did not even have compulsory conscription. Two or three years would elapse before newly established American forces could go into action. For all that time, Britain would have had to wage war alone without starving, tiring, or making peace. The actual final campaign of invading the Continent and defeating Germany's formidable armed forces would require another two or three years. Furthermore, beyond all these enormous and perhaps even unfeasible preparations and sacrifices, there was still no guarantee of ultimate victory. The financial waste, material devastation, and loss of human life would be incalculable. World War I was still on everyone's mind. Its millions of cripples, widows, and orphans still walked the streets. That four-year war had caused 8.5 million combat deaths, and many more perished from hunger and disease. Another war of that scale, lasting even up to six years and ravaging the lands with technology much more devastating, would surely claim ten million lives, or twenty, if not even more.

That fear was real and burdened people's minds as a deep concern. At the Sudeten Crisis, two years previously, the French physician and novelist, Louis-Ferdinand Céline, expressed the fear that another war would create twenty-five million casualties and would bring about "the end of the breed".[14] And when the eve of D-day finally arrived in 1944, Churchill was downcast in profound fear and expressed the same apprehension. D.R. Goodwin writes:[15]

> Unable to purge himself of his abiding fear that catastrophe could accompany a direct assault on the Continent he told Lord Moran that he believed 'man might destroy man and wipe out civilization'. Europe would be left desolate and he would be held responsible.

A monstrous death toll and devastation were predictable in

1940 by anyone imagining the entry of the United States into the war, even without the knowledge of the involvement of the Soviet Union, of Japan, and of the atomic bomb.

In 1940, the consideration of this scenario must have rendered the alternative of concluding a non-vindictive, compromise peace with Germany very attractive. It fell upon Winston Churchill to decide for one or the other course, and so he did. After the American President had been re-elected in November, Churchill proposed his thoughts to him. No persuasion was needed, however, for the President had already made up his own mind months before. Their unanimous decision was that this perilous hour left no choice but to accept the sacrifices, no matter how great, of a war without parallel in history.

If one had questioned a German citizen that autumn about his reaction, he would have appeared both somber and bewildered. He would have been sadly disappointed about the undesired war going on while its pursuit was in no one's interest. He also would have confessed his mystification about the origin of so much hostility against his country, this time and in the previous war as well. He even might have shown incomprehension about the purpose of the war and wondered how the issue of Danzig and the treatment of Germans in Poland could possibly escalate into a world war within the short time span of a few months. Then again, he likely would have shrugged his shoulders in resignation and referred to the United States' declaration of war in World War I against Germany in order to rescue the Allies. It should not surprise anyone, he might have said, if America would do it again.

THE RESULTS

In consequence of Churchill and Roosevelt's decision, peace was not concluded in 1940 but five years later. The six-year war left the World prostrate. The Soviet Union's victory made it one of the world's two superpowers. The Soviet ideology and tyrannical might overwhelmed much of eastern Asia, and it's belligerent metastases spread to many countries around the globe. Europe's largest country, Germany, heretofore its only creditable barrier against the Red Empire, was ruined, dismembered, and emasculated. The eastern European satellite countries, the home of about 125 million people, at that time equaling 83 percent of the population of the United States, was subjugated and forced to idolize the hated god in the Kremlin. The same, no less, continued to be true for most of the two hundred million people living within the Soviet Union. The peace of 1945 was followed by nearly forty-five years of Cold War. Nuclear confrontation was a new, blood-chilling phenomenon and led to the concept of "mutual assured annihilation". For more than a generation, an armaments race devoured the fruits of people's work on both sides of the global divide. Murderous wars were fought in Korea and Vietnam, and the four wars Israel fought for its very existence were unlikely to have occurred without the East-West conflict. The insanity of ideological fanaticism degenerated into the killing fields in Laos. All of this was the outflow of Stalin's victory of 1945, which promoted the unrestricted spread of the communist epidemic.

If we were able to speak to Mr. Churchill and Mr. Roosevelt today, we might point out to them that something went wrong with their plans of 1940 and with their victory in 1945. Churchill would likely answer that he was aware of that fact early on, and that is the reason why he titled his book about the end of the Second World War "Triumph and Tragedy". They might agree with us that this kind of outcome was unexpected and undesired. They would probably say it with the chagrin of a surgeon whose patient suffered from life-threatening complications after a magnificent operation. They might explain that, like everybody else, they chiefly looked after the interest of their own countries rather than after those of the European Continent. With an embarrassment for which he was not otherwise known, Roosevelt might add that in those days his knowledge of the European Continent, its geography, people, and problems was limited. They might also understandably state that, based on the facts available to them in 1940, they had no other choice but to launch into another five years of war.

The conclusion of such a review will most likely confirm the correctness of their actions, no matter their ill aftereffects. But there might also be a minority opinion disapproving of their lack to rec-ognize the fact that Europe was suffering not from one, but rather from two raging cancers, and that the elimination of one cancer and the preservation of the other was inevitably a prescription for disaster—ask a surgeon. Who knows, having been men of good will and sound intelligence, they might even agree with us today in that retrospective diagnosis.

Was there, really, an acceptable alternative to their decision to prolong the war by several years? After all, a patient suffering from two simultaneous cancers is in dire straits. Quite likely, there is no cure for him in the first place. There seem to be only two pos-sible answers that have some degree of realism: (1) they should have accepted Chamberlain's 1939 opinion, which was to let the predictable and inevitable war between Germany and the Soviet Union occur without interference and to keep the western powers out of it. This would have allowed the two devils to slaughter one another and would have—if God were willing to help a little—protected the other European countries against their aggression. (2) If that advice was not followed, then Britain could have made peace in 1940 so as to allow Hitler to attack Stalin unimpeded and again, for Britain and the United States not to interfere so as to achieve the same ultimate outcome.

Such alternatives are not likely to hold up in serious debate. They are perhaps only chin-stroking ruminations about hypothetically substituting the tragic outcome of that war with one that was a little less objectionable. We will never know how the world would have fared if Churchill had been willing to make peace in 1940. How much subjugation and disaster would Hitler have inflicted upon the people of Eastern Europe? Would he have been assassinated by the German Resistance and if so, how soon? Would the Holocaust have occurred? Would there have ensued a Cold War, or actual military conflicts, or a nuclear confrontation? However that might be, even in spite of a peace concluded in 1940, the prognosis would still have been unfavorable. There was no established court that could have aided in sorting out the differ-ences dividing the European nations, in punishing the guilty, and in relieving mutual fears. On the contrary, there continued to be a deluge of uncontrolled dread and phobias in the world, and mankind had not yet learned to control those treacherous dangers that hide in the wrath-of-the-just and which rest on its holy fervor, its passionate and exaggerated denunciations, and its punitive suspension of moral taboos. Have we learned it since?

COUNTRY IDYLL

DURING THE FALL VACATION OF 1940, I spent another week or two in the hospitality of the Wallersbrunn farm. Dieter and Gila were already there while, for whatever reason, our parents remained in Berlin. I was considered old enough to travel alone and was proud of my independence.

On the train, I eavesdropped on an unexpected conversation. The train stopped in every country town and at numerous rural stations, as it was chiefly used by local folks for commuting trips. I was sitting in one of those duplex compartments, where one can hear the conversations on the other side of the partition without seeing the speakers.

A farmer boarded the other half of the compartment and found himself among old acquaintances. I heard one of them welcome him back and then ask him for the reason of his return. As it turned out, this man had taken advantage of the government offer to settle in the Province of Posen by taking possession of a farm previously owned by a Polish farmer. At this point, it was the policy of the German government to make it 100 percent German by expelling the Poles and replacing them with German settlers. For the poor among German country folk, this was a tempting opportunity to better themselves.

I listened with growing amazement to what seemed to be a remarkably bold conversation. What the man said amounted to a fearless criticism of government policy, and he wasn't even lowering his voice, let alone looking around the partition to check who was listening.

"I couldn't take it," he said and went on to describe how he had moved into a house and farm, where every clothes hook, saw horse, pitch fork, or children's swing that hung from the tree told him about the family that had lived there before. Whatever items he found left behind had obviously belonged to someone else; someone who was a farmer just like himself, and with whom he felt a common bond. Speaking as he did in the Low German dialect, it felt as though I was listening to the "common man," or to the soul of the people. The conversation ended when one of them got off at the next stop.

I was eleven years old then, a marvelous age when the mind is wide open to absorb all the new impressions of life—beautiful ones to enjoy, strange ones to wonder about, and some of them merely to store away for the moment perhaps to be forgotten or to be retrieved and wondered about in some distant future. One of them was this Mecklenburg peasant who spoke so freely on the train.

I think it was Dieter who picked me up at the train station in the country town of Teterow.

Before his return to Berlin a day or two later, Dieter told me about that mishap with the motorcycle. It had happened down in the village where the farm laborers lived. Some geese had gotten in his way causing him to skid or something. Luckily, he only had a few scratches and Mr. von Wallersbrunn's motorcycle needed no major repairs either. It had been an embarrassing incident for him, though, and entrusting me with the story seemed to make him feel better about it. In spite of our age difference, we were almost becoming partners.

The elderly couple, the original owners, didn't live there any longer. They had moved away to live in Hungary, I was told. What an odd place to choose, I thought. Why didn't they stay on this beautiful estate? It would have been disrespectful for me to question what adults were doing and, so, I left it at that. It didn't concern me anyway, except that by now I knew that they were Jewish, and to me their quiet departure was much like that of the Rosenbergs.

I have very pleasant memories of that vacation. Much like Wisconsin, the province of Mecklenburg is end moraine country and is sculpted by the glaciers of the ice age. It is a potpourri of hills, knolls, rocky outcroppings, farms, forests, wetlands, and numerous lakes, large and small. Blue bachelor buttons and crimson poppies at the edge of ripening corn fields are part of the scenery as much as the song of the larks, the "keewit" of the swallows, and the clatter of the storks on top of the barns.

Gila and I would take the young Wallersbrunn daughter for strolls through the fields. One particular stroll, a walk along a trail through a forest of young birches, remains a fond memory. There were farm tasks for me, too. One day, it is hard to believe, I was asked to take a horse-drawn wagon to pick something up—I have forgotten what it was—and bring it back to the farm from a half a mile away, all by myself. I had never handled a horse before.

And one evening, at dusk, Mr. von Wallersbrunn took me along hunting. We walked in total silence through the fields at dusk and climbed up one of those hunting high stands at the edge of a forest waiting for deer to come out and graze or, instead perhaps, a wild boar. Once I coughed and he whispered a reprimand. Perhaps I chased them away; in any event, he did not shoot any prey that night.

And yes, there is another thought in my mind attached to that autumn vacation, one that did not occur to me until many years later. An afterthought, really. It's about Hungary. You see, Hungary was no sanctuary for that old Jewish couple either. As we know today, they were doomed there as well. But then, among those who had enjoyed the idyllic Wallersbrunn estate, they were not the only ones who were.

Pinching Mosquitoes

Molly and I were sitting on the top rung of the carpet rail and were shooting the breeze. Her straightforward way of thinking had produced a disagreement with her father. She said, "I asked him, 'But Dad, how are you going to do that? These Poles have always lived there. It's their home! It surely wouldn't be right for us to just walk in there and throw them out on the barnyard and tell them to beat it, would it?' And do you know what his answer was, Peter? He said, 'Now look, Gerda, if a mosquito bites you and you pinch it between your fingers," she brought up her hand and demonstrated the pinching between two fingers, "then you're not concerned about that mosquito either, are you now?"

Molly stared at me quizzically, as if to say, "Can you believe he said that?"

Before the passions of this war had finally calmed, millions and millions of people—rural and city-folk alike, young and old, people like you and me—were to be uprooted and tossed out of their ancestral lands in self-righteous or vengeful anger, or bombed into oblivion in gigantic air assaults on their cities, or annihilated in gas chambers, or banned to the Gulag never to be heard from again. All of this was done to human beings as if they were mosquitoes unworthy of moral concern. It was as if the warring nations were trying to outdo one another in this macabre contest, and it is not at all certain who ended up winning top prize.

As Molly and I were talking about it on the carpet-beating rail, little did we know that the pinching of human mosquitoes had just barely begun.

LETTERS[16]

Jan. 7, 1941

My dear Dieterchen,

Today we received your post card... The same night when you left, Friedrich arrived. It was 3:00 A.M. when he rang the doorbell... His furlough is for a fortnight. Too bad you two missed each other... With all the snowdrifts, whoever is able to should stay at home... We are thinking so much of you, my Dieterchen... Hope you will soon receive our package, so you remain strong.

Mom

February 5, 1941

My dear Dieterchen,

Thanks for the cigars... How was your inspection?... And you are the leader of the choir! Well, have fun, you don't know how much longer you can enjoy this peaceful quiet. It is safe to assume that no later than four weeks from now the war will start again somewhere, perhaps in Greece. And nobody knows whether you won't be involved. So, take advantage of your time so long as you still can. Horace said, "Carpe diem." Enjoy (actually pluck) the day. I had better translate that for you, in case you can't...

Daddy

February 25, 1941

Dear Dieter,

Many, many thanks for the two marks. It arrived promptly on the morning of my birthday... I got a torpedo boat, the cruiser "*Leipzig*" and the vest pocket battleship

"Deutschland," a photo album, a terrific pocketknife...

Peter

Dear Dieter,

We have now learned how to do the Viennese Waltz. Boy, is that terrific! The other day, we had to do fifty-five turns without stopping. At the end we collapsed into the nearest chairs..

Gila

My dear Dieterchen,

Your forthcoming birthday is causing much head scratching... It is difficult to buy anything these days. You were supposed to get a cake from me, my Dieterchen, but a fruitcake, which you like best, is impossible because it won't keep. The same is true for the traditional butter cream torte. But some day there will be peace again! It looks like the U-boat warfare is really taking off now! We hope it will be successful. Daddy, who usually has been pessimistic, has now become quite an optimist. Well, we'll have to wait and see.

Mom

My dear Boy,

I am placing the greatest hope in the U-boats... Three months of that should finish the British. If, in addition, by then our land forces have reached the Suez Canal and perhaps also Gibraltar, then the Englishman is out of options and can no longer stop us from crossing over to England. I am very optimistic. Say hello to Friedrich!...

Daddy

February 28, 1941

My dear Dieterchen,

So now, my dear boy, my very very best wishes for your birthday, your first one away from home. I wonder whether your thoughts might wander back to when you were little, when (on the eve of your birthdays) you fell asleep with your little heart so full of anticipation, or to your more recent birthdays here at home. Our greatest wish is, of course, that during this next year nothing may "happen" to you, that you make it through the war intact and return to us in good health. And then, of course, we wish you success in your career and that you'll soon be promoted corporal and then get your commission so that you no longer have to address your big brother with "lieutenant, sir!"...but if you have a moment send your thoughts home to us as our thoughts will be with you the whole day.

And now once more, *mein lieber guter Junge*, our innermost wishes. Remain the fine and decent fellow and comrade that you are today. Preserve your ideals. Being thirty years older than you, I can assure you that it is indeed possible to preserve one's ideals. I have weathered many a storm myself and my own ideals have survived undiminished.

Daddy

March 9, 1941

My good Dieterchen,

I wonder whether you and Friedrich might have spent another nice weekend together today and yesterday. Perhaps you already celebrated your birthday?... I guess you know how much we are thinking of you and talking about you. Our great and silent wish is that you remain well through the next year and be protected against all dangers!... May it become a beautiful year with many happy hours for you! These are life's most beautiful years! Hopefully your days as a soldier will gradually become easier, and it is good that Friedrich is near you. For us, it is reassuring to know that the two of you are together. Only, both of you must never act rashly, such as when trying to help one another. But what good are all my words and worries? We can only ask that God be with you two and hope that our good and loving thoughts will somehow help you both. In my thoughts, I take you in my arms, my darling, the way I always have on your birthday and tell you of all my love, and all the wishes that fill my heart for my good Dieterchen.

This week, Daddy and I went to see "Gregory and

Henry". Paul Wegener's role (as the Pope) was fantastic. The other actors were also grand, and the stage set was very good. From start to finish, it was a wonderful evening. Afterwards, we wanted to eat dinner at the Adlon where one can still buy a decent meal—fish or something—for affordable prices... Unfortunately, I had forgotten to take along our ration cards...so we had to abandon the idea. But we'll do it another day. I was in the Philharmonic, too, for a very beautiful concert! For my taste, the Philharmonic is still tops, no matter how good other orchestras may be. Originally, this concert was supposed to be conducted by Furtwängler but he was prevented by a skiing accident and so Clemens Kraus, whose conducting was also wonderful, replaced him.

For the rest, we're doing well. Peter finished his plane today and suspended it in his room... Gisela is repairing runs in her stockings at present, something she has become quite adept at. Tomorrow she will have another dancing lesson. Today she went to see the film "Wedding Night," but then didn't. I guess they didn't let her in. I didn't forbid her to go because she would have gone to see it secretly. I heard it doesn't have much of a plot anyway. Are they giving you enough to eat, *mein Junging?*... By the way, your skis have arrived, so you needn't worry about them. Now many loving kisses, my darling!

Mom

Victorious Spring

My chamber in our apartment must have been the smallest one in the world. To use Dieter's words, "When you close the door behind you, you are looking out the window." It was just barely long enough for the bed. But it was my kingdom. A two-shelf bookcase stood on the chest of drawers. There were several of my favorite books, like the trappers-and-Indians adventures narrated by an author named Karl May, undoubtedly the favorite reading of every boy in those days. Also, I inherited *"Huckleberry Finn"* and *"Leather*

Stocking" from my brothers, and a bible was there, too. At one time, I started to read it but never got very far. The language was so stilted, and most of it was mysterious. What was so wrong about eating an apple? I went back to Karl May.

Suspended from the ceiling was the Me-109 fighter plane I had constructed, off to one side halfway over the books, so it wouldn't hit your head. My real treasure, though, were those marvelous toy ship models die-cast of some metal alloy. The catalogue displayed every ship of the German Navy and many of the British and French Navies as well. A destroyer was about three inches long and a battleship was about eight inches, the way I remember. They were rich in detail and you could turn the gun turrets. I had accumulated quite a fleet, including the two battleships *"Scharnhorst"* and *"Gneisenau"*. Of course, in real life they were small by international standards, displacing only 26,000 tons. But we had just completed our first real battleship of the 35,000-ton size, the way other countries had them. It was the *"Bismarck,"* and a sister ship, the *"Tirpitz,"* was soon to follow. As soon as they were available in model size, I would try to get them.

It was an exciting spring. Our U-boats, now ganging up in wolf packs, were sinking several 100,000 tons worth of enemy vessels every month. Then, in March, a marvelous military campaign began in the Libyan Desert where the British had nearly forced the Italian forces to surrender. The commander, Gen. Erwin Rommel, quickly became a household name and a national hero as the *Afrika-Korps* recaptured Benghasi and Tobruk and stormed on to the Egyptian border in the direction of the Suez Canal.

Simultaneously, our troops invaded Greece to evict the British forces installed there. They had sixty thousand men in Northern Greece and more on the island of Crete. This was another campaign, which they had forced on us, just like the one in Norway. According to the news reports, they were trying to get to us via "the soft underbelly of Europe". In addition, everyone knew there was another reason. Mussolini had unnecessarily stirred up trouble in the Balkans, a restless area that we had wanted to keep quiet and peaceful, by having his Italian Army occupy Albania and then declaring war on Greece. He was certainly not a desirable comrade-in-arms, *IL Duce*, as he was heading for defeat both in Libya and Greece and was forcing us to step in to rescue him. Somehow, Yugoslavia had to be invaded by us too because the British supposedly had been instigating mischief there as well. I am not certain the public fully understood the reasoning behind that invasion. Instead, this war had developed into a raging wild-fire, that one watched helplessly and it was anybody's guess why it spread in one direction or another. At any rate, once again, these were rapid two-week engagements, and the British were unceremoniously ejected from the Continent. To me, there was also a certain romantic element about it all to think that our brave troops, many of whom had before never left their home towns, now were able to visit the Acropolis and all the other ancient sites. People were talking about events and men I had hardly ever heard of before, such as the Battles of Thermopylae and Salamis, as well as ancient leaders such as Xerxes, Leonidas, and Themistocles.

As if that was not enough, four weeks later there followed not one, but two magnificent victories all at the same time. Our splendid new battleship, the *"Bismarck,"* my most favorite ship in the world, had encountered the British battle cruiser *"Hood"* and after a short battle had sunk her. Meanwhile, our paratroopers, in a reckless and death-defying attack, had landed on the island of Crete and in only a few days had defeated the much superior British forces supported by the Royal Navy. It was the first airborne campaign in history, and the immense daring and valor of the Airborne Division was breathtaking.

It was an intoxicating season, that spring of 1941. We celebrated victories and gallantries on the high seas, in Africa, in exotic Greece, and on the legendary Mediterranean island of Crete. Victories, victories, victories. The Suez Canal was probably next. One could see the light at the end of the tunnel. The English would stop their silly war and make peace.

There was only one painful reversal. Soon after the sinking of the "*Hood*," an RAF plane torpedoed the "*Bismarck*" and, hunted down by the British, she was scuttled on May 27.

Every night, as I went to bed and said my prayer, I had asked God to protect the "*Bismarck*" and its crew. Then I ceased in those efforts for I was forced to realize that my prayers had not been heard. As for the ship's model, I have never seen it. I think it was not for sale.

THE ONLY ESCAPE

AFTER CHURCHILL AND ROOSEVELT'S DECISION, there was another fateful one that was arrived at in the year 1940. This one was made by Hitler. He announced it to his generals on December 18. It was the decision to attack the Soviet Union.

When that massive campaign commenced on June 22, 1941, some people began to suspect that he was suffering from megalomania, and ever since, common judgment has been that the decision was a fatal blunder. Attention is, however, directed at two different judgments on the matter. Ponting expresses one;[17] Suvorov expresses the other.[18] Each points to Germany's fatal dilemma at that stage of the war and both, in a similar way, claiming that the assault on the Soviet Union, as desperate a gamble as it was, represented Germany's only chance of salvage.

There is no question that Hitler had been obsessed all along by the conviction that in order to safeguard Germany's food supply, he had to conquer large parts of Eastern Europe. Simultaneously, in order to protect civilized mankind, he had to annihilate the "Jewish-Bolshevik" empire. Had Britain made peace in 1940 and had the German Resistance not killed him in the meantime, he most certainly still would have pounced upon Stalin's empire in 1941, based on this obsession alone.

Yet, by the end of 1940, the pieces on the international chessboard had moved into a constellation that, in a most foreboding and urgent way, forced him into an attack on Russia, even if that had otherwise not been his intention.

To follow Ponting's line of thought, Churchill's recalcitrance not to make peace betrayed his reliance upon the military support of the United States, a notion validated by President Roosevelt's actions. While Germany's prospect of having to face the full power of the United States was calamitous in itself, it was made even more perilous by Stalin's recent expansionism in the east. The Red Army had rebuilt its strength since autumn of 1939, and Stalin had taken advantage of Hitler's preoccupation in Western Europe to send the Red Army to make huge territorial acquisitions from Finland to Rumania. His latest request, proposed by Foreign Commissar Molotov in November of 1940, was the further addition of Bulgaria and Turkey to the Soviet sphere of influence. After exhibiting such astounding imperialism, Stalin's future actions were easy to predict. Once Germany was engaged in war against the United States and Britain—an event expected by the end of 1942 or soon thereafter—it was to be anticipated that Stalin would repeat what he had just done in Poland: he would claim his share by moving in from the east. Germany would then be caught in the dreadful nightmare of a two-front war again, as she had been a generation before. Now there existed only one conceivable escape, and that was, if you will, a Schlieffen Plan in reverse. The two-year delay, required for the mobilization of America's military-industrial might, offered the chance of a preemptive and victorious strike against the Soviet Union. According to this way of thinking, Hitler's failure to execute such campaign would have led inexorably to Germany's destruction and the subjugation of large parts, if not all, of Europe by the Bolsheviks.

Suvorov's reasoning is much more direct, factual, and indeed chilling. It regards the German attack as a last minute, desperate strike to escape impending disaster.

In June of 1941, so he argues, Stalin was in the final stages of preparing for a devastating assault upon Hitler's realm. In the two years between the summer of 1939, the end of the Great Purges, and the summer of 1941, he had recreated the badly decimated Soviet armed forces on an unprecedented scale. Where Hitler based his blitzkrieg method on four panzer groups, each counting between six hundred and one thousand tanks, the Soviets had sixteen assault armies, everyone having between one thousand and twenty five hundred tanks. Recently published World War II statistics confirm this immense degree of Soviet superiority (Fig. 2). The westward movement of this unparalleled mass of armed forces to the border began in February of 1941, and in April and May it reached enormous dimensions. Hundreds of thousands of troops were moved from remote regions, such as the Volga, the Urals, and the Caucasus, to the west. On June 13, final orders were issued for 191 divisions to assume their front-line positions, raising the gigantic mass of the Red Army that had poured to the border in the spring of 1941 to reach an accumulation of 247 divisions.

Fig. 2. Russian and German Armored Fighting Vehicle Strength and Front-line Combat Aircraft on the Eastern Front in June 1941:

	German	Russian
Tanks	3,671	28,800
Aircraft	2,130	8,100

From John Ellis, *World War II*, A Statistical Survey. Facts on File, Inc. New York, 1993, pp. 230, 233.

Suvorov believes that the completion of deployment was marked for July 10,[19] but that the surprise assault upon the Germans along the long front-line, from the Baltic to the Black Sea, was to be launched already four days before, on Sunday, July 6.[20] Hitler's sudden offensive on June 22 was said to have out-stripped Stalin's by literally two weeks.[21]

The envisioned military strategy, as evidenced in preceding maneuvers, was to conduct a surprise air attack. It was designed to have the vastly superior Soviet air force attack and destroy the *Luftwaffe* squadrons on the ground, followed by the landing of paratroopers and airborne corps on the German airfields and other strategic targets. Simultaneously, ground offensives, spearheaded by thousands of tanks, would penetrate the German lines and carry out what was called "operations in depth," a procedure not much different from Hitler's blitzkrieg. The superiority of the Red Army, in numbers and materiel, was nothing short of overwhelm-ing and was further aided by a Soviet air force, which, by then, would have acquired free reign in the skies. There is little doubt that the *Wehrmacht*, hit by surprise and with such overwhelming vehemence, would have quickly faced defeat.

In the first days of May 1941, the pro-German orientation of Soviet propaganda made an about turn. *Pravda* spoke of the suf-fering of the working people in European countries conquered by Hitler's imperialist forces, of their desire for peace, and of how they rightfully looked toward the Red Army as a bulwark of interna-tional peace. It is reasonable to assume that, as Stalin's forces would pour into Central Europe, the working people in country-after-country were expected to request liberation by the Red Army, quite possibly all the way to Gibraltar. No request would have been closer to Stalin's heart. In his 1938 book, *History of the Communist Party of the Soviet Union, a Brief Instructional Course*,[22] he had stated that the struggle against capitalist encirclement would be contin-ued until the last country on earth had become a republic within the Union of the Socialist Soviet Republics.

An essential aspect of Stalin's strategy, as seen by Suvorov, was a massive attack on what was in fact Hitler's Achilles heel. It was located in an area within Stalin's easy reach.   Germany's apparently invincible *Wehrmacht* could be asphyxiated within a brief period of warfare if the Red Army seized the Rumanian oil fields at Ploiesti. Rumania and Ploiesti were for Stalin what Norway and Narvik had been for the British. After the Soviet Union had annexed Bessarabia from Rumania in the summer of 1940, Ploiesti was located merely 180 kilometers from the Russian border. Deployed at that very border was Stalin's most powerful striking force, his Ninth Army. It was staffed by elite officers, had the latest types of weapons including tanks and planes, numbered 250,000 men, and its 3,341 tanks were just about equal to all the tanks the entire German *Wehrmacht* possessed. Had that army been given the chance of launching its surprise attack, Hitler's victorious war would have suffered sudden death in Rumania.

One can of course argue that Stalin had no choice but to mobilize his forces in view of an expected German invasion. It is also not unreasonable to say that, since offense is the best defense, a Soviet surprise attack on the Germans was mandatory. However, that argument was, of course, valid for both sides. If that was so, then the mutual fear and threat left neither Stalin nor Hitler any choice but to launch that murderous campaign. The vital question, then, was not whether to attack, but who threw the first punch.

Had Stalin had that chance, we all would have been at the Kremlin's feet, and for many decades we would have been forced to pay homage to the new prophet—all of us, from Belfast to Jerusalem and from Gibraltar to Helsinki. It did not happen, according to Suvorov, because Hitler beat Stalin to the punch, and hence the Red Dictator ended up conquering only half of Europe.

If one considers this interpretation to be correct, then the judgment, according to which Hitler's decision to attack the Soviet Union was a fatal blunder, is utterly mistaken. Rather, it was as if the Israelites and Philistines confronted one another on a field of battle once again. On June 22, 1941, David slung his rock before Goliath could slay him.

BITTER BRAVERY

If these were indeed Hitler's motivations, a public opinion survey in 1941 would have shown that the German citizens were unaware of most of them. That is to say, they had no idea that conquest and enslavement of Eastern Europe was their government's intention; they didn't know—and in fact, never knew—of Hitler's second and secret track of war in the pursuit of ethnic and racial cleansing; and none of them obviously realized that the eastern campaign was forced upon them by the emerging peril of America's entry into the war as described above. But they did indeed sense the chronic and growing menace emanating from Russia and were willing to be convinced by their leaders that this was a prudent time to deal with it.

If one had solicited their opinion about the war up to that point, they would have stated that the sole justification for it had been the protection of the suppressed German minority in Poland; that the war should have ended after the twenty-eight-day Polish campaign; that everything that happened afterwards—the campaigns in Norway, France, Belgium, the Netherlands, Luxembourg, the Balkans, and North Africa, and in the air and on the seas—was caused by the declaration of war by Britain and France with a minor contribution by Mussolini's Italy; and that since the end of the Polish campaign, Germany had been forced into a defensive war, which it neither caused nor wanted.

As of 22 June 1941, the psychology of the German people changed fundamentally. There was no doubt that Germany was now the attacker, but the attack was seen as a life-saving preemptive strike. Popular vision of Stalin and his godless empire evoked immense fear and abhorrence. His designs to enslave all of Europe, either by conquest or by revolution, and to spread Communism across the world, were no secrets. A cataclysmic conflict between East and West, between Bolshevism and European civilization, was believed to be threatening as soon as Stalin thought that his time to strike had come. A preemptive strike, at a time when Germany was strong and Stalin was still supposedly unprepared, was an irrefutable conclusion. In that sense, the attack resembled lancing a boil. It was a violent and ugly, but necessary and curative event.

At the same time, in popular view, it was a decision that was guaranteed to find worldwide approval. If there had ever been a war to please God and all of mankind and, in fact, the Russians themselves, this most certainly was that war. Far from being a vain self-deception, this was a conviction spread among people in many, if not in all European countries. It has been documented in the case of France and the Vatican, reflected in the volunteers from countries such as Norway and Belgium who fought side-by-side with the German troops on the Eastern Front, and seen in the photographs of Ukrainian women tossing flowers on the paths of the advancing German troops.

This intellectual and moral, perhaps even religious, approval of the attack on the USSR, however, represented only part of the German psychology in 1941 and afterwards. Much greater was an apprehension that was deep, awesome, and relentless. Soviet Russian power, in numbers, fanaticism, climate, and a never-ending territory, was known to be enormous. From one day to the next, the definition of the war had painfully changed. No longer was it a chivalrous contest with Britain fought with a mixture of righteous indignation and slam-bang bravado in a strife of rivalry. Rather, the war had turned into a grim and deadly struggle over the question of survival and doom. People knew that there was no way to make a compromise peace or to conclude a settlement, not with Stalin. Also, the light at the end of the tunnel—the light of peace—had disappeared. The Germans were not numerous enough to defeat the Reds all the way to the Pacific. Instead, a permanent defense line would have to be constructed and manned east of Moscow or perhaps in the Ural mountains, while in the west, further years of fighting and bloodletting would be necessary in defense against Britain and perhaps the United States.

In German eyes it was bewildering to watch the disaster unfold that had grown out of the just and human concern over the plight of the ethnic Germans in Poland. If there had been a chance to inquire about their opinion at that time, they would have complained of feeling like helpless creatures caught in the fury of a hurricane. The best they could do was to roll with the punches and to try to survive until the elements would somehow come to rest.

They were very brave, but it was a bitter kind of bravery. It was one that caused people to button up against the cold, against the Siberian chill that went straight through their bones. It was one that caused restless sleep. It was one of sadness, because bravery becomes heartbreaking when hope is fading.

Then again, they derived a measure of encouragement from the trust in the wisdom of their leader. He was entering his ninth year in power, and everything he had attempted in peacetime was crowned by success, while in war, he had led every military campaign to a breathtaking triumph.

COMBAT, HORSEPLAY, AND LOVE

FRIEDRICH AND DIETER WERE FIGHTING in the Center Section of the Eastern Front. Friedrich was wounded in the face and lost a tooth. This, we learned later, happened while "combing a forest". It was an action much hated because enemy soldiers would be lying on the ground playing dead and then turn around and shoot at close range. Both Friedrich and Dieter distinguished themselves and earned the Iron Cross for bravery. Friedrich, in addition, was listed in the Honor Roll of the German Army. In the battle near Smolensk, among the prisoners taken by their regiment, there was a celebrity: Stalin's son. These were restless and exciting times. Mother, meanwhile, woke up at night frequently. The boys mailed a brief note every day and if a day was missed, she was very still.

In the fall, Dieter returned home for further training as an officer candidate at a military school in Wünsdorf, south of Berlin, and so we saw much of him. We would always have a little horse-play, he and I. All I had to do was egg him on a little, and with the gentlest of all big brother smiles, he would submit to a wrestling or boxing match. It was violent enough that we'd always have to straighten out the carpets and the furniture at the conclusion.

Many times he would bring his friends along. We quickly grew awfully fond of them, and their visits were looked at as special occasions. There were three of them, Eben, Rasmus, and Dautwiz by their last names. All of them were bright, spirited, and well-mannered young men. Mother took them into her heart as though they were her own, but actually, all of us did, and the fondness was mutual. The way I remember, all three of them came from the country and their parents were landowners, if they did not indeed belong to the landed gentry. In fact, Eben's father had supposedly dropped the aristocratic "von" from his name as a voluntary concession to this age where, he felt, social privilege should be earned, not inherited. Hans-Günther Rasmus was a year or so older, and he had grown up in West Prussia—that province of mixed Polish and German population that had just been returned to Germany.

Whenever the grown-ups were speaking of the "elite" in those days, I was thinking of these three comrades of Dieter's. They were everything that I looked up to. They were handsome, athletic, well bred, respectful, and idealistic. They wore the uniform with patriotic pride. They were a dashing lot whom the girls adored. There was zest in their laughter. They were the cream of the crop. They were the best of our youth. In my eyes, they were the elite.

The expected quick victory over Russia did not materialize. No preparations for winter warfare had been made. A warm clothes drive for our troops was conducted, and Mother sewed an old sheepskin into a vest and mailed it along with other clothes to Friedrich who was back at the Eastern Front. The winter was brutal. It was forty degrees below zero in Russia.

Meanwhile, life at home retained many of its peacetime features. Gila continued to enjoy her dance lessons but was lovesick over a boy who did not return her feelings. Mother continued to go to the *Philharmonie* once a month during season. Sometimes she was even accompanied by Dad who would impishly express his puzzlement afterwards as to why the bows did not "all go up and down at the same time". Having turned twelve, I had entered the third year of high school and was struggling with Latin and Geometry.

About this time, Dieter rendered two quiet decisions from which I benefited in the short and long run. I had been approached to become a leader in the junior league of the Hitler Youth, so as to follow in the footsteps of my brothers. It filled me with pride and I was eager to oblige, but instead Dieter unceremoniously averted it. "Skip it; you're wasting your time," he said.

While this was of only minor significance, as our experience in that youth group was rather friendly and in no way radical or very ideological, his other decision was the source of decades of enjoyment. Every Thursday I traveled by streetcar and subway to Miss von der Heyde, my piano teacher. She was quite motherly and gave concerts at times, so I heard. But she was also a temperamental woman, and I feared that trip all week. There was, however, an easy solution: I would just discontinue taking piano lessons the way my brothers and sister had done. But when I approached Mother about my intention, she replied that Dieter had talked to her about it already. He had asked her to not let me stop; later on, I would be sorry I did. He had confessed to her his regret of having done so himself. Despite my disappointment, it was easy for me to acquiesce. To me, Dieter's advice was unchallengeable.

In November, Friedrich returned home for recuperation from a bullet wound to the skull. It was right on top of his head. The bullet got stuck in the bone and didn't injure the brain. It happened in a forest, east of Leningrad.

Son, I Says...

Mrs. Karg would usually be on her knees, washing the wide marble steps inside the large oaken entrance door, when Mother returned home from the market. The Kargs lived below us, in the Janitor's small basement apartment. Mr. Karg was an elderly man suffering from Parkinsonism, and he was believed to be a copious beer drinker. They had a son of Dieter's age whose name was Heinz.

Heinz Karg was a trained locksmith, but now he, too, was in the Army and out at the Eastern Front. Every young man was at the Eastern Front.

Mrs. Karg was a simple woman with limited schooling who had been poor all her life. She spoke with a thick, earthy Berlin dialect. She was also a lonesome woman, as her husband was well on his way into senility. In her chest, her heart was beating for Heinz; he was all she had.

She needed someone to talk to about Heinz, what he had written or said, where he was, and all those things, and she had taken to my mother. There was a human kinship between them that bridged all social barriers. "Did you have mail?" was an anxious question each would ask the other with a sense of urgency that renewed itself every single day.

She would usually omit the "good morning" or any other polite expression of initiating a conversation for fear of using the wrong form of address. As Mother shouldered her way through the heavy door holding a shopping net in each hand, Mrs. Karg would just straighten up on her knees and, never letting go of her scouring rag, would open the flood gates of her heart.

"*Der Junge sacht: 'Mutter,' sachter, 'du denkst viel an mir.' - 'Junge,' sach ick, 'ick kann nich' anders.' - Sachter: 'Mutter,' sachter, 'bezwing' dir doch.'*"

Inadequate as any attempt at translating dialect may be, this is what she said, "The boy says, 'Mother,' he says, 'you're thinkin' of me often.' - 'Son,' I says, 'I can't help it.' —Says he, 'Mother,' he says, 'gotta force yourself.'"

VIOLETS AND TULIPS

One day, we decided that the garden was in desperate need of help. To be a garden there had to be a lawn and flowers. There were several of us. Otmar Wagner, the boy from across the street, Molly, Maria, and Fiti, too, I am certain. Fiti—short for Friedrich—was Molly's little brother. He, too, was a late arrival in his family, the way I was, being ten years younger than she. Fiti was in on most everything I did, in and around the house. For years he played on the floor by my feet while I did my homework, and I suppose I was much more of a big brother to him than was Walter.

It was quite a project. At dusk we stole through neighboring properties, plucking off flowers and, adding them to some of the phlox and marguerites of our own, we made little bouquets, which we then sold to the tenants of our building. I fail to recall which one of us came up with this novel idea of earning money. Anyway, with the revenue thus collected, we bought flower bulbs and grass seed. We doggedly tilled the whole garden on our side of the building, raked and smoothed its surface, and landscaped everything with criss-crossing paths and with several circular flowerbeds in the center. I was in charge of the artistic design, I remember, but I also loved the feel and smell of the moist earth. On many an evening, I would stand by the dining room window looking out and admiring our handiwork. "That's the peasant blood in you," Mother said.

In the final stages of the project, as we were putting on the finishing touches, Molly and I were standing by the brick-mounted fence, just about where the Easter Bunny had once laid his eggs, and Molly said,

"I want those violets."

It was in full view of the back windows of the neighboring apartment building, and the violets in question grew about a foot inside their property.

"Come on, Peter, dig them out. Just one or two."

I looked up the four stories of open kitchen and bathroom windows and indicated to her that we really had enough plantings in our garden. Molly wasn't about to change her mind. I refused and answered:

"You get 'em."

She countered that I was a boy, and so it was my job.

"Gosh," I said, "if you want them so badly, why don't you get them yourself?"

"Because," she replied, "I have to go to confession; you don't, that's why."

Now that was disarming logic. Disregarding my erstwhile apprehension and the open kitchen windows, I boldly reached through the fence and dug them out. We gave them a place of honor.

I continued to tend the garden during the next few years. Perhaps it was an oasis of peace and gentleness in a world that was so violent and was slowly turning into mountains of rubble. I even added to it. There was a narrow patch of ground in front of the house, fenced in from the street underneath a tall arbor vitae, in front of Mrs. Karg's basement window. A year or so later, I planted a thick cluster of tulips under that tree. Heaven knows where one could still get tulip bulbs. Red ones, I remember. At the violent end of the war, they became a tiny focus of sentimentality.

PART TRUSTING, PART BROWBEATEN

As the days grew shorter that year, I saw people in the crowds on the streets wearing a big, yellow, six-cornered star on their over-coats, bearing in its center the inscription "*Jude*". The blind next door, when rarely seen outside their premises, wore it too. And their housekeeper, a short, hunched man with a protruding and drooping lower lip and a big, curved nose, did too. When he crossed the street some kid would always say, "Boy, does he look Jewish."

There were many stores and restaurants, too, now display-ing signs stating, "Jews not served here." I heard the authorities were ordering the proprietors to do so.

In my memory, these events, much like those of the Kristallnacht three years before, are shrouded in silence. Neither my teachers, nor my parents, nor any other adults made comments about it that I can still remember.

Such defamation occurring today would generate public outrage. But at that time, there was no stir. One must wonder why. Public opinion polls were not conducted in Germany then, so this question has no answers that could be proven to be true. But I will make some suggestions.

It has been humorously said that revolutions cannot occur in Germany because the law forbids them. A similar version is that revolts cannot get out of control because of the signs on public grounds, which instruct the citizens to keep off the grass. In a more serious way, judgment has been voiced that Germans were too submissive to authority. Yet, in any society, German or otherwise, public discipline is composed of several components. Citizens are law-abiding because they believe it to be proper and necessary, and it is a source of civil pride. There is a belief that a state of need or crisis demands the action of experts—the doctor, the police, the engineer—and that a laymen's interference would be foolish and he should stay out of the way. There is an engrained social sense against those who disregard public law and order. And in many settings, civil disobedience is seen as reflecting wantonness, insolence, cynicism, selfishness, and disrespect. In critical situations, such as an offence against the crew in an airplane, it is seen as downright criminal. Thus, what outsiders view as fearful obedience may actually be no more than appropriate restraint or self-imposed discipline.

Then, in older and traditional societies, there were elements of esteem and reverence not only for the King or Queen but also for the respected notables and personages of society. This was an age-old trust, often a pious trust, in the benevolent expertise of authority. It went so far, according to ancient attitudes, to accept occasional bouts of royal temper as a matter of course. It is an attitude unfamiliar in modern, liberal, and democratic societies and certainly in America. But in those old days and in those countries it was normal for citizens to accept royal temper without ever doubting the King's benevolence and fatherly love. It was as normal to them as it was to put up with hailstorms and pestilence, which were visited upon mortals from time to time by, yes indeed, a just and loving God. A childlike trust prevailed in the power and knowledge of their king, their clergymen, their doctor, their parents and elders, and their expert craftsmen each in his field. This trust gave rise to the powerful attitude of respect, a fundamental force in the proper functioning of their old-fashioned society. Even if a man were convinced of his doctor's error, he would have lacked the courage to say so because of his respect for him. In much the same way, to question the king was renounced in their culture as being unseemly, disloyal, and bratty. The desire to speak up was repelled by a potent behavioral taboo.

Throughout hundreds of generations their society had consisted of a father-like ruler and subjects who, like children, were part trusting and part browbeaten. This had been their traditional social structure which was considered to be natural, was shared by most of the older nations around the world, and, in spite of recent liberal and democratic challenges, many of its attitudes were still alive and well in people's minds.

Of course, there also was the element of fear. In the escapist spectator psychology, a person might see someone being issued a traffic ticket or suffer a more serious misfortune, and, instead of feeling compassion, merely steal away thinking, "Thank God, it wasn't me." It is not an uncommon reaction in situations of intimidation, such as under a strict government, which is cracking the whip and where no opposition is tolerated. This is particularly true in a police state, as the communist and fascist dictatorships were called, where nobody dared to open his mouth. Mr. Volkmann, the reader might remember, spent three months in a concentration camp because "he said something."

With regard to the anti-Jewish measures, traditional anti-Semitism did not help either; yet, its influence was probably weaker than the cultural attitudes and taboos just described. Popular anti-Semitism in Germany, as opposed to that thundered forth by the government, had been indistinguishable from that common in other countries and was probably much milder than it was in the United States at that time; that is to say, it was verbal, mild-to-moderate, and without action.

The results of two American opinion polls,[23] taken at that time regarding sentiments toward the Jews, reflect the way I remember public feelings in Germany as well. In a 1938 Roper opinion poll, Americans were asked to select what kind of people they objected to. Respondents disliking the Jews had, with 35 percent, the largest number. In another Roper poll a year later, in 1939, 53 percent of the respondents agreed with the statement that Jews were different from all other people, and that business and social restrictions should be imposed on them. I trust such a poll obtained in Germany would have given similar results. Most people had reservations about them as they were feared of exerting an aggressive and usurping influence in the cultural and business world. They were indeed believed to be somehow different from the rest of us, and it was thought that much of it had to do with the fact that they did not have a country of their own. I heard people talk about the idea of finding a country for them and where on the globe that might be.

Then again, such grave judgment seemed to be limited to theoretical discussions about the problems of the world, which one might contemplate over a glass beer, only to be forgotten when real life resumed. Intermarriage between Jews and Gentiles had been quite common, and there were numerous other facts, at least in Germany, which likewise spoke of easy mutual acceptance.

In fact, as the war progressed and grew steadily more violent, anti-Semitism was displaced by much more pressing concerns and, therefore, faded. But at this time, in the fall of 1941, as the Jews' wearing the yellow star brought their persecuted existence and plight to public display, it was possible that the silent suffering emanating from them was easier to ignore on the basis of the fact that they were "them" and not "us".

All of these considerations reflect fundamental elements of social psychology, yet, in their entirety, they likely accounted for less than 50 percent of the apparent indifference that people showed toward the Jews that fall. As it repeated itself a few months later in the United States with regard to the treatment of the

Japanese-Americans, the weightiest reason was the smoke-screen effect of the erupting passions of the war. The subdued minority's suffering and fate was crowded out of view by the violence and fears of war and blurred away from the focus of public attention.

As we saw them walking silently in the rushed crowds in the streets with the yellow star on their overcoats, nobody realized that their freedom would last only three or four more months. There was nobody in the world then, neither in Germany nor elsewhere, suspecting that this mean-spirited pogrom would end drastically different from all the other pogroms of the past. Indeed, as the tragedy progressed year-by-year far away in Poland and the Soviet Union, complete incredulity greeted occasional rumors and messages. This did not occur only in Germany, London, and Washington, but initially even in the Jewish ghetto of Warsaw.

In my own life, and likely in that of most people of that time, the persecution of the Jews occupied only a very small fragment of the exciting and frightening events of the year 1941. I will relate two of my own experiences and a third one, told to me by my father years later. In reading about these three episodes, it is important to remember that at that time, in the fall of 1941, the Holocaust had already begun. The gas chambers, to be sure, had not been developed yet, but the first stage of the Holocaust, the mass executions of Jews behind the Eastern Front, had been in full progress since late June of that year, and 100,000, if not twice that number, had already been killed. It was at that time, in Berlin, that parents were disturbed about the naughty pranks of teenage girls, and a Jewish gardener worried about the pumpkins in his garden. The innocence and naïve banality of these events provide a vague image of how the people and the government lived a world apart and how incredibly ignorant everybody was of the evolving catastrophe.

STERN VON RIO

My sister Gila was being reprimanded frequently. Her eye operation had corrected her squint and her stuttering had largely disappeared. But it was still obvious that the challenges of growing up were harder for her and that she enjoyed fewer joys than other children her age. Quite innocently, she blundered into trouble or conflict, and, if there was an altercation, it was invariably she who lost and got hurt. I was becoming quite adept in diagnosing the gathering storm long before anybody else knew it was coming. As I abhorred hostility, I often quietly intervened early, in a way that would deflect the course of events both to protect her and to preserve tranquility.

Yet, I was also naive and a tattletale, and so it came that, greatly impressed and amused, I shared with Mother the story of an exploit, which Gila had told me about in private.

Loitering among the crowds at night, whenever they—she and other girls—met a person bearing the Star of David, they blurted out the beginning of the latest hit song entitled *Star of Rio*, only to giggle their way hastily into the safety of darkness.

One might forgivingly observe that reinterpreting that yellow star in the romantic light of a schmaltzy popular song and a moving picture about of an exotic South American city was, after all, rather benign and perhaps even, if anything, a compliment. But still, to make fun of strangers and adults in this manner was, of course, disrespectful, and this, I suppose, gave the girls the delicious feeling of being naughty.

I, for my part, enjoyed the cleverness of switching the meaning of the word "star" the way one enjoys a clever pun. To me, it seemed a perfectly natural way to be amused, and it must have been for the girls as well, so long as we lacked the maturity to know that this was much too grave and sad a matter to be joked about.

I felt badly for having been responsible for Gila's ensuing reprimand, and I suppose that is why this minor episode has lingered in my memory. She was told to avoid the company of those girls, and that it was cruel to make fun of other people's plight.

THE JEWISH GARDNER AND THE PUMPKIN

We were sitting on the top of the carpet rail again, Molly and I. Suddenly, there was a rustling in the elderberry bushes on the other side of the fence; two hands gripped the top edge, and then the gardener's face appeared. He read us the riot act on cutting up pumpkins.

He was right. In fact, I had done that myself a day or two before, while retrieving a ball. Near his compost piles, the gardener was growing several large pumpkins. Pumpkins were uncommon in Germany and I had never before seen them in real life and wanted to know how they tasted. So, with my pocketknife, I had cut out a small wedge. Now I sat there, eyes cast down, abashed, the sinner who got caught. Molly, on the other hand, saw no reason to share that attitude.

Molly was a good girl. My parents liked her in spite of her mischievous and rebellious ways. They viewed her as being honest and decent and solid stuff right down to the core. They were right. But that is not to say that she was a saint or something. When attacked she would bloody well defend herself, utilizing every tactical advantage that presented itself.

Molly made an instant diagnosis of the situation and felt called upon to defend her young friend against this evil gardener. Also, she had no difficulty recognizing a weapon, which she could not refuse.

"Peter," she said, facing me rather than him, "when people like that talk to you, you don't even listen." Looking at me, she pointed at him with the back of her head.

The gardener fell silent as he stared at her insolence while she let him have it without mercy.

"They are Jews, you know that. They should be grateful for being permitted to live in that mansion; he has the nerve, accosting us!"

I thought I would die. I had never known anyone talking to an adult like that. I had never known an adolescent like her brazen-faced enough to talk about an adult in his presence, not facing him, but rather referring to him with the back of her head. I could have crawled into a hole in the ground to hide. No need, though. The gardener had let himself down from the fence and disappeared. Her brutal counter-offensive was a smashing success and she knew it.

"How can you talk like that?" I whispered. She grinned.

That was too good a story not to tell at suppertime. My parents looked at one another. I still see Father shaking his head.

"That's her dad," Mother said.

"Sure," Dad nodded, "that's where it comes from."

Terror in His Eyes

The Town Hall Square of the district of Steglitz was connected with the Düppel-Markt via a short street. There, about two houses from the market, was our small hardware store. The Düppel-Markt was a large expanse that was usually vacant, except for two days a week when it was the site of the produce and fish markets.

It was many years after the war that my father told me about an encounter which took place there, at about this time of my story.

It was winter, and night had fallen by the time stores were closing. Father was returning home from work. He was crossing the Market Square, which was desolate, and, because of the blackout, totally dark. A man approached, and in spite of the darkness, Father recognized the outline of the owner of the hardware store.

"*Er war so ein grundanständiger Mensch,*" Father related to me. "He was such a fine and decent man. I had known him for years; and now he was the victim of this terrible persecution; and one was so powerless, so completely powerless to help him. I think that's why I had this sudden urge to at least tell him how I felt. The night was pitch black and nobody could see us. I walked straight up to him, but you see, he didn't recognize me at first and tried to walk away. Then he stood still and stared at me, and I will never forget the naked terror in his eyes. He must have believed me to be from the Gestapo. His eyes were wide and he seemed petrified. Can you imagine the fear these people lived in? I'll never forget his face that night, as long as I live. Of course, then he did recognize me, and he relaxed. I took his hand and pressed it for a moment, and we just looked at each other. I didn't say anything, what could I have said? He didn't either. We just stood there, silently in the darkness, and then we each went our way. But, Heavens, I will never forget that fear in his eyes."

Harsh Internment

Then, one day, the Jews were no longer there. Some government agency moved into the Home for the Blind next door. The authorities described them as a security risk. Sympathizing as they were with "international Jewry"—to me, that entity was located in the general direction of Paris, London, and New York—many Jews would turn into saboteurs and spies or, in fact, even form a Fifth Column; they might allow light to shine from their windows at night in order to guide enemy planes and commit other dangerous acts. One couldn't take chances, not at a critical time like this. They were placed in internment camps where they could do no harm.

I had heard about internment. The Swiss had interned Uncle Hans, the archeologist, during the previous war. They had played a lot of chess there. This, now, appeared to be a little different, though. I once saw a group of Jews shoveling snow in the street wearing prison garb and guarded by soldiers with rifles. The treatment they received was apparently quite harsh.

It seems that this was the only time I saw them after they had been rounded up—which was done secretly in the dark of the night—but it is difficult to be certain. Their disappearance, because it was so silent, was hardly noticed by people whose attention was fully absorbed by the spectacles of bombed-out and burning apartment buildings, by the lack of sleep from the nightly air raids, by the queuing up at the markets and stores and replacing broken windows, and above all, of course, by their gnawing fear for their men at the Eastern Front. The merciless Russian winter, so impressively depicted in the newsreels, had frozen the battle lines and cynically arrested our victory march on Moscow. It caused motorized equipment to malfunction and brought general awareness to the fact that, all of a sudden, our military position had become vulnerable. The enemy's T-34 tanks were much superior to ours and we were forced to use eighty-eight millimeter anti-aircraft guns to brake their armor. Their multiple rocket launchers, the so-called Stalin-organs, caused a terrifying drumfire effect and outclassed our own artillery. Within a short period of time, this had become the most intense, far-reaching and frightening war. There could have been no more perfect smoke screen for anyone who had something to hide.

But such reflections arise out of hindsight. In those days, nobody spoke of a smoke screen, and I think that while many people expected the Jews to be in for a rough time, nobody conceived of anything criminal, let alone a "genocide", a word that did not even exist in those days because it had never happened before. Had it been possible to sample public opinion, one probably would have learned that people assumed that obviously a mass internment of this nature, carried out by the authorities of one of the most civilized countries, much like the treatment of prisoners-of-war, would be in keeping with that reputation and with international law.

Others might have felt that, at a time when millions of men and women were being drafted and sent to camps, barracks, and the battle field, it was not the end of the world for the Jews also to leave the comfort of their homes for a year or two and to put up with the life in camps.

With or without whispered suspicions, and with or without reassuring self-deceptions, average people believed that the Jews, having been safely put away somewhere for the duration of the war, received acceptable treatment but possibly enjoyed few comforts. If one had been able to point at instances of uncivilized treatment, their likely response would have been that over-eager local bosses sometimes got carried away, and such excesses were unavoidable, as Hitler was too busy to keep his eyes everywhere.[24] Then again, some of them, blissfully ignorant of the oppression and impoverishment the Jews had endured for the preceding nine years, probably assuaged their conscience with the excuse that the Jews had always been so rich and that there was nothing wrong for them to suffer a little now too.

A Comparison

B Y PECULIAR HISTORICAL COINCIDENCE, the apprehension of the Japanese-Americans and that of the German Jews took place at about the same time. Up to the point of this internment, the American and German people were thus faced with much the same sudden experience. It is tempting to look into the Japanese Relocation Program in the expectation that the reaction of a free, democratic, and responsible nation facing a similar challenge could have served as a model.

Regrettably, on the surface at least, that comparison is neither fair nor helpful. There was nothing in the American conduct that could usefully serve as a model to other nations. That was so because the state of mind of the Americans soon after the Japanese attack was unhinged and had no resemblance to that of the Germans. True, in both cases there was a preexisting, chronic, mild to moderate racial prejudice, here against Japanese and Orientals and there against the Jews; but superimposed on it, the Americans suffered an acute outburst of fear and fury, which was not present in Germany. If there ever was a good example of the eruption of acute anger with its three stages of trauma, denunciation, and violence, it prevailed in the United States after the attack on Pearl Harbor. Unsubstantiated fears, passionate fervor, maledictions, furious damnation of everything Japanese, and thus, impulsive and unrestrained reasoning, as well as unquestioned self-righteousness consumed the land. All of this united to affect all levels of society including clergymen, columnists, governors, and members of Congress.[25] Even the American Civil Liberties Union and the Supreme Court refused to intervene.[26] As a consequence the government overreacted by suspending basic constitutional principles. The unmerciful impact of the Japanese surprise attack knocked a great nation out of emotional kilter, a transient condition against which no country in the world could claim to be immune and which the world has judged understandable and probably forgivable.

No such situation existed in Germany. The quiet Jews had not launched an attack, there was no sudden angry reaction against

them, and they were apprehended "by night and fog" without public agitation or clamor. Thus, the German and American frames of
mind were located at opposite ends of the scale and their public
reactions were not comparable.

  Nonetheless, on a different level a useful comparison can
indeed be drawn. There are reports written by high-ranking,
responsible officials such as Secretary of War Henry L. Stimson,[27]
FBI Chief J. Edgar Hoover,[28] Attorney General Francis Biddle,[29] and
Chief of the War Relocation Authority Milton Eisenhower,[30] which
reflect sincere awareness of the unconstitutionality of the program
and genuine concern for the interned individuals. It seems obvious, therefore, that away from the activists there was a silent
majority of Americans who regretted the execution of Executive
Order 9066 and who kept a cool head but were unable to swim
against the torrent. Impotent, they stood silently by as their fellow
citizens disappeared behind barbed wire, much the way the
Germans are known to have done at the same time. I feel that this
silent group of Americans and the German citizens shared much
the same attitudes and thoughts.

  They were both rendered powerless, here by the storm of
public outrage and there by the fetters of the police state. There
existed genuine fears of the rise of a Fifth Column engaging in sab-
otage and even sober citizens had to admit that there indeed was
a security problem and that one could not take any chances. There
was preexisting, low to moderate racial prejudice, which made it
easier to take refuge in indifference toward the rights of that
minority. In both countries, proud patriots thought theirs was one
of the most civilized lands in the world and would not have
remotely considered the possibility of their government conducting such a confinement program in a disreputable or criminal
manner. Finally, and this is presumably the most important psychological aspect, their attention was quickly being carried away
by the actions and battles and passions of the war. The fate of the
small ethnic minority vanished behind the smoke screen of the
greatest war there had ever been.

  There is, of course, no way to substantiate such an estimate
of public opinion on both sides of the ocean a half a century later.

Stalin carried out the uprooting and deportation of undesired ethnic groups, such as the Tatars and Chechens, on a much larger scale; and an incredibly brutal and massive deportation program was part of Mao's Cultural Revolution. So it appears it can be instituted anywhere in the world, the victims helplessly suffering the consequences and witnesses standing by, unable to interfere or even to voice their opinion.

Once the camp gates closed behind the Japanese-Americans on one side, and behind the Jews on the other side of the ocean, the victims were concealed in the blind spot of the public eye. In neither country did the people know what was transpiring in the camps. They had to wait two or three years in order to learn what happened there and whether their country's honor had been saved. Then, indeed, the gods of fortune dealt more gently with the Americans.

PART 4

THE EVIL CURSE

BACKSTAGE

AT THIS POINT OF THESE EVENTS, their narration faces a peculiar choice. Imagine you are the manager of a stage on which a tense and dramatic play is being performed. Imagine further, that during the performance a vicious murder is being committed behind the scenes. Should you now allow the play to continue and postpone informing the audience of the crime until the end? Or should you stop the performance to describe the crime and what other details might be known to the viewers; and then, with apologies for the interruption, resume the play? In the latter case, the play's spell would likely dissipate. The audience might lose interest in it or watch it only half-heartedly, being distracted by thoughts of the happenings backstage. Clearly, from the standpoint of the producer, the first option would be preferable because it would save the success of the play.

History created a similar double-drama between 1941 and 1945. A gigantic war was being waged on the stage for all mankind to watch during the first half, whereas during the second half the Holocaust suddenly was erupting and unrolling in silence behind the scenes. The way history evolved, the war was allowed to brutally play out to its end without interruption, and the world learned about the second drama not until the final curtains were rung down on it.

The Holocaust did not touch my life then. In fact, that was true for almost all people across Europe. If this story were told without mention of it until reaching the year 1945 when the news of it broke, and only then reported it, it would be a truthful description of the actual sequence of events the way they were experienced.

Nonetheless, my account has arrived at the point of time when that second drama did indeed commence and, despite the fear of unduly distracting the reader, I shall relate it now. We will leave the stage of my story to look into that incredible massacre which took place outside the arena.

Unusual

The history of the Jews is four thousand years old. Around 1225 B.C., they escaped from Egypt. They were expelled from Jerusalem in 589 B.C. They were once more expelled from Jerusalem in 70 A.D. They were expelled from England in 1290 A.D. They were expelled from various cities in Germany, Italy, Poland, and Lithuania in the fifteenth century. They were expelled from Spain in 1492 and from Russia in 1550. After 1515, they were quarantined in ghettos all over Europe. During the last thousand years, they have been subjected to riots, pogroms, and massacres on at least seventy-five occasions in twenty-three countries. At one time or another, they were accused of causing the Black Death by poisoning the wells; of being tormentors and thieves; of stealing the consecrated Host and torturing it; of serving the Devil; of having concealed tails; of having committed deicide; of usurping our Western culture; of praying at the altar of Mammon; of being cynical capitalists here and subversive fanatics there; and of conspiring to dominate the world. Such accusations can be separated into different categories. I have counted twenty-five categories, but there are more.

They have survived two millennia of disdainful and angry persecution. Yet, the world's two largest religious faiths are derivatives of Judaism. On man's march into modernity, they almost single-handedly opened the doors into the new realms of banking, capitalism, socialism, publishing, and different branches of the entertainment industry. They have supplied supreme composers, artists, and scientists and one could easily count fifteen categories of similar cultural disciplines where the subtraction of their creativeness, genius, and Nobel Prizes would leave the world much poorer. Jews have, indeed, a most unusual history.

FOUR ROOTS

How were the Jews different from other peoples to be predestined for such an exceptional fate during the past two millennia? The search readily leads to four distinctions.

The oldest one was the Judaic religion. In Hellenistic and even earlier times, it was truly a unique faith. It alone was monotheistic. With 613 Mosaic laws including 365 prohibitions, it was more rigorous and regulative in every sphere of life than other faiths. In a way, it was seen as proud, haughty, and avers to ecumenical openness. It was a religion that was believed to be incapable of blending into Hellenism and mainstream Roman civilization, which was the general trend in that era. Rather, it preferred to remain separate. Some observers in those ancient days might have rejected them in the belief that they were a fervent sect or cult.

Their second distinction was literacy. Their stubborn resistance to abandoning their ancient culture in favor of the overwhelming wave of Hellenism led to the introduction of universal schooling that was to ascertain the widest possible exposure to the Holy Scriptures. This occurred in the last two pre-Christian centuries. Thus, the Jews became an almost fully literate nation not only in a world that was not so at that time, but in a world that was not going to be so for the next 1800 years and they maintained this amazing accomplishment for the next two millennia. Literacy, of course, increases knowledge, civilization, and economic power. It raises you on a horse among pedestrians. The literate Jew was apt to be superior to his contemporaries in any task or contest. He was also invincible, individually and as a group, not only because he could better defend himself but also because he had become indispensable. His worst enemies could not dispose of him, because they needed his expertise.

The third difference was the diaspora. The Jewish communities were spread among other nations from Babylon to Spain and from Alexandria to Cologne. This had already been partially present for several pre-Christian centuries and was finalized after 70 A.D. Despite being geographically dispersed, they remained ethnically, culturally, and religiously united because of the power of their faith and because the art of writing permitted them to communicate and to form a network. They did not disappear into the melting pot of their host nations—not after five generations, not after ten, and not after one thousand years. They did not melt because their separate status was locked in place. That was so because their religion was non-yielding (as would be true for most religions), and even more importantly, their literacy made them the stronger culture. Stronger cultures resist blending into weaker ones.

The fourth distinction was forced upon them by the animosity of their hosts. It arose out of a Mosaic prohibition to practice usury, a word meaning lending money at interest. Both Christianity and Islam inherited the proscription from the Torah. It was an economic impediment, because an economy needs credit, and without interest the availability of credit was stifled. There was, however, an exception since a clause in Deuteronomy 23:20 permitted Jews to charge interest from strangers. As the Christian church advanced into the status of a state church, a situation was created where Jews were the only ones permitted to lend money to gentiles at interest. This in itself was not the reason for the derogatory perception of the money-lending Jew, but rather the fact that progressive injunctions excluded them from any *other* trade or employment from which to make a living. Thus, the Jews had little choice but to sustain themselves by a trade very much at the bottom of social esteem. Indeed, even over a thousand years later, in the fifteenth century, Jews living in France and Italy had little other chance to earn a living.[1] Yet, a merciful fate granted them two advantages: their schooling allowed them to master the necessary arithmetic; and their connections throughout an international religious network gave them access to funds for larger loans, as might be requested by kings wishing to fight wars or to build a castle. And so, out of this age-old occupational confinement imposed upon them, there grew public disesteem, to be sure, but there also grew a well founded expertise in the realm of finance, in the management of the business of royal households, for the founding of the Bank of England, for opening the door to modern commercialism, for financing the building of railroads and other major projects, and for supplying, still today, many outstanding leaders in the world's financial realm.

Such, then, are the four parameters that have governed Jewish existence during much of the past two thousand years. It is not unreasonable to view them as root causes for their incredible history. None of them—not their religion, not their literacy, not the Diaspora, and not their money lending—are in any way offensive. And yet, the intractable hostility against them might have been predicted, for the combination of the four contained vigorous and indestructible seedcorns of conflict, as will be shown.

A SIMPLE RECIPE

A foreign organism living within the body of a host organism is an exceptional and risky manner of coexistence. Under favorable circumstances, the host may view the foreign organism as a symbiotic partner. They will both benefit. But it may conversely see him as a parasite. In that case, the way human psychology works, there is no limit to the viciousness of the host's revulsion. In the extreme, he may indeed perceive the stranger as a demon and may wish to exorcise and exterminate him.

It may not be an exaggeration to suspect that in the diaspora the Jews lived in the ever-present danger of provoking xenophobia and of being perceived as parasites. Throughout the centuries, it was as if they rested on a teeterboard that could tip the wrong way at any time. Being permanent strangers whose separateness seemed immutable, they lived in a world where, even in friendly symbiosis, xenophobic resentment was never far away.

If you wish to create a society riven by recurrent, intractable inner antagonism, today or a thousand years ago, in my country or in yours, then I recommend you follow this simple recipe: you should implant people of a dynamic and progressive civilization as colonists in a land of less dynamism and progress; you should make sure that the colonists and the host people are of different ethnic origin, or of different religions, or of different languages, or, better yet, combine all of these; you, then, should seal the barrel and let it ferment. Without fail, there will be resentment, bitterness, contempt, envy, jealousy, and animosity handed down from generation to generation. You can even aggravate the antagonism at will into outright riots and massacres by instilling one further agent: subject the indigenous population to great pain and suffering, perhaps by war, or the plague, or a famine. As the misfortune rises in vehemence and becomes unbearable, it will create fury and a scapegoat psychology among the suffering people. They will combine and unleash themselves upon those thought to be the mean-spirited source of all misery.

This happened to the Jews in the crusader riots in 1296 A.D. in France and the Rhineland, in 1348 at the time of the Black Death in many countries, around 1492 in the Spanish Inquisition, in 1648 in the Cossack Rebellion, and again in the 1880s in Russia. The recipe is effective not only with regard to the Jews. The outburst of brutality against the Germans in Bohemia and Moravia in the Hussite Wars in the fifteenth century was a classic example of it. In a milder form, it was more recently directed against other German settlements in Eastern Europe. With a slightly different background, it raged between the Turks and Greeks after World War I and between the Hindus and Pakistanis in 1947. Perfect examples, again, were the massive massacres of ethnic Chinese in Indonesia in 1965 and in similar subsequent outbursts. It can happen anywhere in this troubled world. It does so not so much because people are evil, but rather because the recipe is fail-safe. Once instituted, the process will run off obediently, according to the laws that are embedded somewhere in the depth of human psychology.

NEW ROOTS

Hypothetically at least, it is possible to explain most of the changing faces of anti-Semitism on the basis of these four factors all the way until the thirteenth century, perhaps even to the eighteenth century. After that time, the logic of this hypothesis fades. The Renaissance, the age of the Enlightenment, and the French Revolution diminished the differences between Jews and gentiles. Growing secularism weakened the impact of sectarian contrast. General literacy was spreading across Europe. A well-meaning policy of Jewish emancipation and assimilation abolished anti-Jewish restrictions and allowed them to become productive members of every aspect of modern society. More and more, they lived like regular citizens and were no longer in a ghetto or a diaspora. Therefore, their separateness appeared to be no longer immutable. Their marks of distinction were fading and, consequently, so should have anti-Semitism. But it didn't. Seventy-five years after the French Revolution, the emancipated Jews were despairing, and they rightfully exclaimed, "We must leave this continent. There is no other way. We must have our own country." Instead of receding, anti-Semitism had once again become virulent. That was so because it had grown new and different roots.

About three centuries ago began the modern age that propelled our civilization in science, technology, industry, social structure, and the ways of human life into a new future. It created an outpouring of thought and creativity in philosophy, literature, art, and music. It lifted us up and carried us away like a huge tidal wave, and we can still see no end of it today. Not only did the Jews ride that wave along with the gentiles, but they did so always up near its very crest. Along with all the new forces and changes that the wave of modernism has brought into our world, from its depths there also grew the roots of a new wave of anti-Semitism.

In order to reduce this multi-faceted process into a simplified, tangible formula, one might divide it into two aspects. First, the Jews rode too close to the wave's leading edge for them to escape the suspicion that they were responsible for the painful changes associated with it. That was a perilous suspicion for some of the social and economic changes were revolutionary and violent. They evoked offense, indignation, and fear, and it was ill omened to be held responsible for them. Secondly, they escaped from the ghetto and poured into the previously inaccessible world of flourishing arts and culture with so much vigor and success that the gentile establishment felt overtrumped and crowded out.

Without much difficulty, one can go another step further and trace these two mechanisms back to a common denominator. The result is aptly expressed in the aphorism: "Jews are like other people, only more so."[2] That is to say, if a person has more adrenaline coursing through his veins than his fellow men, he will most certainly be found at the cutting edge of progress and an intimidating competitor. The source of that extra amount of adrenaline being obvious, the whole phenomenon can then be seen as a consequence of the simple fact that the Jews were a persecuted race.

No Brakes

The vehemence of anti-Jewish resentment in the late nineteenth and early twentieth centuries was astounding. It was pervasive. It came "from aristocrats and populists; from industry, from the farms; from the academy and the gutter; from music and literature and, not least, from science."[3] It was shared across the nations. In France, the land of the Dreyfus Affair, the brilliance and triumphs of Jewish prodigies were seen "as an act of violence."[4] With bitterness and sadness, André Gide, the French novelist and writer, in 1914 deplored the "takeover of French culture" by the Jews. He believed French literature written by Jews lacked in significance and said, "It would be far better, whenever the Frenchman comes to lack sufficient strength, for him to disappear rather than to let an uncouth person play his part in his stead and his name."[5]

In Germany and Austria, the sensation of defeat was similar. Richard Wagner complained that the Jews were progressively
"taking over" the citadel of German culture, especially music.[6] In
1873, Wilhelm Marr, who coined the term "anti-Semitism," published a popular book, which stated that the Jews had become "the
first major power in the West," and that Germany had degenerated too far to withstand Jewish superiority.[7] The historian Heinrich
von Treitschke wrote, "The Jews are our misfortune," and a petition
to the Berlin government spoke of "alien domination."[8]

In England, J. A. Hobson, in publications around the turn of
the century, charged the Jews with "taking advantage of any weak-
ness" of their host societies and of letting British troops fight and
die in the Boer War to serve their personal interests in the South
African diamond mines. He claimed them to be economic parasites in imperialism and that, through their control of international
capitalism, they were able to "set their face against" any major
plans of European governments. Ominously, he said, "United by
the strongest bonds of organization...controlled...chiefly by men of
a single and peculiar race...they are in a unique position to control
the policy of nations."[9] His perception, then, was that of a powerful entity that, serving only its own greed, was hidden in the
background from where it was able to direct, by remote control,
the governments of nations.

Anti-Semitism, at that time, was like a fever that had
befallen Europe. But fever from what? There was defeatism, sadness, and resignation in Gide's words. There was also bitter
defeatism in Marr's statement. Treitschke's "misfortune" was an
expression of dismay. The term "alien domination" again was an
admission of defeat and humiliation. When they spoke of leftist
radicalism, Marxism, and subversive Jews, they were circumscrib-
ing the words fear and panic. The meaning was identical when
they pointed at Jews as the silent financiers who controlled world
capital. The underlying denominator was fear—fear of the Jews'
ascendancy and immense power, and fear of being invaded, overwhelmed, and superseded by them. Panic may even border on the
irrational. He who suspects a powerful force hiding in the background, invisible in the mist, pursuing him or directing him by

remote control, is dangerously close to paranoia.

Thus, there is good reason to interpret the vehement anti-Semitism prior to the First World War as resulting from a rapidly rising wave of dismay and apprehension at the sight of the explosive Jewish ascendancy. That interpretation would be in agreement with an empirical rule, according to which most anger and violence is spawned by anxiety and fear.

A tragic aspect of this treacherous crisis was the absence of an escape route. The Jews could not possibly go back to the ghetto. In spite of the antagonism directed against them, they had no choice but to continue to thrust forward. Anti-Jewish resentment, on the other hand, was without doubt sincere and unaware of any moral challenge. After all, it was universal and age-old. Their aggressive invasion and overpowering of European nations seemed undeniable. In all innocence, a non-Jew might have asked to know why an upright man should ever apologize for his anti-Semitism. By God, weren't they surely a disagreeable and dangerous lot?

There were no brakes. The only hope was that the vehement confrontation would run its course without violence and eventually somehow abate.

But then came the Great War. Then came the Treaties of Versailles and St. Germain. Then came "Jewish-Bolshevism."

Ten Times Ten

On the ladder of pain and anger, that ten-stage scale of progressive suffering described early in this text, the pain suffered by a Frenchman or an Englishman by the end of World War I had probably reached the eighth rung. "Your name stinks. Your presence is an outrage." At least they were victors; that helped. For the German, on the other hand, after his superhuman sacrifices and loss of the war, anger and despair, without question, rose to the tenth level. It would have even risen higher had the ladder not been so short.

For Germany to have lost all of her colonies would seem insignificant today. Thirty years later, every colonial power was forced to do so. In those days, however, it was a demotion of dire proportions. They did not even leave one little island. No, they took it all. This loss rates, one might estimate, another ten rungs on the ladder of pain.

The peace treaty further decreed for Germany to surrender her entire navy and almost all of her merchant fleet. The material loss was immense and the loss in pride was devastating. When Franklin D. Roosevelt, twenty-one years later, thought Hitler might gain control of the Royal Navy, he considered this reason enough for the United States to enter the war. The loss of her fleets might have amounted to another ten rungs on the German scale of anguish.

Territorial amputations from both Germany and Austria were even more difficult to endure. Few punishments are less tolerable than to give up land over which the proud flag of your country once flew, where people spoke your language, where centuries of your history are embedded, and where generations of your ancestors are resting in the cemeteries. Nothing is more likely to provoke another war. France's holy right to recapture Alsace-Lorraine from Germany was hailed in all Western Allied countries. For Germany and Austria in 1919, this count again generated ten tormenting rungs of grief.

I count another ten rungs of hatred for the reparations, another ten for the billion-fold inflation it produced, and yet another ten for the occupation of the industrial territory of the Ruhr by French and Belgian troops five years after the war. And as we speak of anguish and suffering and despair, we must not forget another item that Germany shared with all other countries. It was the unemployment and hunger associated with the flagging economy of the 1920s, the stock market crash in 1929, and the Great Depression that followed.

But the load of grief was still heavier. There were two more burdens and, truly, they were particularly grave. One was the so-called war-guilt clause of the Versailles Treaty, which declared Germany solely and criminally guilty of the war and all its sufferings and resulted in her virtual excommunication from the family of nations. Psychologically, that is a most satisfying action for the victor because after the opponent has been physically defeated this "finishes him off" morally to boot. "Before all mankind, yes, indeed before God you are declared evil and an outcast. We banish you from civilized society." It is an extremely powerful and hateful weapon. It resembles stepping on the face of the fallen enemy. But for Germany, it was even worse than that. Up until then, she had been vying for the cultural, educational, industrial, and scientific leadership in the world. She had been a rising star on the firmament of nations. The degree of her degradation was monstrous. Germany did not descend into the mud of humiliation by falling from a horse. Rather, she fell from the stars.

The last and most important item of all was, in fact, a veritable nightmare that prevailed for the subsequent seven decades. It was, of course, the specter of the rise of Bolshevism—a phenomenon, which in the public mind was perceived as a menace so evil and powerful as to lack any parallel in history, except perhaps the invasions of the Mongolian Hordes or of the Huns before them.

This enumeration does not attempt to judge the wisdom of Allied actions nor the truth behind German fears or beliefs. Instead, it is merely meant to cast light on how, rightly or wrongly, the world was perceived in their injured hearts. In a manner of illustration, it states that there were ten major grievances that each reached the tenth rung, the maximum level, of distress.

To whatever degree this illustration reflects reality, this was the time, if there ever was one, where a population was submitted to that excessive degree of suffering that would incense, at least in the less rational ones among them, a fury and a scapegoat psychology that, in turn, would, according to the ancient recipe, unleash itself upon a minority that was thought to be the malignant source of it all.

There was no doubt that minority was. It was all over the newspapers across the world. It was not the nobility, the generals, the rich, the industrialists, the Catholics, nor the Protestants. It was the Jews. Everybody was aghast at their dreadful and demonic role in Lenin's Cheka and his Red Army, and in revolutions elsewhere. Woe to them whose name had attached itself to the frightful word of Bolshevism.

And yet, in spite of all of this, the tenfold despair of the German people and the potential imputation of the Jews did not result, as will be shown, in the outburst of popular anti-Semitism that should have been expected.

Different Curves

There is no indication that Hitler's anti-Semitism was different from anybody else's, during the First World War and prior to it. It seems to have abruptly risen at the end of the war to a level of a paranoid obsession. From that point forward, it never changed until his death. As illustrated in Fig. 3, one could plot his anti-Semitism on a chart, the degree measured on a scale of zero to ten, against time measured from 1910 until 1945. It would start at the level of two; then in 1918, it would rise to the level of ten and remain there until 1945. Anti-Semitism in the Western World would presumably also have started at level two, then have risen to four or five between 1917 and 1922 because of the disturbing reports from Russia, and then have receded back to two. During the Great Depression in the 1930s, widespread hardship probably caused a new wave of such resentment in Europe and the United

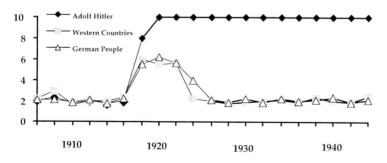

ASSUMED CHANGES OF ANTI-SEMITISM

Fig. 3. This graph is to illustrate the alleged difference between Hitler's anti-Semitism and that of the German people.

States.Among the Germans, it is surprising that despite their extreme distress and indignation just described at the grassroots level, the curve was identical with that of other countries. In fact, before the First World War, anti-Semitism was on the decline in Germany and was much lower than in France, Austria-Hungary, or Russia. At the elections for the German Reichstag in 1907, only 2.5 percent of the votes were given to anti-Semitic parties.[10] After the temporary rise in the immediate post-war years to perhaps the level five, it fell back again to level two. One can be quite certain of that fact, as in the 1924 elections Hitler's party won 6.6 percent of the popular vote, and in 1928 a mere 2.6 percent. It was only after the outbreak of the world economic crisis, in 1930, that he won 18.3 percent.[11] *Der Stürmer*, the viciously anti-Jewish weekly, in the whole year of 1927 sold all of thirteen thousand copies, slightly more than a thousand a month in a nation of seventy million. Thus, dissecting anti-Semitism into "pathological" and "customary" varieties reveals the little known difference that existed between Hitler's curve and that of the rest of the country. Unquestionably, the enormous misfortune of the recent war and its aftermath introduced a predictable poison pill into the relationship between the Jews and the Germans, but it poisoned only a small radical splinter group.

A World of Violence

In our view, the Holocaust has assumed a rank of ultimate human evil. In the eyes of many, it overshadows all other destructive and atrocious events of that time. It would be wrong, though, to see it as a single structure, as a solitary tower, for it resembles instead the most prominent summit within a mountain range. It is as if there existed, through most of that century, a geological fault giving rise to a long series of large and small volcanoes, building huge mountains and belching up the fiery wrath of the underworld. The Holocaust transpired in the turmoil of a morally unhinged world, for there seemed to be mega-killings wherever you looked.

The First World War caused over eight million combat deaths. In the Third Armenian Massacre in 1914/15, 1.75 million

Armenians were expelled from their homeland and an estimated 600,000 died on the forced migration from starvation or were killed by soldiers or police.[12] The terror of Lenin's revolution was attended by four million deaths from hostility and epidemics in addition to millions wiped out by famine. At the end of the Greco-Turkish War in 1922, victorious Turkish troops killed thirty thousand Greeks in the port city of Izmir. With no less than twenty million civilian victims, Stalin brought about the most incomprehensible mass murder of all times.

During the collapse of Poland in 1939, the Poles caused bloodshed among the Belorussian and Ukrainian minorities in Eastern Poland for which these minorities retaliated in kind. In the early 1940s, Ukrainian national forces killed eighty thousand Poles.[13] From 1941 until 1943, the extremist Ustasha government of Croatia, in a desire to reserve Croatia for the Croatians and Roman Catholics, is said to have killed 500,000 Orthodox Serbs.[14] Behind the German front-line in the Soviet Union, up to 175,000 Soviet partisans were waging war against the Germans and their allies. In exerting terroristic pressure upon the local population so as to undermine their collaboration, they are estimated to have killed at least forty thousand of their own people.[15]

At the Teheran Conference of Allied leaders in November of 1943, Stalin proposed over a toast to kill fifty thousand German military officers at the end of the war to which Roosevelt, in good humor, agreed. At the Yalta Conference in February 1945, Roosevelt suggested to Stalin to repeat that toast.[16]

In the summer of 1944, Churchill, enraged about the new German V-1 rockets, called for a "cold-blooded calculation" regarding the use of poison gas. He wanted to "drench" the Ruhr area and other German cities with it but yielded to warnings of possible German retaliation.[17]

Some Americans thought all Japanese surviving the war should be exterminated.[18] A similar sentiment was expressed by Col. Burton Andrus, prison warden at the Nuremberg Trials, when in talking about his hate of the Germans he said, "It's too bad we could not have exterminated them and given that beautiful country to someone who was worthy."[19]

In Tunisia in 1943, Gen. Eisenhower complained about the difficulties of dealing with several hundred thousand prisoners-of-war. "It is a pity," he wrote to Army Chief of Staff Gen. George C. Marshall, "we could not have killed more."[20] But two years later he could. When peace came and German troops laid down their arms by the millions, the United States Army, under his command, enclosed them in "cages" of such a nature that an incredibly large number of them perished.

From Eastern Europe, both inside and outside of German borders, fourteen million Germans were expelled in the manner of ethnic cleansing. Of them, two million died from exposure, from hostile military action, and from man-to-man and man-to-woman violence.[21]

The bombing of civilian population centers was initially done in the context of military operations, but it rapidly escaped control to the point where it was clearly meant to bring about demoralization by causing utter devastation and mass civilian casualties. The British-launched mass bombing of Germany in May of 1940,[22] was, in turn, responded by Germany with enormous raids on Britain. Mastering the technology of constructing forever more destructive air fleets, the Americans and British then propelled this art to an order where one could turn city after city into wastelands of rubble. Two successive British attacks on Hamburg in July of 1943 caused a firestorm with temperatures over 1,400 degrees Fahrenheit and the death of 42,000 civilians.[23] The attacks on Dresden, in February of 1945, were no doubt the most violent air attack upon Germany. They incinerated an unknown number of inhabitants and refugees, estimates running between 70,000 to 250,000 people within twenty-four hours. Somewhere between 750,000 and one million German civilians perished as a result of Allied Air raids.[24] The air raid on Tokyo on March 10, 1945 killed 120,000 people in the three hours between 12:30 and 3:30 A.M. The firestorm tossed the huge, low-flying B-29 planes several hundred feet up and down; the bomber crews could smell burning flesh and felt as if they were witnessing Dante's inferno.[25] Perfected in this manner, these attacks were then repeated on Nagoya, Osaka, and Kobe, killing another 100,000 civilians.[26]

For the bomb that fell on Hiroshima on August 6, 1945, it took not three hours but a mere second to cause the early and late deaths of 200,000 people. Before the *Enola Gay* left for this mission, the chaplain prayed with the crew. He said, "We shall go forward trusting in Thee, knowing that we are in Thy care now and forever. In the Name of Jesus Christ. Amen."[27]

To this day, sober judgment has correctly maintained that, of the alternatives available at that time, the use of this bomb, for the Japanese no less than for the Allies, was the quickest and the least inhumane method of ending the war. It was indeed, in Churchill's words, "a miracle of deliverance."[28] Yet, the chaplain's well-meant words, as well as Churchill's correct diagnosis, illustrate just the same to what degree moral and religious righteousness of that angry war had entered the realm of insanity.

The enumeration of mega-killings continues into the 1960s and 1970s with the millions of victims of Mao's Proletarian Cultural Revolution and Pol Pot's unspeakable terror among his Cambodian people.

Yes, most of these were meant to serve a beneficial purpose. It is usually a patriotic purpose that intends to defend, rescue, or glorify one's country, whether the presumed enemy is seen as foreign or as an alleged infestation at home. But none of these barbaric programs could ever be launched if man could not become possessed by anger and fury. In the illusion of self-righteousness and God's blessing and within the torrent of hot fervor and demonization, the gate into barbarianism is tossed wide open. Once we have passed through it, we are in a world where savagery has no limits. There, the laws of civilization and morality have been suspended and our holy scriptures are meaningless.

From these mountains of immense violence, the Holocaust has stood out as the most prominent one. It was so indeed, not only because of its own dimension and horror, but because there seemed to be justifications which, in the light of wartime morality, allowed many of the others, despite the magnitude of their cruelty, to be excused. The most important one of these were actions carried out by the military in the pursuit of war. The attacks on Dresden, Tokyo, and Hiroshima, for example, could be seen as attempts to end the war rather than as acts of savagery, while the gas chambers in Auschwitz obviously lacked such excuse. If one is willing to subtract these, then the Holocaust is left standing in great solitude, being surmounted only by Stalin's death toll of twenty million helpless souls.

It differed from anything previously known. The count of six million victims was so excessively high that many initially rejected it in disbelief. The method of gassing people to death in chamber after chamber was seen as a weird invention of scientists gone mad. The notion of an attempt to eradicate an entire ethnic group or race, generating the new word genocide, seemed to belong into an alien, diabolical, and futuristic world. The photographs and records of it were numerous and explicit, while none of the world's other crimes had been documented or undergone prominent publication over the whole world in a like manner. Its ghastliness went beyond description and was powerful enough on the mind of the onlooker to create a definitive and immutable judgment against the perpetrator.

The Messiah Never Came

It is assumed that it was during the first two months of 1941 that Hitler reached the decision of how a final solution of the Jewish problem was to be accomplished. He abandoned the idea of resettling the Jews in some remote country in favor of exterminating them altogether. The idea of using huge chambers in which to gas them to death had not matured yet. Instead, he ordered the formation of indoctrinated and loyal killing squads, which, on the heels of the invading armies, would round up the Jews and shoot them. They were the *Einsatzgruppen*, the special duty groups or mobile killing squads, which were recruited from the SS, the *Gestapo*, and the police. Initially, their number was small, only three thousand men altogether, and they were deployed in four groups—A to D— along the Eastern Front.

The indigenous anti-Jewish sentiment in the eastern countries must have been enormous since the *Einsatzgruppen* were apparently able to solicit willing help from the local population and to enlist thousands of them into ethnic SS units. Considering the large number of their victims, the total force of German and non-German units must have been far in excess of the initial three thousand. In the reports, Latvian, Lithuanian, and Ukrainian forces are most frequently mentioned. Of 100,000 Ukrainian volunteers, the SS is said to have accepted only 30,000.[29] In addition, the Rumanians, being described as the most brutal of them all, operated on their own, separate from the *Einsatzgruppen*.[30]

* * *

Between October and December 1941, Groups A to D reported killing 125,000, 45,000, 75,000 and 55,000 respectively.[31] Small detachments killed tens of thousands. In Riga, twenty-two men are said to have killed 10,600 Jews. In Kiev (Babi Yar), two small detachments are reported to have killed over 30,000.[32] A notorious killing ground was Ponary, not far from Vilna (Vilnius) in Lithuania. Within the first three months of the eastern campaign, 20,000 of Vilna's 60,000 Jewish inhabitants met their death there. By the end of 1941, the death toll at Ponary had risen to 47,000.[33] They were all executed by a bullet, one by one. The fatal terror repeated itself in Riga, Kovno (Kaunas), Minsk, Bialystok, and in hundreds of smaller towns, and was inflicted by German, Lithuanian, White Russian, and Ukrainian squads.[34] On October 23, 1941, a massacre was carried out by Rumanians in Odessa in which 20,000 to 30,000 Jews, who were caged in four warehouses, were burned to death. The Rumanians killed 200,000 Jews in Bessarabia.[35]

* * *

Sheer terror struck those who were temporarily spared by the repeated killing waves. Dawidowicz reports about the Jews in the Vilna ghetto who were issued "permits" for those employed in industries supporting the German war effort. The permit covered three family members, no matter how big the families were. There was no secret that lack of the permit meant death at Ponary. Of Vilna's 22,500 ghetto residents, 10,000 were left without permit. Many of these went into hiding. On October 24, 1941, all permit holders were forced from the ghetto and the Lithuanian police proceeded to search for hideouts. As they broke into the houses, stores, and shops, the hunted in their hiding places observed desperate silence. "Suddenly...a baby starts crying... We are lost. A desperate attempt to shove sugar into the baby's mouth doesn't help. They stop its mouth with pillows. The mother weeps. In the wild terror people demand that the baby be strangled..."

They were not discovered, but 7,500 others were. They disappeared in Ponary.[36]

* * *

The deployment of the *Einsatzgruppen* continued through 1942. During that phase they killed another 900,000 victims.[37] They had adopted the Soviet technique of conducting mass executions. It was termed the sardine method. The victims had to lay themselves face down, next to one another, at the bottom of the pit. They were then executed with a shot in the nape of the neck. The next layer had to lie on top of the corpses head over feet. They were killed and stacked there five to six layers deep.[38]

After preliminary testing in the fall of 1941, however, six death camps were equipped in Poland for mass killings in gas chambers. Automobile exhaust gasses were soon abandoned in favor of the disinfectant gas Zyklon B or hydrogen cyanide. Of the six camps, two became functional in the winter of 1941/42, one in April 1942, one in June, one in July and one in October 1942. They were in operation nine, twelve, sixteen, sixteen, seventeen, and thirty-nine months respectively. Auschwitz, with thirty-nine months, has been known as the most infamous one.

A minority of the fresh arrivals was assigned to work. The remainder went to the gas chambers. They had to undress. Women had their hair cut off. They were then herded into the "shower rooms" where they stood packed densely with no room to move.

The gas killed them in ten to thirty minutes. The bodies persisted standing upright, "like pillars of basalt...not having any space to fall."[39]

* * *

In March of 1942, Jews from the ghetto at Lublin went to Belzec, and Slovakian Jews to Auschwitz. In July 1942, the first shipments from the Warsaw ghetto arrived in Treblinka. In February of 1943, Jews were sent from Bialystok and Berlin followed by those from Greece, Holland, Luxembourg, Vienna, and Prague. In April 1943, young Jews in Warsaw decided to make a last, violent stand and their uprising led to the destruction of the Warsaw ghetto by German, Latvian, and Ukrainian *Waffen-SS* troops. In the summer of 1943, more and more ghettos underwent "liquidation" by transferring their people to one of the six killing centers. In the fall, there followed those left over in Minsk, Vilna, Riga, and all other White Russian ghettos; while, at the same time, from the west there came the Jews from Denmark, France, and Rome. In the spring of 1944, Jews were collected in Athens and Hungary, who so far had been spared. In August and September 1944, as Stalin's armies were approaching, the Lodz ghetto was sent to the gas chambers, followed by more from Slovakia and France. At the eleventh hour of that war, in December of 1944, Jews from Budapest were taken for extermination to Austria.

* * *

The uprising in Warsaw in April 1943 was a desperate and suicidal, last-stand battle meant to wreak vengeance and to redeem the honor of the Jewish people. The young men proudly went on the road to their death rather than be led like sheep to the slaughter.[40] But that violent defiance was an exception.

They laid themselves down to be shot in the mass graves, stoically, and in the same manner they went into the gas chambers. Yes, they were deceived to believe that they were merely being "resettled"and that the gas chambers were shower rooms, but their credulity went only so far. One killing squad commander commented,"Strange is the calmness with which the delinquents allow themselves to be shot, and that goes for non-Jews as well as Jews. Their fear of death appears to have been blunted by a kind of indifference, which has been created in the course of twenty years of Soviet rule."[41]

Various reasons have been suggested, some citing the influence of lessons Jews learned from their religion and painful history. Quite likely, the docility and compliance toward the powers of the authorities was a characteristic not limited to them alone but was prevalent in the cultures of Central and Eastern Europe in general. Any defiance against the rulers, so it was believed, had always been and will always be fruitless. Instead, in their firm religious faith, they took refuge in piety, saw God's hand in everything, and proceeded toward their end "wrapped in prayer shawls and reciting psalms."[42] Hasidic Jews related tales of deliverance and hoped for the coming of the Messiah.[43]

*   *   *

It was a nightmare so abhorrent that death must have been an act of deliverance. Surprisingly, despite the industrialized nature of the killing process, there was ample room for individual cruelty. Sadism was put forth in a degree so excessive and in varieties so exotic that in today's world, one would assume the perpetrators were under the influence of drugs. Without pharmacological alteration, it seems the human brain is incapable of functioning that way. But they were not on drugs. There was some other kind of poison in the air that made those who breathed it violate the most elementary instincts nature has bestowed upon us.

A train of freight cars arrived in Auschwitz. It carried 6,700 Jews of whom 1,450 were dead on arrival. Two hundred Ukrainian guards beat the survivors to the ground with leather whips and forced them to disrobe. The entire naked contingent was then herded to the gas chambers. Prisoners were flogged to death for such trivial offenses as trying to retain a wedding ring or drinking water without permission.

A prisoner was incessantly beaten for refusal to squeal on a comrade until he finally collapsed. "The accepted camp procedure when a prisoner became unconscious was that the beating continued until he was dead."[44]

Rudolf Vrba wrote:

> I followed him into the dimly lit room; and I then stopped suddenly. Every available inch of space was occupied by bodies, all piled neatly in rows of ten. There must have been at least four hundred of them.... I saw that a lorry had drawn up outside the outer door. Four husky Poles came in, the men who made the birds fly, and Fred, his note book ready, joined them. One man glanced at an arm and called the tattooed number out to Fred who jotted it down. Another opened the dead mouth with a pair of pliers, hauled out a few gold teeth and dumped them with a clank into a tin can beside him. The remaining two picked up the corpse and sent it whirling through the door toward the lorry. They worked swiftly, rhythmically, like a closely-knit team. The number was called, the teeth came out, the flight began and Fred, all business now, surveyed the operation like an experienced foreman, watching for flaws that might snaggle the smooth machinery.[45]

* * *

The system ruling Auschwitz, and likely all other annihilation camps, was simple, diabolical, and faultlessly immutable. It was headed by an SS commander and his officers and NCOs who were devout disciples of a their false prophet, Adolf Hitler. They were imbued by a fervent faith in the sacred mission conferred on him by Providence. They were convinced of the righteousness of their task, which was the salvation of civilization and of their fatherland, by the exorcism of the fiendish race of the Jews. They went about it with the zeal and moral conviction that is otherwise known only from wars, where it is the accepted mandate of generals and their men to plan and execute massive, lethal, and destructive actions on their enemies so as to provide freedom and bliss to their own country. Consecrated to this task, the SS team rigidly supervised the flawless progress of the bestial crusade. Their noble purpose, as they saw it, was reassuring their conscience. At the same time, the system allowed them, for the most part, to keep their own hands clean since, in an inexorable manner, it compelled the prisoners to do the inhumane and ghoulish work themselves.

That was so because the immediate, hands-on portion of the management was delegated to overseers called Kapos. As described by Vrba, many of these, prisoners themselves, had been professional criminals in the past whereas others—communists or anti-Nazis—were imprisoned only for political reasons. Not all, but many of them, were Jews and they came from various countries. They were forced to supervise much of the transfer of the victims to the gas chambers, the emptying of the gas chambers, and the loading and operation of the crematorium. They had to execute the verbal abuse and flogging of their fellow prisoners in order to chase them into faster work. They were the ones to decide which prisoners were strong enough to do physical labor and which were too sick or emaciated and therefore had to be delivered to the "hospital" where they were done away with by intracardiac phenol injections. As all other prisoners who were selected for labor rather than for the gas chambers, they were themselves, by a constant threat of the death penalty, cowed into submission to a morbid scheme that gave them no other choice but to execute the assigned, repugnant tasks.

Add to this sketch an ocean of despair, hopelessness, horror, fanaticism, sadism, and savagery, and you may have gained a faint glimpse of one of the most violent eruptions of man-made evil.

*　*　*

The literature penetrates only rarely through the wall of secrecy surrounding these terrible events, to provide a glimpse at the reactions among German witnesses or of the executioners themselves. There are reports of a "nerve clinic" and an "SS-hospital" for SS-men "whose minds have collapsed through having to shoot women and children."[46] The SS Gen. Bach-Zelewski has testified about a visit of SS-chief Himmler at an execution of one hundred Jews in Minsk. Himmler apparently could not force himself to watch and expressed his revulsion. The SS-general thereupon seized the opportunity to point to the deeply shaken firing squad and to say,"These men are finished for the rest of their lives. What kind of followers are we training here? Either neurotics or savages."[47]

Several military officers who were decorated for bravery and previously loyal, and who were stationed on the Eastern Front, grew disabused and joined the German resistance after either having become accidental witnesses of such mass atrocities or having learned about them otherwise.[48] One of them was Col. Stauffenberg, who carried out the unsuccessful attempt to kill Hitler in 1944.

There was Kurt Gerstein, a mining engineer and committed Christian, who in 1941 joined the *Waffen-SS* in order to become "a spy for God."[49] A year later, as the head of the Technical Disinfection Service of the *Waffen-SS* and a specialist on cyanide disinfectants, he was dispatched on a tour through four concentration camps in Poland. What he saw there drove him into despair. He was told by the commandant,"There are not ten people alive who have seen or will see as much as you."[50] He is the author of detailed descriptions of the conditions and events he saw in the camps. A mere lieutenant, he could not be expected to interfere with the process. Instead, he made persistent attempts to inform the world of his eyewitness knowledge via the Swedish government and the Vatican, and hoped to have the Royal Air Force drop leaflets to inform the German people of it. He was met with disbelief; his efforts came to nothing.

Propaganda minister Josef Goebbels, one of Hitler's closest associates, did not discover the true meaning of the term Final Solution until March of 1942. Writing in his diary, he called it barbaric but deserved. "If we did not fight the Jew, they would destroy us. It's a life-and-death struggle between the Aryan race and the Jewish bacillus."

Then, of course, there was the testimony of Rudolf Höss, the commandant of Auschwitz. He said, "I am entirely normal." He stated that he led a normal family life.[51] When Himmler informed him of the "Führer Order" (a term coming close to meaning God's commandment) to convert Auschwitz into an extermination facility, he could only reply "Yes, sir." As a member of the elite SS, the idea of disobeying an order was unthinkable. He had never conceived of being held responsible for his work at Auschwitz. Responsibility had always rested on the man who gave the orders. "We were all...trained to obey orders without even thinking..."[52] As Abraham had been willing to follow orders to sacrifice his son Isaac,[53] so these men, too, viewed absolute obedience, even if it meant following insane orders, as an indispensable prerequisite of absolute loyalty. Indeed, loyalty, especially in a cult-like atmosphere, had always been one of the most sacred virtues.

*   *   *

In those days, rumors and clandestine reports of the Final Solution found few believers. In the winter at the end of 1941, two Jews escaped from the Chelmno camp and managed to reach the Warsaw ghetto. Their terrifying accounts of the mass gassing of people were disbelieved and rejected; their listeners suspected that their fright had caused them to lose their senses. The information was judged implausible and was suppressed.[54]

Similarly, news reached the Warsaw ghetto in January 1942 of the mass shootings in Ponary, with estimates of about fifty thousand victims. The Warsaw underground leaders dismissed the warning that this might represent the beginning of a program of annihilating Polish Jewry. The Vilna Jews, they felt, had perhaps brought this upon themselves by supporting the Soviets. The Germans would never dare to carry out such mass killings in Warsaw, a European capital.[55]

Rumors about death camps were disbelieved "all over Europe" by Jews and non-Jews alike.[56] Kurt Gerstein's eyewitness reports to Baron von Otter, secretary of the Swedish Legation in Berlin, were received with doubts.[57] Even more so, when Gerstein conveyed the information to such anti-German men as the Dutch resistance, their reaction was one of "utter incredulity."[58]

In the United States, first reports of the extermination program, obtained via Jewish members of the Polish National Committee in London, arrived in May 1942. They were published in the Boston Globe and New York Times but only as short and inconspicuous news items.[59] President Roosevelt was briefed through several reports and interviews about the events but exerted little and late initiative. "The political landscape," that is to say, mounting American anti-Semitism, was unfavorable to emphasizing the matter either in words or deeds, and this was true with respect to the Congress, the church leaders, the intellectual community and even influential Jews.[60] As a consequence, the American nation as a whole was essentially uninformed about the disaster befalling the European Jewry. At the end of the war, many Americans were unwilling to accept what they read in the papers and saw in pictures and newsreels, and were apt to denounce it as propaganda.[61]

*   *   *

Working in the National Central Security Office (RSHA), SS-Col. Adolf Eichmann was section chief in charge of Jewish affairs. Under Heydrich's supervision, he was given administrative responsibility of the Holocaust at the age of thirty-six. He was tried and executed in Israel in 1962.

SS-Gen. Reinhard Heydrich was Chief of the RSHA, which included the Security Service and *Gestapo*, and he was the leading force behind the police state measures against opponents of the regime and the Jews. Hitler ordered him, verbally through Himmler, to set up the machinery of the Final Solution, a job that largely fell into Eichmann's section. Heydrich was also appointed acting "Protector" of Bohemia and Moravia and was there, in fact, a benign and not unpopular dictator. The British arranged for his assassination in May of 1942.

Ernst Kaltenbrunner replaced Heydrich as Chief of the RSHA. He was convicted at the Nuremberg Trials and hanged in 1946.

Heinrich Himmler was head of the SS including all of its subdivisions such as the RSHA and *Waffen-SS*. He had overall operational control over the *Einsatzgruppen* and all concentration and extermination camps. Feared by all, he himself was a trembling servant to Hitler. He committed suicide in May of 1945.

The man without whom there would have been no peacetime persecution of the Jews, no Second World War, and no Holocaust was Adolf Hitler. He committed suicide on April 30, 1945.

The Legacy

If a traveler were to visit Germany today and if he had the chance to speak to a German citizen about these events in a private, heart-to-heart manner, he would encounter a somber and grave sentiment and a spirit of profound atonement. It is a feeling of collective disgrace, and perhaps even contrition. Contrition, of course, is a word that emphasizes the admission of guilt and most Germans who lived during the war would find the concept of personal guilt difficult to accept because they had as little knowledge or involvement in the crime as did the citizens of any other country. For most, therefore, the atonement is instead one of shameful recognition of collective liability and the responsibility to render retribution.

The general atonement is a sincere feeling, which is coupled with a mature and heartfelt readiness to acknowledge the facts of a grievous past and to deal with it in an upright manner. One might compare this sincere readiness with the similar attitude among the white community of North America who have turned their backs on their past of anti-Negro racism. However, there is a difference, for in Germany, the implied national humiliation renders this attitude immensely traumatic. It has subjugated patriotism and as such it is probably unique in the world. Patriotism is the principle for which millions of mothers and fathers have sacrificed their sons in wars. Patriotism is why multitudes of men have fought and died for their country for centuries. Patriotism rises magnificently in victory but even in defeat it settles in as patriotic spite. Patriotism is considered glorious and sacred the world over. I know of no country where patriotism is in disrepute except in Germany. There, one might find fervent patriotism perhaps in championship games on the soccer field, but not otherwise. It has fallen victim to the grievous shame imposed by the Holocaust.

Looking back at the Second World War, one might correctly conclude that Germany's decline was not so much imposed on the battlefields at Stalingrad, El Alamein, or in Normandy under the impact of her enemies' arms, as it was by that self-inflicted evil curse at Auschwitz.

PART 5

THE TURNING OF THE TIDE

Two Proud Lieutenants

I<small>T MUST HAVE BEEN IN</small> M<small>ARCH OF</small> 1942, when Dieter's training in Wünsdorf was completed, and he received his lieutenant's commission. Before being sent back to the front, he served several weeks with the Reserve Battalion in Stralsund—the Baltic town where I was born, where Grandmother lived, and not far from Uncle Siegfried's farm. The train ride to Berlin being only two hours long, he was still able, on some weekends, to travel down to visit us. As before, the two of us engaged in horseplay; he played "*Taboo*," "*Nightmonster*," and other tunes on the piano; and he also went to parties where, I understand, the girls went for him in a big way.

Starting in April, Friedrich was stationed at the School for Fast Troops in Krampnitz, not far from Potsdam. He spent almost a year there training officer candidates. Hence, on some weekends in April and May, Dieter and Friedrich were both home on leave, and we were all united again. Dieter made sure his older brother noticed that he too, now, was wearing the smart lieutenant's uni-

form, sword and all. "Yeah," Friedrich said returning the insolent grin, "you caught up with me, darn it."

One day, we all gathered in the living room and Dieter's girlfriend, a photographer, took pictures of us, all the family together. I still have one of them.

FAITH AND HERESY

One weekend, friends and relatives were visiting. The conversation unavoidably revolved around the war and politics. As was common, when people in the closed circle of like-minded friends felt safe to speak their minds, they must have had quite a time exchanging anti-government comments, rumors, and jokes.

Some of the subdued criticism was, you might say, routine and in no way different from those in other countries. The news reports were suspected of being heavily doctored and untruthful. Goebbels was always a favorite target in political jokes, not only because everybody knew about his falsifying the truth, but also because of his small size, his clubfoot, and his theatrical singsong voice. Party bosses were despised as uncouth as well as corrupt. The police, I heard, had caught one of them with a pig in his trunk, slaughtered on the black market.

Obviously, though, there were graver complaints as well. The Party's atheism and its annoying anti-church attitude cast an ill shadow over the whole regime. Himmler and his *Gestapo* had a sinister reputation, and people rumored about their illegal intrusions. While the *Waffen-SS* divisions, steadily growing in number, were generally excepted from such aspersions and were rather correctly seen as elite units of exceptional bravery and patriotism, they, nonetheless, were resented as Himmler's private army that stood aloof from the regular army, air force, and navy. People knew that they were, at times, called upon to execute unsavory tasks, such as the unforgiving police actions against partisans. It was a widely held opinion that the war had to be won first, but surely, the first thing afterwards had to be the elimination of the SS. The Party and Himmler's SS forces were clearly "the other camp," where a person had to watch out and keep his thoughts to himself.

There was, of course, no notion of the Holocaust. At this time, it was in its early stages, and its secrets were not discovered until the end of the war.

Hitler, on the other hand, peculiarly maintained the reputation of an honest and decent man, a well-intentioned helmsman who tried his best to steer the ship through the hurricane. Yet, he did not entirely escape censure either. Mother never had much use for his invoking "Providence" in his speeches. "What does he mean by Providence if he doesn't believe in God?" she asked. Somebody had heard that the Catholic Church had excommunicated him. And then, of course, when he invaded the Soviet Union, perhaps, or declared war on the United States, one might have heard people whisper that he was suffering from *Grössenwahn*, from megalomania; not that he was immoral, mind you, but just a man with too much power who had gone loony.

I don't know what they spoke about at that get-together in our home. I was not present, maybe away on my bicycle, who knows. But I heard about it later. Dieter had suddenly spoken up.

"Listen," he had said, "you can't talk that way. If what you say is true, we shouldn't be out there fighting. It's pretty rough out there, you know, and you have to believe in your country and what you're fighting for. Otherwise you just can't do it." They quickly changed the subject.

Their regiment was still deployed up in the Leningrad area where Friedrich had been wounded in November. One day, not long before Dieter returned there, we were talking about the *Afrika Korps*. It might have been related to Gen. Rommel's new offensive that May which later was to take him to El Alamein. Dieter confessed that he would much prefer fighting in Africa than in Russia. I have never forgotten his reason for it. Between the British and the Germans, he said wistfully, prisoners and captors were said to be exchanging addresses so that they could get together after the war.

Whether or not his information was correct, the feelings it expressed were shared widely during the war. There was no real hostility against the British. On the contrary, there was a desire to end this unwanted war and the hope for reconciliation with them, once peace had returned.

A QUESTION OF DOOM

The war was raging on. After the attack on Pearl Harbor the previous December, the Japanese had been making a clean sweep across Southeast Asia. Obeying the Tripartite Pact between Japan, Italy, and Germany, Hitler and Mussolini had declared war on the United States. Like the Japanese, the German forces made huge advances as well. Rommel's *Afrika-Korps* was routing the British across North Africa while, on the Eastern Front, our troops reached Stalingrad on the Volga River and farther south the oil fields near Maikop and the Caucasus. Mountain troops hoisted the German flag on Mt. Elbrus, the Caucasus's highest peak.

But all was not well. The previous winter had already brought a shocking reversal. For everyone to see, our troops had been entirely unprepared for the campaign in Russia's brutal winter that paralyzed equipment, personnel, and the spirit of élan. Many people and many soldiers knew then that the era of *blitzkrieg* and quick victories was over.

British air attacks on all major German cities had become so numerous and destructive that the government instituted a voluntary program allowing evacuation of city children, along with their teachers, to smaller towns and resorts where they were housed in hotels not needed much now by tourists. It sounded exciting, and I would have liked to go along, but my parents did not agree. They suspected it to be a program designed to remove children from the influence of their parents so as to better indoctrinate them in the Party's ideology.

Our summer offensives were murderous, both sides deployed unprecedented concentrations of armor and materiel. Casualties were mounting. The mass killings of the *Einsatzgruppen* being unknown, people thought brutality was limited to the enemy. The Russians did not take wounded men prisoner; they shot them. They shot everyone in a field hospital including the doctor meeting them with a Red Cross flag.[1] I heard about soldiers who preferred death to becoming a prisoner-of-war and who saved their last bullet for themselves. The image of the Russians, prevalent among Germans, was similar to that so eloquently expressed by Churchill of the Hun-like Germans. A spine-chilling terror took possession of them. They felt that they had made contact with a foe who was made up of a sea of mindless peasants radicalized by Bolshevism and commanded by a brutal dictator. They saw in the east a monster, which was alien to the western world, dumb but immense, backward but mechanized, primitive but fierce, and bleeding but not falling.

No propaganda and no threat by the *Gestapo* could have been more effective for the nation to close ranks than the collision with Stalin's empire. No matter what objections one might have had to our own government, they suddenly had become petty and irrelevant. There was only one problem on this earth, only one peril confronting civilization; that peril was mortal and it wore the face of Joseph Stalin.

IF YOU'RE NOT AFRAID

July 25, 1942
My dear little Peter,

Many thanks for your sweet postcard. I enjoyed it very much. Enjoy your vacation there, and say hello to everyone including Minna (Grandma's live-in maid). At the moment, I'm lying in my tent because outside it's raining cats and dogs. The slacks have arrived and the packages with Mom's cakes, too. They tasted "fantastic". ...you could give her a call and tell her I'm putting in a request for more of them. Too bad I'm no longer stationed in Stralsund because you could be visiting me now and then, the way Karl-Hermann did. If you're not afraid of soldiers, why don't you go to the Prinz Moritz Barracks and convey my respectful greetings to Maj. Seidel. All you have to do is mention your name there and no question everybody is going to be nice to you. You might tell him we're presently being regrouped near Mga. Another one you can visit is Capt. Gless, A Company. The best time is 11:00 A.M., that's when everybody is there. Just tell the guard where you want to go, he'll take you there. All right, Popowisch, that's it for today. Stay out of trouble, I always did.

A loving hello!

Your brother Dieter

A BOTTLE OF CHAMPAGNE

September 21, 1942
Madame,

My heart-felt thanks for your and your family's wishes on my birthday and also for the package. It made me mightily happy, the fact that you thought of me. It is so good to receive news from home, out here in this Workers' and Peasants' Paradise.

Dieter and I celebrated my birthday together.

Actually, it was the day before. We sat down in a trench, drank a bottle of champagne and smoked several good cigarettes. Our spirits were low because shortly before we had lost several of our best friends, as Dieter, I'm sure, has already reported to you. Dautwiz... and Eben have both fallen. There was an attack on my birthday, too. Unfortunately, things didn't quite work out as planned either.

By the way, Dieter and I see each other quite often, in spite of the fact that he is in the first battalion and I am at regimental HQ. On orders of my C.O. and over my objections, I'm being sent to a convalescent center at Pernau, Estonia. I'll miss Dieter a lot. To you, Madame, and your esteemed family, many greetings.

Devotedly yours,

Hans-Günther Rasmus

Tomorrow I'll Write You

September 24, 1942
My dear parents,

You are really supplying me generously. Yesterday I received the package from Friedrich. Boy, was I happy about it. From you, dear Mom, three small packages have arrived and in addition the first of the large ones. ...I'm in a great rush because we're leaving this area... It was really nice here. I don't know where we're headed and I shouldn't be telling you anyway... I'm convinced the Russians can't hold out much longer. No news otherwise... Rasmus was immediately returned to the front even though he had not recovered completely. But the colonel promptly sent him to Pernau where our division has a convalescent center. So now I am the last one of those who came out here...

A photo of my bunker, dear Mom, I couldn't possibly send you. There aren't enough films...for all the bunkers I've lived in... If Friedrich could lay his hands on a pistol, he should try to mail it to me from his office as official mail...

Tomorrow I'll try to write you right away where we are. We're off! Many heart-felt greetings,

Your Dieter

LETTER FROM ESTONIA

Pernau, Oct. 1, 1942
Madame,

I have just received word from a corporal of Dieter's company that Dieter was seriously wounded on 25 September. A shrapnel wound of the head. I hope I'm not the messenger of this news. I am presently out of touch with the regiment...and that's why I am turning to you, Madame, to give me news at the earliest possible time of his condition and his present whereabouts. I know it may be insensitive to ask this of a grieved mother but, you see, we're talking about my last and my best comrade in the regiment. I was given to understand that soon after he was wounded he was transported by plane to Germany. I hope that is accurate.

My stay here is to last another ten days; however, (in my heart) I don't have a quiet minute any more. By the way, a short time after Dieter was wounded, his superior, First Lt. Preuss also was wounded seriously. Our proud regiment is in sad shape.

With the warmest greetings, also for your esteemed family, Madame, I am devotedly yours,

Hans-Günther Rasmus

VERMISST

Our letters were returned with the notation "*Vermisst*," missing-in-action. Father, using connections through the Ministry of Agriculture, was able to contact Divisional Headquarters by telephone via the Army High Command, as well as the Reserve Battalion, but neither had information beyond the fact that Dieter had been wounded.

There was, however, one report—I have forgotten its source - which we clung to and recited frequently because we had nothing else to go by. It stated that someone had found him lying on the ground after the battle, had paused and said, "Well, Dieter, so they got you too."

Mother's voice still reverberates in my ear today, the way she recounted the story, time and again, to concerned friends, "And then Dieter said, 'No, I'm not dead! I'm alive!'" All her despair, her pain, and her trembling hope were vibrating these words. She repeated it often, for months and even years when people inquired. "No, no," she would say, "he said, 'I'm not dead, I'm alive!' don't you see?"

The way the story went on, they picked him up to take him to the aid station, but he never arrived. Not until months later did this letter arrive from the medical officer who had examined him.

> February 12, 1943
> Esteemed Sir,
>
> It is very late that I am responding to your request for a report about the fate of your son Dieter. I had hoped that further investigations would yield something definite to give you certainty. Let me start at the beginning.
>
> On September 24, Dieter was brought to my aid post. He had a shrapnel wound at the back of his head. It was nighttime, there was pouring rain, and the aid post consisted merely of a shed covered with tree branches. Thus, a detailed examination was impossible and was, in fact, not advisable because of the danger of infection. It was obvious, though, that the shrapnel had entered the brain. Nonetheless, he was conscious and when I asked him how he felt, he recognized me and asked, "How long before the ambulance arrives?" (The aid post was located in the midst

of swamps and the nearest access point for vehicles was two and a half kilometers away. Thus, transport by ambulance was out of the question.) After administering the necessary injections, we could fortunately turn him over to a group of ration carriers returning to the rear so he could at least rapidly be taken to the collection station. From there he would have been taken to the mentioned vehicle park and on to the collection station of the Fifth Mountain Infantry Division... Two weeks later, immediately after we were relieved, I visited all of the collection stations in question to inquire about the fate of the wounded we had cared for ... Despite repeated searches, none of their logs listed the name Dieter Nennhaus... By coincidence, weeks later, I learned from an ambulance driver that when walking through a cemetery he had seen a fresh grave bearing the name Lt. Nennhaus... I sent two men... (to the area) in order... to confirm this. Unfortunately, two days ago they returned without success because the front section where the cemetery is located is either in no man's land or in Russian hands...

Wagner

A note attached to this letter indicates that, soon afterwards, the doctor was killed in action.

Not Ten Years, Not Twenty

A month after receipt of this letter, in March of 1943, we held a somber counsel, all of us including Friedrich. There was no hope. Nobody, we said, survived a brain injury like that, and nobody survived being a Soviet prisoner-of-war either, even if well. We unanimously agreed to put the obituary notice in the paper. There were pages full of them now, every day. Our announcement began with the words: "We no longer doubt..."

Mother did, though. In her heart she felt him to be alive. She was a little superstitious and believed in telepathy. In the darkness and silence of night, unable to sleep, she could feel how

Dieter was thinking of her, she said, from somewhere far away in Russia... On many a morning, I heard her quietly say, "Last night, his thoughts came home. Yes, he was thinking of us. I know he did, I could feel it."

For decades after the war, there prevailed in Germany the notion of secret Soviet labor camps, in which the Red Regime was supposedly concealing massive numbers of prisoners who were never permitted to write to their families or otherwise send out a sign of life. They were called "*Schweigelager*," Muted Camps. That name, *Schweigelager*, was a haunting and dreadful word. The belief in their existence was probably never entirely given up until the Soviet Regime finally collapsed. Thus, even though there was no sign of life coming from Dieter, there still existed the possibility of his languishing in a Muted Camp. In her faithful heart, Mother never gave up hope, not after ten years and not after twenty, that Dieter might return some day, ring the door bell, stand there, and say, "I'm back, Mother."

TEARS

Dieter's loss was grievous and sorrowful. When alone and nobody could see me, I did a lot of crying. In school with the boys, I flew off the handle at the slightest provocation. Miss von der Heyde just mentioned Dieter's name, and there I was, bawling. There was little she could do about it. She chose for me to play a piece from "*Winterreise*," a very melancholic melody by Schubert.

I wasn't the only one. We all cried. We were heartbroken. Returning from school, when I pushed the heavy entrance door open and entered the cool, dim inside of the building, I took a deep breath and braced myself; it was like entering a mortuary. Mother would have red eyes and would barely smile when opening the door. It was hard for me to see her that way, and I went out of my way to help her with house chores. It seems this was still so a year later. The pain and heartbreak just did not want to fade.

One day, I was in the study and, through the open sliding door, I heard someone sob in the living room, uncontrollably sob. I furtively looked around the corner. It was Dad. He was standing by the tiled furnace warming his back. He blew his nose and wiped his eyes. He thought he was alone. Never before had I seen a man cry.

At times, I would sit at the piano and try the tunes Dieter used to play: "*Taboo*," "*Night monster*," and "*A little white house by the great blue sea*," even though my style was so much poorer than his. Or perhaps, I would play "*Ich hatt' einen Kameraden*," that haunting song of the Fallen Comrade. Once, Gila came in the room and whispered angrily for me to stop it. "You've got Mother crying in the kitchen!"

I still have a sketchpad that I used that year. Like the piano, sketching provided some relief. There is a sketch of a grave, a helmet hanging from the cross. Another one is labeled "Stalingrad," the city were that tragic battle was fought at that time. It showed a cityscape in ruins and on fire and a soldier firing a machine-gun from a pile of rubble. The sadness lasted for years, and I kept returning to the same theme. A later sketch, a melancholic drawing, shows a desolate wintry plain and a solitary tree, underneath it a disabled tank and again a grave. Snow covers everything, the land, the barren tree branches, the tank, and the cross.

It was still cold outside. Mother was fussing around in the living room putting things in order. Friedrich, on leave for the weekend, was warming his back on the furnace. Nobody spoke a word. Then she stopped near him, turned toward him, and pressed her face into his uniform. He put his arms around her, laid his cheek on her hair, and gently stroked her back. I can still see them standing there. There was no sound.

Faith in Science

The tide of martial fortune had turned; there were Rommel's reversal at El Alamein, the landing of American troops in North Africa, and then the incredible disaster at Stalingrad. It did not look good. People began to wonder. They badly needed a morale booster.

There were rumors of "new weapons," some kind of super-bomb perhaps. Yes, a super-weapon would do it, would help us stave off the threatening deluge of the Red Army. We turned to our scientists for hope; everybody was kept in awe by the near miracles they had already wrought.

Science had given us synthetic rubber and gasoline hydrolyzed from coal. When there was need, scientists became inventive. We learned about that in Physics class. There was shortage of soap, so now they made soap from bones of cattle and hogs.

The sulfonamides were a new class of drugs that killed bacteria and cured infections. They had also developed a new gas now, Zyklon B it was called, a lethal gas, that was to replace the electric chair, because it was so humane. One would place the criminal into a chamber and then blow the gas into it; he would feel no pain. A gas chamber, it was called. They were working on jet engines too, now, making planes fly even faster. There was exciting scientific progress, wherever one looked. Anyhow, we had good reason to have faith in our scientists and placed our hopes in them.

HE IS MY BROTHER

I was, on this Sunday morning, not merely the only boy on the Krampnitz Training Grounds but also the proudest and the most excited. There were soldiers everywhere, and they all snappily saluted my big brother. I climbed on and under tanks and armored personnel carriers, and, finally, he took me to the shooting range.

"Of course, *Herr Oberleutnant!*" said the corporal casting a big, benevolent smile, first at me and then at Friedrich, who seemed as proud of his little brother as the little brother was of him. I got on my belly behind the machine-gun and fired away. I had seen it many times on the newsreel but never realized how much a machine-gun comes to life when one squeezes that trigger. It gave off a frightening din, it vibrated fiercely in my hands, a strange smell hit my nose, and the butt was painfully hammering against my shoulder. But with everybody looking on, this was no time to be timid about it, and so, giving them a sample of what the enemy could expect from me, I ferociously fired away.

Friedrich was convinced of my valor sooner than I expected, though, for he stepped forward and said smilingly, "Well fine, Peter, yes, terrific, I guess that will do. That's expensive stuff, you know."

Total War

His voice was shrill and his message was spine chilling. In my ear it is still as real as though it were today. Speaking in the Berlin *Sportpalast*, which was packed with Party functionaries, Goebbels, the master orator and propaganda minister, had slowly built up to this incisive climax by enumerating a series of setbacks and reverses. Then it came, loud, startling, alarming:

"*Gefahr—ist im Verzuge!*"—"Danger—" he waited a second to allow the cry to reverberate in the large arena and to let it sink in, "is in the offing!" Another brief pause of reverberation before he followed through, *"Es muss schnell—und unerbittlich gehandelt werden!"*—"We must act with speed—and inexorable resolve!" He proclaimed Total War, "war even more total and more radical than anyone can as yet imagine."

His speech set in motion a massive program to mobilize a vast new work force for the war industry, largely from the ranks of housewives. Women were to volunteer for this noble effort and, indeed, they did in large numbers. Not until several weeks later—I remember, we were standing in the hallway near the kitchen—did Mother tell me that she had at last worked up enough courage to sign up after all. I suppose it had been a difficult decision, because she had never worked as a laborer in a factory before, or perhaps there had been other reservations. But now, she had made up her mind. "You know, I can't let Friedrich fight alone. They need support."

A Small Bomb With a Silent Fuse

ATTEMPTS MADE BY THE GERMAN RESISTANCE to depose Hitler, or to kill him, evolved in two sequences. There were five such attempts between the fall of 1938 and the summer of 1940 and six between March of 1943 and July 1944. Initially, their purpose was to stop him from initiating a war and after that had failed, to prevent him from launching a campaign against France in November 1939, which was judged militarily insane and which he indeed canceled.

The ensuing three-year pause grew from the fact that now there was nothing left to do but to fight the war, which the Resistance had been unsuccessful in preventing and, also, from the conviction that it was utterly impossible to remove a leader whose miraculous victories had made him unassailable. By then, the people of the Resistance had resigned in the belief that Hitler was Germany's lot to bear.

In the second phase, whose preparations were actually beginning in 1942, the motivations were different and belonged in three categories. Fragmentary knowledge of the mass killings of the *Einsatzgruppen* had reached a progressively increasing number of people in the regular Army, to a degree where their criminal nature became obvious. Secondly, even without such knowledge, many were alarmed by the disastrous flaws in Hitler's military leadership, especially so after the catastrophe of the battle of Stalingrad, and recognized the urgent need to remove him from power. By 1944, finally, although the conspirators felt his assassination would no longer change the impending disaster of their country and would have little practical effect, they still believed that for purely moral reasons—much like the last stand taken by the young Jews in the Warsaw ghetto — it had to be attempted, just the same, so as to save the honor of their country.

The decision to undertake such a task was impeded by various adverse circumstances. Hitler was almost inaccessible and was surrounded by a hermetic security apparatus. Several requests to obtain cooperation from the British and Americans had failed, and it was correctly feared that Churchill and Roosevelt would agree to nothing less than reducing Germany to a subservient nation irrespective of the nature of the German government. Among the majority of the German people and the younger officer corps, there prevailed continued faith and trust in Hitler's good will and competence, even late into the war. A coup attempt was certain to face public incredulity and condemnation. The crisis of the war was so deadly as to make the risk of a palace revolution or civil war difficult to accept. The merciless conflict with Stalin ruled out any chance of a negotiated settlement, even if Hitler left and the country established a normal government. Roosevelt and Churchill's demand at Casablanca, in January of 1943, for an unconditional surrender indicated the same attitude on their part and thus, all escape routes in the west were blocked as well. And lastly, under the martial circumstances, a coup d'état could only be carried out by the military, but many among the officer corps were possessed by the old code of patriotism, loyalty, and obedience, much more than by any political or conspiratorial talents or ambitions.

Nevertheless, the Resistance was a broad network with centers in the Foreign Office, the *Abwehr* (military intelligence and counter-espionage), the clergy, of course, and in the middle and upper ranks of the Army, including Hitler's headquarters in East Prussia. One conspiratorial focus was active in the headquarters of the Army Group Center in Smolensk. Almost all of the military members of the Resistance belonged in the nobility. They were convinced Christians and idealists who were deeply impressed by the gravity of the disaster at hand and by their moral obligation to take action.

Lt. Col. Henning von Tresckow was the senior operations officer at the Smolensk Headquarters. At that time he was forty-one years old. In the summer of 1942, he reached the conclusion that the only feasible method of assassinating Hitler was by means of explosives. He approached Rudolf von Gersdorff, an intelligence officer and a co-conspirator, who had connections with the *Abwehr* in Berlin. He asked him to search for explosives that, unlike available German devices, were small and had a silent fuse. Gersdorff found sophisticated bombs captured from the British that satisfied these criteria. Over the course of several months, he was able to divert a quantity of them from the *Abwehr* to Smolensk where they conducted secret experiments with it.

After repeated refusals, Hitler at last accepted an invitation to visit the Army Group Center HQ on March 13, 1943, flying from his supreme command post at the Wolf's Lair in East Prussia in the Führer plane, a FW 200 Condor. In Berlin, the Resistance went into action to prepare for the take-over of power once Hitler was dead. Tresckow was able to persuade one of the members of Hitler's group, a man by the name of Brandt, to take along a package containing"two bottles of Cointreau"for a friend of his at the Wolf's Lair. As the Führer boarded the plane for his return flight, the silent British fuse was set for thirty minutes. The bomb would go off when the plane was near Minsk.

Hitler arrived safely in East Prussia. The device had not ignited.

Tresckow sent his aide, Lt. Fabian von Schlabrendorff, by regular courier plane, the next day, to Hitler's headquarters to retrieve the "Cointreau" under some pretense from Brandt, before anybody opened the package. Schlabrendorff took the bomb to the Resistance group in Berlin. There, the group realized that a new opportunity presented itself within a week to make another attempt with the same device. March 21 was Hero's Memorial Day, on which occasion Hitler was to be present at a ceremony, which included a visit at an exhibition of captured Soviet war materials. This exhibit was prepared by the intelligence section of Rudolf von Gersdorff, who himself was to guide Hitler through it. Gersdorff had lost his wife and had no descendants. He volunteered to carry the bomb and to blow himself up along with Hitler. As the tour began, he reached in his pocket to set the ten-minute fuse, all the while being under the eyes of numerous vigilant SS security men.

Nobody ever understood what suddenly altered Hitler's will. He rushed through the exhibit, failing to be retained even by Reich Marshall Göring's comments and was out on the street after only two minutes. Gersdorff managed to escape into a lavatory in time to defuse the device.

This was the first of four successive suicide missions planned to kill Hitler during the next twelve months. For different reasons none of them ever reached the point of execution.

Sixteen months later, on July 20, 1944, Col. Claus von Stauffenberg exploded a bomb in Hitler's map room at the Wolf's Lair, which also failed to kill him. Lt. Col. von Tresckow, having played a role in that attempt as well and facing the predictable vengeance of the SS-State, killed himself the day after.

Lt. Schlabrendorff was arrested, tortured, and put in a concentration camp. In February of 1945, he was brought into the courtroom of the infamous hanging judge, Roland Freisler, but the trial proceedings were interrupted by an air raid. A direct hit on the court-building killed Freisler. Lt. Schlabrendorff survived the war.

Rudolf von Gersdorff's further adventures vibrantly illustrate the two conflicting sides in the hearts of the Resistance men; one that loved their fatherland, and one that condemned its government. In the summer of 1944 he was Chief of Staff of an army in France. The assassination attempt on July 20 exposed him, too, to the danger of being caught as a member of the Resistance. Instead, however, he was taken prisoner by the Allies. He did not accept that state for what it was, namely the safest refuge against probings by the SS. On the contrary, he escaped from his captors, made it back to the German lines, and led his troops out of an encirclement known as the Falaise Pocket. He was promoted to Major General and received the coveted Knight's Cross. His loyalty to this country remained unperturbed, even though Hitler remained in power. Gersdorff fought to the end of the war and was one of the few members of the Resistance who survived.

STIFFENING RESOLVE

BEFORE FRIEDRICH RETURNED TO THE EASTERN FRONT in early May of 1943, he had left me with a large map of Eastern Europe. I mounted it on the living room wall. A dark green cord, winding around pins, followed the course of the front line from the Arctic to the Caucasus Mountains. Approximately three hundred kilometers south of Moscow, it jutted out in a nose-like eastward projection around the city of Orel. The Twenty-fifth Regiment was deployed there. The city of Kursk, south of it, was in Russian hands.

From this point, a decisive breakthrough was planned. He had told me about the arrival of the new Panther tanks, finally a match for the Russian T-34s, and that our even heavier Tiger tanks were soon to follow.

Three and a half years had passed since the outbreak of the war and victory was becoming more and more elusive. The strain began to show itself in an increasingly embittered determination to forge ahead, no matter what the price. Indeed, the rising specter of possible doom at the hands of Stalin left little choice, even for the faint-hearted or those otherwise critical of the war or of the government. Such a hardened attitude was quite possibly a self-protecting mechanism. It served as an emotional armor, warding off fear or the unbearable feeling of despondency. At times, one could hear anger voiced at those who seemed to stand in the way or who didn't carry their weight in the war effort. Or people might repeat official patriotic slogans, as if reaffirming support for the cause, but it was often merely an act of self-encouragement.

My brother, by nature given to single-minded and loyal devotion to a task, showed this kind of stiffening resolve more than did the rest of our family. He was an eyewitness of the slaughter of the war more than we were at home. His resolve developed after the loss of Dieter and as a result of the catastrophe at Stalingrad, along with the increasingly grim experience of the war anywhere else in the east.

FOCUSED ON WAR AND VICTORY

June 26, 1943
Dear Mom, Dad, and Gila,

What must you be thinking of me that I haven't written in just about a week? ...Perhaps I am a bad son because I write so rarely; (but) my thoughts travel home sooo often... I'm trying to do my duty here as well as I possibly can. Perhaps I'm bull-headed and one-sided because all of my thoughts and actions are exclusively—and I mean exclusively—focused on the war. But I really don't want to be different because in the soldiers who are, like me, bull-headed and one-sided with all their thoughts and actions focused on the war and on victory, in these soldiers lies the certain guaranty of our victory...

But why am I philosophizing; you know how I am and that I always endeavor to do what is good. Good, though, is only that which serves my company. Many of the orders we receive are not good for my company, and then I simply don't do it, or I change it. That way, I believe, I am fulfilling my duty and I am acting in the interest of our good cause. If that bucks the system sometimes, that doesn't bother me. So long as one is upright and decent, it can never be totally wrong. Now enough of that! Just received your letter of the seventeenth. ...Everything is quiet, absolutely quiet... No guerrilla bands far and wide...

...Friedrich

THE BRICKLAYER'S SUSPICION

As Mother entered through the big, oak door, Mrs. Karg straightened up on her knees and told her of a strange occurrence. She had heard it from Heinz, her son, and as she couldn't get it off her mind, she had waited for Mother in order to see what she thought of it.

Heinz, who had lost a leg in Russia, was stationed somewhere in Saxony. One day, a bricklayer friend of his and others of the same trade were detailed for a special job. They were taken into some kind of a compound or prison camp that made them feel ill at ease from the start. At a remote section of it, they were instructed to build a row of peculiar cubicles. They had never built anything similar before and were puzzled. The eerie atmosphere did its part, and so the mason came to imagine prisoners being forced to squat and crouch in these cubicles, for hours perhaps, as a form of punishment or torture. He felt this thought to be sickening, and, after returning to the barracks that night, he told his friend, Heinz Karg, about it. Heinz, too, felt sick. The next time he was home on leave, he told his mother about it. Mrs. Karg, in turn, was affected by it in much the same way.

"You don't think they'd *DO* that, Mrs. Doctor, do you?" she implored Mother. Mother told us. There were grave looks, but if I remember correctly, Mrs. Karg's question was left open.

At that time, this was merely one of many rumors and reports people exchanged in those turbulent days. I did not attribute much significance to it then. I do today.

Obviously, her story was no more than a rumor. It was hearsay, not even of a fact but hearsay of a suspicion. It raised a suspicion of undue violence on a scale so small that it could never compare with the mass killings that were occurring on the world's battlefields every day or, indeed, in the air raids inflicted upon our very city. Nor could we have thought of the supposed victims as innocent people, since prisoners were generally considered felons or lawbreakers. And what kind of numbers were we thinking of: six squatting chambers, or a dozen?

And yet, the mere suspicion of it was revolting enough to be passed along among many citizens of different strata of society. How pristine an image must they have had of their country? How strong must have been their expectations of official decency and propriety, how pure the values, which they thought their country stood for, that a rumor about cruel penal methods in a penitentiary was so surprising and so shocking?

These sentiments reflect our almost pious faith in the honor and righteousness of our country that I remember so well.

AHLBECK

That summer, as the bombing grew worse, my parents let Gisela and me participate in the children's evacuation program. Her school went to Brünn (Brno) in Czechoslovakia, mine to a seaside resort by the name of Ahlbeck, on the island of Usedom off the Baltic coast.

We spent three months there. Our class was lodged just a block or two from the beach, in a hotel called *Haus Augusta Viktoria*, I remember. We had regular classes, there was drill and marching and singing, fun at the beach and in the surf, and some good fellowship and patriotic singing in the evening breeze by the ocean that was warm and wholesome for our young souls.

While there, I was anxiously following the dramatic events on the Eastern Front. The Russians hadn't been sleeping, and when in the battle of Kursk, as the history books call it, the German offensive was launched, they were prepared. It was quickly labeled one of history's most massive battles of materiel. The gigantic German offensive was repulsed. Casualties were enormous. Friedrich was wounded. The brother of Otmar, the boy from across the street, a tank commander, was killed in action near Orel. Molly's brother Walter, fighting farther north, was killed, too, that summer of 1943. The Twenty-fifth Regiment was initially kept in reserve.

July 7, 1943
My dear, good Peter,

Now the great battle has been joined. As yet, we haven't seen action, however. We are located behind the front and are monitoring the events on the map. Progress is being made even though the Russians are offering fierce and heavy resistance. The day before yesterday they launched a heavy counteroffensive with two hundred T-34s. But they crashed headlong into our Tigers, which within a short period dispensed of eighty T-34s. The remainder turned tail. We had no losses...

...Friedrich

July 22, 1943
My dear Peter,

Just a quick note. I am slightly wounded, shrapnel left knee. Bone is probably intact, shrapnel still in the flesh, absolutely no pain, no fever, chow very good, great doctors, German nurses, radio, soft bed. You can see, everything is hunky-dory.

...Friedrich

July 27, 1943
Dear Parents,

Today it's a week since I got here. I feel terrific. Unfortunately, the hospital train isn't here yet... I hope soon! I'd love to sit together and enjoy a glass of wine with you again. And then take a trip up to Peter at the Baltic. And then immediately return to the front. My men need me there badly. There is big trouble at the Orel front. But we must hold out and Ivan must bleed himself to death. Under all circumstances. And that means, every single man counts, including myself, dear Mom! No back talk, there's no other way. Otherwise, we'll all go down the drain. It must! And it will, if everyone pitches in...

...Friedrich

Ahlbeck, August 11, 1943
My dear and good Mutti, dear Gila,

...When I learned about the evacuation of Berlin I felt awfully lonesome for all of you... (The other day we were
informed) that we will be leaving from here on September
20, 1943, to be reunited with our respective schools, which
by then will have been relocated from Berlin... My room-
mates...I like very much, (but) they're irked when I mention,
during a card game, that our troops have knocked out five
hundred tanks, (and) they don't notice that, all of a sudden,
Orel is located east of the front line.

     I was shocked to hear that Otmar's brother was
killed in action... Are you saying Uncle Axel was killed as
well? The other day I read among the Obituaries-of-the-
Fallen that now the third son of Mrs. Weiss has fallen, too. I
didn't cut it out and forgot the first name. But it read, "he followed his brothers Theo Weiss, killed...in France and (?)
Weiss, corporal with the fighter bombers," or something like
that. At the bottom it said, "Fate has tried us sorely."...

         ...Peter

Thus, all the action was occurring far away from our pleasant seaside retreat; yet, for reasons we did not understand then, at
this point the island was also being reclassified as being unsafe for
school children.

There had been rumors, circulating among the local folks,
dealing with those mysterious "new weapons," but we didn't take
them seriously. They claimed that a bomb was being built there, a
bomb so powerful it could wipe out half the island. Today it is no
longer a secret that a remote town by the name of Peenemünde,
barely thirty kilometers to the northwest of us, was the testing site
of the V-rockets, those buzz bombs that were to strike London a
year later. The little town might even be called the birthplace of the
space age.

On August 19, I wrote: "The other day there was an air raid

alarm here twice. Nothing happened. Only in Peenemünde were there some minor fires. Therefore, it is possible that we leave here sooner..."They moved us off the island a few days later. We arrived back in Berlin in the evening hours of August 23. Our parents were at the Stettiner Station to pick us up. It was so good to be home again.

A few hours later, the British arrived for one of the first showings of a brand new generation of air raids on the capital. It was as if they had come with a thousand bombers. The destruction from explosive and incendiary bombing was massive. There were to be many, many more like this during the ensuing twenty months of the war, slowly, but inexorably laying waste to this metropolis, along with most other major and medium sized German cities.

PART 6

APPROACHING DOOM

The First Stage

THE BATTLE OF BRITAIN, sometimes called the London Blitz, took place in the fall and winter of 1940. It was an aerial contest between the *Luftwaffe* and the Royal Air Force. Even today, it is known as a highlight of the war when the Hurricanes and Spitfires thwarted Hitler's attempt to gain superiority in England's skies, and about which Churchill movingly said, "Never in the field of human conflict was so much owed by so many to so few." We have read about the valor of the people of London and of other cities, who unperturbedly accepted the destruction and sacrifice, and whose stubborn spirit could not be broken by the unprecedented ordeal.

A statistical representation of the Battle of Britain is shown in Fig. 4. The diagram depicts the violence of strategic bombing of enemy cities, as measured by the monthly tonnage of bombs dropped. While the main feature pertains not to the Blitz but rather to the Allied bombing of German cities, the Battle of Britain can be recognized as a slight elevation between September of 1940 and February of 1941.[1]

By comparison, even though the British may not have thought so at the time, the German effort impresses the viewer as minuscule and insignificant.

Early on, the proper technology was still in its infancy. Daytime aerial attacks were quickly given up to avoid the heavy losses inflicted by enemy defenses. On the other hand, while night raids were safer to carry out, the darkness rendered accurate targeting virtually impossible. This created for the British the uncomfortable choice of either abandoning that type of warfare altogether, or resorting to the only method of inflicting damage, namely the method known as area bombing. Area bombing was the massive and indiscriminate carpet-bombing of large target areas, such as population centers. Its military mission was not only the destruction of whatever industrial and transport systems happened to be present, but, most importantly, to achieve a maximal amount of killing and devastation, so as to cause terror among the civilian population and to undermine their will to fight.

Fig. 4 Tonnage of Bombs Dropped per Month 1940-45

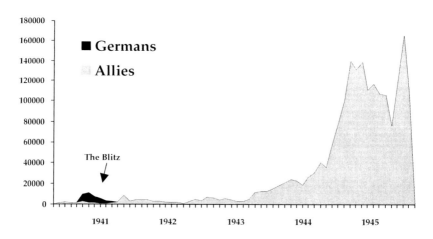

Despite the obvious failure of the German raids to instill such demoralization among the English, Air Marshals Charles Portal and his successor Arthur Travers Harris were convinced of this method's effectiveness in Germany. Even after the *Luftwaffe* had been rendered powerless in 1944 and the Americans freely carried out daytime precision bombing without enemy interference, the RAF adhered to the technique of the vastly lethal annihilation of cities until the very end of the war.

As is evident in the diagram, the intensity of British bombing by 1942 approached that of the Battle of Britain two years before. It was at this time that the German government initiated programs to evacuate children and their teachers from the larger cities. In the fall of 1942, the Eighth American Air Force began operations; and, with the deployment of four-engine Lancaster bombers and the B-17s, the Allied air offensive became truly devastating in 1943. The first firestorm was created in July 1943 in Hamburg, resulting in a death toll of 42,000. During fall and winter, Berlin was the target of sixteen such raids. With the arrival of the long-range P-51 Mustang fighters in February 1944, whose range was great enough to protect the bomber stream all the way to Berlin and with the depletion of German fuel supplies, complete air superiority was achieved over Germany. At that time, as seen in the diagram, the Allied aerial assault achieved monumental proportions.

As a consequence, by the end of the war, virtually all cities were turned into wastelands of rubble and empty facades. The strategic bombing offensive cost the lives of more than fifty thousand British and fifty thousand American airmen. The death toll among the German civilians is estimated between 750,000 and one million.[2]

Short of opinion polls or similar documentation, this graph is shown here as an aide to describe one side of the German mind during the later stages of the war. One can look at the rising curve as reflecting the panic and despair in people's hearts, as one might expect among the passengers of a sinking ship. It would be similar to a graph summarizing the destruction of their homes, schools, work places, churches, hospitals, shops, theaters, concert halls, and all the other material foundations of their civilization. A curve just like it would count the fatalities among the city dwellers. Another chart describing battlefield losses would begin to rise already in 1942, but it would ascend again to enormous heights in 1944 and 1945. And by the same token, then, if panic and desperation could be measured in numbers, a curve recording the public's mounting apprehension would abruptly rise much sooner than in this figure, perhaps in the winter of 1941/1942, when Germany's gigantic eastern campaign froze near Moscow in frightening paralysis. It would soar immensely again during 1944, just as demonstrated here, under the oppressive dread at the vision of soon being surrendered to Stalin's mercy. The figure provides an image of the destruction, killing, and emotional crisis attendant to the steadily progressing shipwreck of a whole nation.

This image of the German mind would be incomplete, however, if it ignored the opposite direction of a brave, recalcitrant spirit. Just as it was present among the Londoners during the Blitz and no doubt the Russians during the German invasion, this foreign onslaught generated an impressive growth of patriotic pride in Germany and evoked unsuspected resilience, endurance, and death-defying defiance. It is in extreme crises such as this, that in any country patriotism becomes truly self-denying and pure.

Fig. 4 also permits a look inside the psychology of war. Once passion, hatred, and righteousness have passed severe judgment upon the evil foe, the destructiveness of vengeance - the way history has recorded it—has become limitless. At this stage of the war, an enraged world was preparing to lay Germany down on the guillotine of reckoning. In the eyes of the Allies, this was more than a war. As Eisenhower termed it, it was a crusade, a term implying its violence as well as its moral rightness. Already years before knowledge of the Holocaust became available, it was seen as a definitive conflict between good and evil, as an Armageddon. Its mission was to settle things once and for all, to achieve, if you will, a final solution of the German problem. When it was all done, it had accomplished the devastation of Germany's centers of population, industry, and culture; the killing of millions of its citizens; the rape and expulsion of many more millions from their ancestral lands; the surgical diminution and segmentation of its territory; its permanent submission under foreign military occupation; and its defamation as an international anathema. History has recorded this verdict as being just and correct. Among all these progressive steps, the first to be completed was the laying waste of the centers of its civilization. Thus, the diagram in Fig. 4 shows the initial stage of the punitive sentence set upon Germany. It outlines the manner in which this was achieved.

Why is the Whole World Against Us?

There were two weeks of fall vacation during which we gladly escaped to Uncle Siegfried's farm. The mood was somber. It wasn't the bombing so much or the setbacks on the African-Italian front, as it was the advances of the Red Army. That development was slowly growing into a general nightmare.

Father's response to the rising apprehension was different from Uncle Siegfried's. Father's mind was analytical. He brought up a question, which, to the Germans, was central to the second half of the war and a question with an unknown answer because it addressed an enigma. He asked me,

"If the whole world hates Communism, and we are the ones carrying the flag in the battle against Communism, why is it that the whole world is against us?"

It was a cryptic question, but one that Father would pose, since it searched for the principle explaining the phenomenon. I could easily see that he had pinpointed a surprising contradiction and shared his puzzlement. But I doubt that it led either of us toward any particular realization, except that the world was obviously, and for mysterious reasons, more afraid of Germany than of the Red Empire. Rather, I would guess, Father's question merely verbalized what most people felt anyway, namely, that the world was in turmoil, and it was making less sense every day.

Uncle Siegfried was made of a more emotional fiber. He was forward and aggressive, and his sense of humor was feared because it was laced with sarcasm. Once, at the end of one of those somber conversations about the outlook of the war in Russia, he said flatly,

"Well, there is nothing we can do. I just hope the guys in Odessa have sense enough to throw lime on them."

Mother, with a sour smile, replied, "Oh Sietz!"

"Well?" he asked and shrugged his shoulders.

Afterwards, I asked Mother what he had meant by that remark. She explained, "There are rumors about mass graves near Odessa, of people killed by the SS. You know, partisans that got caught or hostages killed for their blowing up our supply trains." She went on, seeming a little embarrassed to have such words cross her lips, "and you know, lime causes decomposition. Uncle Siegfried meant, if the Russians were to come back it would be better...well, you know."

Before my mental eyes, I saw the recent newspaper pictures of Katyn. In the forest of Katyn, not far from Smolensk, mass graves had been found of thousands of officers of the Polish Army that were taken prisoner by the Red Army in 1939 and then killed by Stalin's execution squads. An international commission had been brought in to verify the facts, and it remained a major news item for weeks. The reports claimed, at the time, that twelve thousand men had been assassinated. Subsequent estimates have been lower, but to me the word "mass grave," a term I had never heard before, meant these pictures and was associated with that number.

I did not know what to think. That had been Stalin's doing. Everybody knew Stalin. But the SS? The SS did have something adverse about it, but surely, I thought, they couldn't be linked to mass graves.

Uncle Siegfried made one more memorable observation during our visit. It contained an ironic insinuation, one I did not believe but, nonetheless, enjoyed because of his iconoclastic sense of humor. He was indeed the first one I can remember to have ever said it, at this late date, four years after the outbreak of this war. With an almost pugnacious grin on his face he said,

"Peter, do you know what I think about this war-that-has-been-forced-upon-us?"

"No, sir."

"I think," he explained, "we shouldn't have started it in the first place."

The Nest Disintegrating

Almost overnight, our world changed. Much of the furniture and our more valuable belongings, such as the china and silverware, were moved for storage in the country. Some of it went to Fischershof, the farm of my father's sister about fifty kilometers northwest of Berlin, and the remainder to another farm, where I later saw the bookshelves in the barn. Our apartment was largely empty, except for some of the basic living room and bedroom items.

The Fierkes were now living with us. Siegfried Fierke was my closest friend at the time, and they were—to use the new expression—"bombed out". I had mentioned it at home, and Dad had said, "Go tell them they can live here. He is your best friend, isn't he? So now is your chance to prove it. Go tell them to move in. Right, Mother? They can move into our bedroom and the children's room."

I know Dad meant it the way he said it. His attitude of good will was simple and straightforward. Mother agreed with his decision although, I think, in her more practical way of thinking, she arrived at it from a different tack. You never knew what kind of people would come once the authorities began assigning them.

Then, soon after, we more or less all left. The destruction of the city from the air became so massive that everyone, people and offices that were able to, moved away. Father's office was transferred to a small town called Meseritz, about 150 kilometers east of Berlin. I was moved to Potsdam, where I stayed with Uncle Hans and Aunt Lotte and attended high school together with my cousin Joachim. Gila was still in Brünn, preparing for her finals. Mother stayed alone in Berlin, much of the time in the air raid shelter. Dad and I joined her on the weekends.

Good Cousins

My transfer to Potsdam proved to be a welcome one. Achim, as he was called, was a year older than I, and so he usually ended up the winner. But that was all right, our wrestling matches were carried out with growing athletic sophistication and with mutual delight. These contests, too, like those I used to have with Dieter, created the need for restoring the original position of carpets and furniture afterwards.

It was Achim's example that caused me to sign up with the Horsemen's Section of the Hitler Youth, rather than with the ordinary march-'n-sing outfits, and so, for about a year, as the world around us was slowly collapsing, I fulfilled my patriotic duty by currying horses in the stables and mucking out and taking in a fair amount of riding and jumping.

We engaged in scientific experiments, too, Cousin Achim

and I. One of us returned from chemistry class with the intriguing news that intestinal gas was largely methane, and, of course, we knew that methane, or wood gas, was combustible, since most of the cars, busses, and trucks now carried a wood-burning stove to replace the need for gasoline. We agreed that the chemistry teacher's assertion could not be accepted *prima facie* and that it required verification.

The experimental set-up was easily conceived, and it was merely a matter of our being prepared once the opportunity to test the theory presented itself. Not much waiting was required before Achim came rushing into the study with the announcement he had one. I grabbed the matches, he stooped over, and I approached him with a lighted match. Then I said, "Let it go," and he did.

The chemistry teacher was right. A long bluish flame licked lazily along the seam of his pants and then vanished. I laughed, "It worked!" but he was not amused. He had jumped forward and was rubbing his hot seat.

Achim, like myself, was the youngest. The oldest was Barbara who had a position as a librarian at the Prussian State Library in nearby Berlin. Hermann, his brother, about Dieter's age, was the most scholarly and the least bellicose of all the cousins. He excelled in mathematics and physics, had built his first wireless set at the age of eleven, and was now stationed in some Norwegian fjord where, as a member of the Signal Corps, he was monitoring the British.

NOT RESPECTED

The instructor was short and stocky, he wore heavy glasses, he licked his lips frequently as he talked, and he was a glib character. He taught German and History. He catered to our favors with a sense of humor, which chiefly relied on gore and malice for its effect. We faithfully came through with the dirty laughter he was aiming for and readily accepted his entertaining ways, but he was not respected. He also never missed a chance to heap ridicule on Church and Bible. He was with the Party in a big way, and I had the feeling that the other teachers kept their thoughts to themselves when he was around.

He had just finished mocking the preachings of the Church when one of the boys respectfully raised his hand. At the age of fourteen, he already had a somewhat professorial bearing and, as a recent evacuee from Berlin like myself, he had failed so far to be accepted by the group. That obviously did not seem to bother him.

"Sir," he said, "that isn't true. The Bible doesn't say that."

There ensued an argument, which we watched with growing relish. Finally, the teacher, still riding the wave of his latest joke and irritated by his challenger, dismissed him with the words,

"Well, then you can bring the Bible and show it to me." His eyes widened in disbelief as the boy quietly replied,

"I have it with me, sir, and here is the chapter in question," as he pulled out a pocket edition, opened the marked page, and proceeded to quote the passage. That brought the house down. The roar of laughter seemed to support the teacher and allowed him to save face.

THE MATH TEACHER'S THOUGHTS

Mr. Richter was a tall and lanky man with eyes much too kind for a math teacher. We bore him good will and respect. All math teachers, I feel, command respect. They deal with a difficult, intellectual discipline that is subject to scrutiny and proof down to the last decimal point. They deal with facts, and they are by nature honest men.

It was the last day before school closed for Christmas. He

finished a little early to have enough time to express some thoughts about the holiday. I do not recall his exact words, but as he slowly walked up and down before us, sometimes pausing to look at us thoughtfully, he spoke of the meaning of Christmas and that we shouldn't dismiss God from our hearts simply because He seemed old-fashioned. He kept on speaking in this manner, quietly and unobtrusively, but with obvious purpose and determination. Being quite aware of the conflict that existed between Church and State, I admired his courage to speak as he did. He doubtfully made any converts among us heretics, but we listened to him without growing restless, and when he dismissed us, he had lost none of our respect and had gained some of mine.

CHARMING HOMELAND, BECKONING WORLD

Geography was fun. It was fun because Mr. Habermann was. He was one of those teachers one never forgets. As tall as he was, he would shun the teacher's desk and rather sit among us, usually on the first desk in the window row, crowding the boy sitting there a little, with one foot on the floor and the other on his bench. He had a permanent twinkle in his eyes and possessed a remarkable repertory of amusing expressions, with which to keep us chuckling and laughing through most of the hour. In this manner he teased and delighted us through the continents and oceans, the capital cities of South America, the rivers of Siberia, and the meteorological mechanisms that created the monsoon seasons in India and the trade winds in the Atlantic and Pacific Oceans.

Not to overtax us, he would often break the routine with humorous tales of the days, when he used to take his class for week-long hikes through different parts of our picturesque country. In this manner, subtly and unbeknownst to us, he instilled in us a love for the gentle beauty of the streams and forests and val-

leys and castles, the golden grain fields, and the shores and mountain peaks of our homeland. To this day, when I dream of them or
while visiting, once again stand by the roadside watching the flowering meadows billow in the wind, or listening to the hum of the
bees in the ripening fields or to the song of a lark high up in the
sky or perhaps to the distant crowing of a rooster wafting up from
a barnyard in the valley, I often think of Mr. Habermann.

He must have been the most even-tempered man, continuing unperturbedly, as he did, in this cheerful manner, as though it
were peacetime. He gave no indication of knowledge or concern
that our world was slowly disintegrating, except perhaps once. He
mentioned that, some years previously, he had declined an offer to
go to Venezuela.

"Of course, you all know," he stated with an extra twinkle in
his eyes, "how glad I am today that I didn't accept. What would I be
doing there?" He turned his head to look out the window, "Would
have missed out on all of this."

THE TOWN OF THE GREAT KING

Potsdam stood in contrast to Berlin in different ways. A small town
by any standard—all one had to do was look at their quaint little
streetcars—it possessed very much its own beauty, class, and sense
of importance. Sitting astride the Havel River and ringed by its side
arms and lakes and pine, birch, and beech forests, it was studded
with historical gates and arches and the monuments, obelisks, and
imposing edifices of yesteryear. The tree-shaded canal, the abundance of flowers, and the numerous well-kept parks surrounding
ponds and lakes softened their severity. Its prize attraction, of
course, was Sanssouci, that idyllic castle erected in 1747 in the
image of Versailles.

The Francophile king, who had left his mark on the town,

the "Old Fritz" as people still lovingly called him, had been a remarkable man indeed. Little Prussia, an aggressive upstart of a power on the political map of that century, survived almost single-handedly under his dogged leadership the combined onslaught of Sweden, Russia, Austria-Hungary, France, and Holland, plus the majority of the other German states. That was the Seven-Years-War that was intertwined in America with the French and Indian War. When after seven years a peace treaty was signed, his Prussia prevailed undiminished, while once mighty Austria was exhausted and France lost Canada to the British.

He was called "the Great," Frederick the Great, but he was more than just a stubborn warrior. He was a philosopher at heart and enjoyed a long friendship with Voltaire. He was an author, played the flute, and even tried his hand on composition. As a product of the Age of Enlightenment, he must have been an eminently fair and tolerant ruler.

I always liked the story about the miller. There was a windmill that stood a stone's throw away from the castle. The windmill creaked, and the creaking apparently disturbed the King when he was trying to concentrate, or, perhaps even more so, when he was trying to play the flute. One day, it must have been a trying day for him, Frederick, in a state of exasperation, sent a messenger to the miller with the order to turn the blooming thing off. The miller's answer, so the story goes, was that the windmill was his own property and so nobody could tell him to turn it off, not even the King. Frederick the Great, the absolute ruler, did not take offense to the lack of deference and acquiesced, for he knew the miller was right. This was an almost humorous story in a country where one did not talk back to the King.

One of the political jokes, I remember, referred to Frederick's religious tolerance, which granted equal rights to adherents of all religions. He was credited with the quote, "Let everyone be happy in his own fashion," using the French word "façon," as he spoke French better than German. The word was, in fact, adopted into the German language, but was then spelled "Fasson". The story was that Hitler had complained to God about his being misunderstood. "After all," he said, "like Frederick the Great, I, too, only wish everybody to be happy according to his own Fasson.""True, Adolf," answered the Lord, "but you see, there is a difference. Frederick spelled the word with 'ç,' while you spell it with 'SS'."

Respite in Belgium

Late in 1943 Friedrich was detailed to Belgium to participate in the creation and training of a new division of the *Waffen-SS*. Among our friends and relatives this caused some raising of eyebrows. The public's respect for their bravery was indeed whole-hearted, but they never lost their stigma of being Himmler's private army. The *Heer*, the name for the regular Army, and the *Waffen-SS* were rivals who cooperated on the battlefield but otherwise observed a strict line of separation.

It is not unlikely—at least so I heard at home—that the SS was trying to "steal" promising young Army officers by taking them on loan for a while and to treat them to a little propaganda, temptation, and indoctrination.

Friedrich was utterly unhappy and frustrated there and complained of being put on ice with sharply curtailed responsibilities and of being generally treated as an outsider. From our viewpoint, however, being on ice was better than being on the Eastern Front. After all, Belgium in those days was one of the safest places in Europe. And we were not aware, then, that he did form an unusual friendship in that little Belgian town of Westerlo.

Mortal Violence

The obituary pages told a grim story. There used to be one name per notice. Then there came those containing an additional phrase such as "...joined his brother Gerhard in death on the battlefield..." But now, there appeared notices, which were very long, listing five, six, or even more names, entire families wiped out all the way down to "Karin, five, and Jürgen, two," people who perished in the ferocious air raids. There were pages after pages of them.

Crews were working everywhere. Many of them were composed of women clearing away rubble to free the trapped from the shelters and to make way for streetcars and traffic. Mother, witnessing it on her way to and from work every day, once said, "You know, these women of Berlin are really something else." She still didn't feel like a Berliner herself. "There they are, up all night with the air raid, and now, on their way to the factory, the street is blocked. So they all get out and help the workmen clear the tracks, joking and kidding all the way. 'What our men can do, we can do any day,' they say and laugh."

In the face of adversity and destruction, obviously delivered with the intent to demoralize, there was a mood of high-spirited defiance. Goebbels helped as much as he could. His message was: in this most crucial hour (he spoke of the "labor pains of the New Era"), history was looking down on us to see if we had the mettle. By gosh, people seemed to say, we have!

It had been a long time since the constantly broken windowpanes had been replaced with new ones. For a while, wire-mesh reinforced cellophane was used instead. Then this became scarce, too, and people boarded up their windows; their rooms only dimly lit through a small slit in the center covered with cellophane.

The faces in the air raid shelter, when I spent the Saturday nights at home in Berlin, they were different too, now. No more of the sleepy, dozing expressions or casual conversations. The heavy thuds of exploding bombs transmitted through the foundation walls like sudden shuddering quakes had everybody sit straight up, their features taut and tense and their wide eyes fixed at some point of the ceiling. Every thud was followed by a crackling noise upstairs in our apartment as the stucco splattered over the carpet-less floor.

A neighbor came down the basement steps and shouted, "Your top floor is on fire!"

The din had calmed a little. We all rushed upstairs with our buckets. Flashlights pierced the smoke-filled darkness. It was in one of the rooms of the two high school teachers. We quickly put it out. Just the rug had caught fire and some furniture.

During the last year of the war a special radio station, called the "*Drahtfunk*," kept the populace informed about the location of the various invading air armadas. Thus, people had advance warning and could better adjust their chores and shopping trips to the irregular schedule of death and destruction. A slow up-and-down cadence of tones indicated that the station was on the air and that the planes were approaching again.

Intermittent bulletins were issued every ten to fifteen minutes.

"Enemy aircraft are approaching the Dutch and Belgian coast." Soon one could recognize two or three lines of attack, as they approached different target areas between the coast in the north and the Alps in the south. Finally, the announcer would tersely list a number of cities over which there was "heavy enemy activity".

The bulletins would also provide an idea of the magnitude of the expected assault. I recall one that roughly stated, "First aircraft formations have reached the western outskirts of the nation's capital. The bomber stream stretches across the North German Plain and its end is as yet not in sight over the English Channel." The announcer was describing an air armada the length of one time zone.

Mother soon took to spending the nights in Potsdam with us. Potsdam was spared, having been hit only by a few stray bombs. But we got up there just the same, when Berlin was struck again.

One night, Achim and I were standing outside, eager to watch some of the action. Suddenly, with the drone of aircraft overhead, a huge Lancaster bomber was caught in the beam of a searchlight. Within five seconds, half a dozen more search lights locked on to it, and it glistened brightly at the crossing point of their beams. A barrage of shells exploded nearby. Then, no longer than twenty seconds later, the huge plane exploded in a dramatic, fully illuminated display of mortal violence in the black sky.

The next morning, daylight had a strange and eerie cast. The sky was clear and blue, but the sun was hidden behind a huge, towering cloudbank across the eastern sky. It was brownish-gray and it wasn't clouds. It was the smoke rising from a metropolis in flames.

THE SMELL OF APOCALYPSE

In spite of the brutal nature of the air attacks delivered by the British and Americans whose target, obviously and for all to see, was the civilian population, there was a strange lack of hostility against them. Somebody's son in the neighborhood had been in the *Afrika-Korps*. He was now writing letters from a POW camp in the United States. People kept talking about it. Each Sunday, so he had written, they were listening on the radio to a concert given by the New York Philharmonic. Lord Almighty, were the Americans fortunate to still be living in a world of sanity, we were thinking. There was peace and normalcy over there in the west of us; they were civilized people. The air raids did not seem to contradict that. They had no choice; they had to bomb us, their enemies, *c'est la guerre*. Besides, we had done it to them, for the same reason.

There was an undercurrent of feeling that the alignments in this war were all wrong. We were engaged in a desperate struggle in the East trying to fend off approaching peril. Was it conceivable that the western Allies were unaware of that? They should have joined forces with us against the common enemy. Unless my memory deceives me, I think there was such a feeling of kinship with the West and such readiness for reconciliation and camaraderie that we would have forgiven them, the Americans and the British, for what we thought was their role in causing this war and welcomed them with open arms had they passed through our cities on their way to reinforce the hard pressed Eastern Front. We would have cleared the rubble they themselves had created to allow them easier passage and would have cheered them on, even if they had arrived only three days after the last air raid.

So powerful was the fear of the approaching "Bolshevik chaos," so bone-chilling was the mere thought of Siberian labor camps, so terrifying was the idea of "eastern hordes" invading the heart of Europe that everything else seemed trivial. Danzig and the Polish Corridor were now trivial; Himmler and the SS and the *Gestapo* didn't even come close to being relevant any longer; and even the air raids, they were trivial now too, if one looked eastward and saw what was coming.

New Year's Resolution

January 1944
Dear parents, dear Peter,

...Exactly on New Year's Eve we were entrained...and traveled south... At midnight I gave a short speech (and said)
that the year '44 would become the hardest one so far in the
history of this war, that very shortly now the most gigantic
battle of all ages ever fought by a nation would begin, that
we want to stand together bravely and in inexorable determination, and that as the champions of a better ideology
we are invincible so long as we remain united... We then
drank to (the health of) our families and to a great, heroic
year 1944...

Friedrich

The Pastor's Game Plan

Aunt Lotte warmly recommended the Rev. von der Heydt. It was
decided the Rev. Garten, our pastor in Berlin, would confirm me in
spring, but I would take catechism classes in Potsdam. Aunt Lotte
took religious matters very seriously, much more than Mother did.
She went to church not just occasionally but every Sunday, on certain holidays even twice. Uncle Siegfried, who never went to
church, was always ready with some unloving remark about his
sister's piousness.

The Rev. von der Heydt was indeed a good choice. Not over
fifty, he was a handsome man with sincere eyes that looked
straight at you with open-hearted warmth, and he had the gift not
only to convey his message to us boys but also to kindle in our
hearts the flame of Christian idealism. Looking back, there is no
doubt in my mind that in those days that were so trying for the
clergy, this was a man of their elite.

One day, he asked us, "Are you boys leaders in the Hitler
Youth?" I said I wasn't. He looked at me with just a touch of dis-
approval and then explained, "We must show them that we
Christians are the best, you see?"

Today, one would say that he was trying to work through the system. One, also, would have to conclude that at this late date, a year and a half before the catastrophic end, he must have had a very benign view of the errors of "the system," as well as of the state of the war. In his appraisal, one has to assume, the political system was expected to prevail for many years to come so that his efforts would eventually, through us, help improve its imperfections. The way I remember the public mood, that kind of blissful ignorance and brave optimism was, indeed, quite characteristic of the time. In fact, blissful ignorance and brave optimism might well be marks of mass psychology at wartime anywhere.

TWIN PEAKS

In my view of life and the world, God occupied the summit of all authority. God was the ultimate reference point, the highest judge, and the supreme commander to whom all principles and values were subordinate.

Then one day, I made a peculiar discovery. Having been so deeply and so personally involved in this war, there was no denying that what my heart was really beating for every day, every week, every month, and what I was adoring with all my youthful idealism, what I was praying for every night before falling asleep was that precious and glorious and sacred something called "my country". If ever there was a moral summit, a high principle to live and die for, it surely was our country, our beloved fatherland. But then, were there two summits up there?

There most certainly were. There was no doubt whatsoever that I could recognize two summits. Which one was higher? I knew that God had to be. "God is the highest," I said to myself, but it did not work. There was no use trying to fool myself. I could see it with my own inner eyes; Fatherland was just as high as God. At least as high.

We were singing patriotic hymns and anthems just as haunting and revered as the religious ones we sang in church, with words no less solemn and devoted. I knew of martyrs who had died for their faith and for God, but that was history and a long time ago. Perhaps some of our present churchmen, those belonging to the Confessing Church who risked being put away by the *Gestapo* for forthrightly speaking out from the pulpit against the Government's atheism, perhaps they would be willing to die for God. But otherwise, I could think of no one personally who had laid his life on the line for God while, on the other hand, there were so many who were proudly dying for our imperiled country every day. It really was a *Heilig Vaterland*, a holy fatherland.

The disturbing aspect of this discovery, of course, lay in the potential predicament of serving two masters. In the unlikely event of a conflict between the two, would I be able to follow God and forsake my country? Again, there was no use in trying to deceive myself. Never, never in this world could I turn my back on my country, but neither would I want to act against God. It really was a cruel choice to ask of anyone.

The way I remember, I left it at that. It was, after all, a highly theoretical predicament, wasn't it? What strange corners your thoughts could wander into if you allowed them to roam! Fortunately for us, I thought, the twin peaks had always been in harmony with one another. God and Country—in a mysterious way they somehow belonged together, much the way I looked at my parents: they were two, but really one.

FRIENDS

Westerlo was a small town in Flanders, not too far from Antwerp. There lived the Arnaut-Hanssen family. They owned a clothing store and had two children, a boy and a girl. In their upstairs room a German officer was billeted. Needless to say, he was not welcome. He was my brother Friedrich. It was not until eleven years later that Monsieur Arnaut-Hanssen told us the story.

They gave him the cold shoulder, and Friedrich kept to himself. There were times, however, when the parents were minding the store and the children were alone at home. The children easily crossed the invisible barrier between friend and foe, being too young to recognize it, and found in Friedrich a welcome playmate and helper with their homework.

"So," related Monsieur Arnaut-Hanssen, "one evening I said to my wife, 'Look, why don't we get a bottle of wine from the cellar and ask him down and see if we can't talk some sense into this misled German warrior. He can't be all that bad.'"

They had a long session that night and many more were to follow with heated discussions about the war, and the National-Socialist State, and whose fault everything was, and who was right, and who was wrong. Neither was able to convince the other, and, until the end some two or three months later, they never agreed on these matters. Yet, they came to respect and like one another as individuals so much so that when the German officer left in spring to return to his unit on the Russian Front, the Arnaut-Hanssen family, young and old, sent him off worrying lest something might happen to him. In fact, they sent him packages of food and clothing for many years after the war had ended.

THE BIG HOPE

Father related a humerous tale. On a train, two travelers came into conversation and one of them said,

"You know, all this talk about secret weapons! I don't think there are any."

"Oh yes, there are," answered the second." I know. You see,

I'm working on the project."The first one was duly impressed."You don't say!" he said. "Well listen, what is it anyway, this new weapon, can you tell me in confidence?"

The second traveler couldn't resist. His voice kept low, he proceeded to explain, "What they do is this: they take very old oak trees, a thousand year-old oak trees; they cut them down and then hollow out the trunk and fill the big cavity with dynamite, and then they seal it. You drop that from a plane and, boy, it causes unbelievable devastation. It makes conventional bombs look like toys."

The first traveler had listened in amazement and now said, "Oh, is that what it is!" He stroked his chin thoughtfully and asked admiringly, "And you say, you are working on it yourself?"

"Why, sure."

"Well, what is it you're doing?"

The man replied, "Me? I'm planting the trees."

Adam, Odin, and Atma

I pulled the booklet out of the shelf in mere curiosity and not knowing that this was a beginning. Heaven only knows how I came upon this inconspicuous volume among the hundreds crowding the bookshelves all around the library.

Uncle Hans, the archeologist, was head of the Brandenburg State Office for the Preservation of Prehistoric Monuments. He was a benign bear of a man who was not against good fellowship. He would, at times, come up with the kind of joke that the ladies would call "fresh" and would relish especially because he delivered the naughty story using cultured and erudite terminology. By and large, however, his interests in life on this earth were only two in number: "his urns," as Aunt Lotte termed it, and chess. Beyond these, he gladly left everything else up to Aunt Lotte's initiative and was quite content in allowing her, in true fashion of the domesticated bear, to lead him.

The booklet was entitled "A Dictionary of the Indo-European Language". In it, I read that the Sanskrit word *atma* (soul), the Greek word *atmos* (steam), the German word *Atem* (breath), the biblical name of Adam, and the name of Odin, the chief deity in Valhalla, were all derivatives of a single parent word in the long extinct Indo-European language. Totally fascinated, I couldn't stop reading. I found pages filled with examples of this kind, and the second section of the booklet consisted of an attempted dictionary of several hundred surmised, extinct word roots. It must have been a very old book, perhaps printed in the nineteenth century. Nowadays, etymological reference books come as thick as a college dictionary and, it seems, provide the genealogy of almost every word.

I have never ceased being fascinated by the science of etymology, and sometimes still, after a lively etymological discussion with a like-minded friend in the cafeteria, or when hitting upon an exciting new word derivation while driving down the expressway, I think of that moment in Uncle Hans' library when it all began.

At that time, of course, Uncle Hans was no longer tending to "his urns" in the museum. Probably fiftyish, he had been drafted into the Army and was in charge of some "Stalag" near Berlin, a prisoner-of-war camp where, so I heard and had no reason to doubt, he was playing chess with captured Allied flyers.

OMINOUS GOODBYE

It was May 1944. Friedrich packed his things and got ready. We sat a while yet together. It was awfully hard on Mother, these last few hours and minutes. His train left from the Zoo Station, eastbound. I would take him there, helping with his luggage. We all agreed that it was best for Mother not to come along. She threw her arms around him and held on. She did not want to let him go. When at last she did, she fought her tears back and said, "Write soon, *mein Junging*. Stay well. And come back, do you hear?" We then left quickly.

I had never known him so reticent and so very grave. He had not seen Berlin in several months, and as we stood on the platform of the streetcar, he watched the old familiar streets pass by. They were no longer recognizable. Trying to cheer him up, I told him a current joke reflecting the local humor of the gallows with regard of the widespread destruction in Berlin but he managed only a thin smile.

Before my eyes, I still see the station platform where I was standing as the train slowly moved out and as he, leaning out of an open window and waving back at me, was becoming smaller and smaller, but still waving his handkerchief until, at last, the train turned away into a bend.

He had looked so somber. My big, manly brother, I thought, had a hard time letting go, too. I turned and proceeded on my way home. I felt choked. Saying goodbye had become such a fateful and ominous, almost frightening experience.

STIFF UPPER LIP

Latvia, June 7, 1944
Dear parents,

A comrade is shortly leaving for Germany. He will take this along. That's faster.

I'm doing well. We're constantly sitting by the radio in the hopes of hearing optimistic news about the (Normandy) Invasion. The order of the hour is: keep a stiff upper lip! Then we'll make it. Of course, the enemy will land elsewhere as well, but we're prepared for that. It is to be hoped that things will become quieter for you now (he was referring to the air war on the cities). Of course, we're expecting bang-bang in the Baltic as well before long. Well, let them come! No pain, no gain! In this greatest battle of world history now unfolding, it's us who will force the decision.

This afternoon I'll go for a swim...in a small river. Now a friend of mine is showing up, he wants me to defeat him in a game of chess. Now heart-felt greetings. Down with England!

Friedrich

LUCKY FELLOW

Hermann had left his Norwegian fjord and had been transferred to France. In Normandy, his right knee was shattered and he was taken prisoner. Soon, Aunt Lotte received mail from him, transmitted via Switzerland. He was in a POW camp in Scotland and was learning how to knit.

"Knit?" I asked. I was told in Scotland the men do the knitting.

IT'S BARBARIC!

Incredibly, there still existed islands of peace in our ocean of war and destruction. Mother, more than ready for a respite, had found one. During the school summer vacation, she took Gila and me to Bad Harzburg, a resort town in the Harz Mountains. Father even joined us there for a few days.

We had breakfast on the tree-shaded lawn, visited nearby caverns, and went on hikes through the forests. It was almost like the unforgettable days in the Black Forest, six years previously; only, we did not sing any more.

On one such walk, I excitedly pointed out a hunting high-stand to Dad, the old hunter. They usually stood concealed at the edge of the woods and during season, the hunter would hide there at dusk and wait for deer to come out of the forest to graze in the clearing. But Father looked sad and expressed disapproval.

"But Dad," I said, "you used to be a…"

He waved me off. He said he had changed. He didn't like hunting any more, he said, not since "this happened" to Dieter. "You raise your rifle and shoot the animal and kill it, just for the thrill of it. It's barbaric, Peter."

Joyful Tranquility

I was lying on a meadow, way up in the mountains, and was looking up in the sky. Around my face, the tall grass and wild flowers were pointing skyward, gently swaying in the clear air. A ladybug crawled up to the tip of a grass blade, unfolded its wings, and fizzed away. I watched the snow-white clouds as they leisurely drifted past and changed contours. A gentle breeze momentarily brushed my skin and made the tall grass stalks around me take a nod or two. All was silent except for the intermittent hum of the bumblebees, gathering honey.

I lay there a long time, taking it all in and forgetting the world. Never again did life and peace and nature join for me in such a perfect union of joyful and harmonious tranquility. It stood, of course, in stark contrast to the brutality of the real world of those war years and that is, I am certain, the reason why it impressed me so deeply. But still today, it remains a nostalgic memory, that meadow on the mountaintop.

SPECTACLE IN THE SKY

From where we were hiking along the road, one had a panoramic view across the northern foothills into the distant plains. The sun was bright and the sky was spotless.

I was the first to detect the plane. It was a huge four-engine bomber, the only plane in sight, no more than three kilometers away and not flying very high. It was headed westbound and did not seem to be in any hurry. We stood and watched in amazement as over the peaceful countryside, on this lovely day, an almost silent drama unfolded itself.

The stately aircraft, reflecting flashes of sunlight, slowly, very slowly banked and dipped its nose earthward. As it picked up speed it left behind a flock of white parachutes. There was a roar followed by a black cloud rising from the forest, and then after a delay we heard a distant crash.

Moments later, in the foothills, Army vehicles were speeding down a road. I proposed that if we hurried, we might get a better view and see some of the action. They would take them prisoner and all. But Mother said no; not only that, she seemed listless afterwards and did not say much anymore.

I thought it was a great spectacle, myself.

CAVE-IN AT THE EASTERN FRONT

July 16, 1944
Dear parents,

The worst is behind us. The situation is slowly settling down. Mad war. We were detrained near Ossipovichi and were immediately engaged in battle and for starters gave a Russian armored corps and an armored brigade a solid beating. Then an armored task force of ours broke through to relieve (the city of) Bobruisk and liberated over 25,000

German soldiers encircled there. In order to bring them back, we were forced to hold our position so long until it was our own turn to be pretty well trapped in Ivan's bag. But then, once again, the Twelfth Panzer Division came through. With lightning speed we showed up near Stolpce, where we broke out... Our losses were tolerable. If we had no honorable mention in the High Command Report, it's only because the whole situation was much too topsy-turvy... We are still slowly moving back, but that's only because our neighbors are sometimes not on the stick...

...Friedrich

MOTHER'S DESPAIR

This date is listed in the history books. The events of this day were startling in themselves, but, in addition, they brought along a profound surprise.

I had always been aware that our patriotism, albeit spontaneous and sincere, was tempered by certain reservations about the Party and the Government. It was as if to say, "Yes, these people have accomplished a lot for our troubled country, and one must give them credit for that; but many of them are against us Christians and are corrupt and not trustworthy, and the Himmler clique is clearly suspect." But there had usually been a positive balance; the good was thought to outweigh the bad. Blame was ascribed to underlings, whereas Hitler himself had retained the reputation of being a sincere, capable, and honorable man.

Unbeknownst to me, during the preceding year or so, in the minds of my parents that balance had shifted, and it was on this day that I found out, how far.

Mother, my sister, and I were paying a visit to Uncle Carl-Johann. A bachelor, he was Mother's cousin and was president of a bank in the city of Hanover. I liked him well because he was my godfather and regularly sent me a twenty-mark bill for Christmas and my birthdays. In spite of being a diabetic, he enjoyed good cooking and was particularly fond of spaghetti, a dish Mother had usually prepared whenever he was in Berlin on business. Because of the bombing, his Hanover office had been relocated to Bad Harzburg, and it was he who had arranged for our stay there.

He lived in a small mansard room, which was unpretentiously furnished with a bed, a chair, a wardrobe, and a washstand. An old radio was playing from the top of the wardrobe. We were ready to leave but then stayed because a News Bulletin was announced.

In my memory I still see myself standing in front of the wardrobe, looking up to the radio set and listening to the shocking news: an attempt had been made to assassinate Hitler, but he had escaped with minor injuries. Once again, the announcer said, Providence had held its protective hand over the nation's leader. Later in the day, he would personally address the German People.

We had all been staring at the receiver with bated breath. When it was over, I felt something was missing. A bulletin of such enormous gravity had to be followed by an emotional release, an outburst of exclamatory comments. But it wasn't. Mother and Uncle Carl-Johann acted as though we had just listened to the weather forecast. They looked at one another and merely said, "*Na ja*—Well." We left a few minutes later.

By the time we emerged on the street, I could no longer control myself. That was all we needed now, a palace revolution. Excitedly I said, "*Mensch, Mutti*, isn't it fantastic the Führer was saved? Gosh, if you imagine what would have happened if he..."

"No, Peter, no!" She barely managed to keep her voice down. I had never seen her like this. She shot around and either grabbed me or even struck my chest with her little fist, I am not certain. In her face there was a mixture of anger and despair and it poured forth from her right there on the street. I had punctured a balloon ready to burst.

"It's terrible! It's a disaster! This was our last chance! Our only chance was getting rid of this scoundrel! Oh God, why didn't it succeed? Now nothing is spared us, nothing, nothing! And now you will see his vengeance, oh, it will be horrible!"

We slowly walked back to our guesthouse. The date was July 20, 1944.

BIALYSTOK!

July 28, 1944
Dear Parents,

I'm doing well. We're positioned near Bialystok. Here the matter has finally come to a stop of sorts. But now all hell is breaking loose in other places. Well, somehow we will succeed...

...Friedrich

August 8, 1944
Dear Parents,

Today, Sunday, quickly a loving note. But...after every sentence I have to answer the damn telephone. We are engaged in battle at the moment, you see. There are two locations along the line held by our division where four fresh Russian divisions have broken through and they are getting a bad whipping. In addition, we are also supporting the divisions to the left and right of us. Here, along a broad front northeast of Bialystok, the (retreating front) line has come to a stop.

I'm doing fine. The divisional command post is far in the rear as I keep telling you. Your mail is getting through. It always makes me very happy. Glad you enjoyed the Harz Mountains. Now I've run out of time. Cheers,

...Friedrich

Rapid Developments

In the meantime, I had returned to Potsdam and a new school year had begun. After English and Latin, at long last, we were now starting out on French, something I had eagerly been looking forward to. I learned to say, "Paris est la capitale de la France."

I resumed my piano lessons, too, with Miss Elfriede Fleck. Grieg was my current favorite, along with some easy Chopin and Brahms.

Amazing how life can go on in its normal tracks, long past losing its relevance. The memories were still fresh of Bärbel's wedding to a medical student named Heinz, a few weeks earlier, when food packages from our relatives in the country had enabled Aunt Lotte to prepare a modest feast.

But time was running out. Cousin Achim was now serving as an auxiliary gunner with the local anti-aircraft system. All over the country, the sixteen year-olds were doing this in their hometowns, while continuing with school. Uncle Siegfried, approaching fifty, was drafted and dispatched to Italy for combat duty, while Aunt Dora took care of the harvest.

Not long after, the Red Army reached the Baltic Coast. Just before it did, the Twelfth Panzer Division was redeployed in the Northern Section to join the German Courland Army in Latvia, which had to be supplied across the sea.

Mobilization of the Young

School lasted only ten days. Early in August, the fourteen and fifteen year-old boys were organized to build fortifications east of Berlin. We slept in barns, marched out every morning into the country cheerfully singing our marching songs with spades shouldered, and dug trenches and tank traps all day.

It was exceptionally hot and humid. We were very thirsty, and our canteens did not last out the day. One evening, on the way back to the village, I could not resist the tempting sight of the clear lake water and drank some, scooped up in my cupped hand. A few weeks later I came down with hepatitis.

Our location happened to be near the country town of Meseritz where Father had spent the last year. So one Sunday, to my surprise, from the hayloft I heard my friends shout for me, and looking down, I recognized my parents standing in the farmyard. They had come for a visit, and I recall the mixed feelings showing on their faces as they observed this army camp of children. I introduced my beaming comrades to them and, very mannerly, they all shook hands with them, clicking their heels smartly and taking the appropriate bow of the head.

Before returning to Meseritz that evening, they must have stopped at our commander's office, some Hitler Youth *Stammführer*, and talked to him.

How to Carve a Knight

There were willow trees lining one of the country lanes where we marched every day. Some of us cut off branches and took them back to the farm to make things out of them. Pretty soon I had launched a major project: to carve the pieces of a chess set from a willow branch. I seemed to have no trouble remembering the shape of a rook, or a bishop, or the queen and king; but the knight was a problem. Every one of my attempted knights looked pitiful. Then, there came unexpected help.

There was some kind of problem with discipline. Some of the boys had chased a teen-age farm girl and touched or grabbed her in an ungentlemanly manner. As a consequence, we were all, several hundred of us, ordered to assemble on the large meadow that we used for flag raising and similar military ceremonies. We were lined up in a quadrangle, in rank and file and at attention, as the camp commander dressed us down. All of a sudden, I heard him shout my name and found myself racing across the grass and coming to a heel-clicking stop in front of him. In order to state an example and to show what draconian measures he was willing to impose so as to restore discipline, he informed us of a grave decision he had reached. Pointing at me he shouted,

"His parents are about to celebrate their silver wedding anniversary, and I had acceded to their request that he be granted a three day leave to return to Berlin for this purpose. But now, after the unheard-of transgressions of some of you, I have been forced to rescind that decision. On that special day of his parents, he cannot be with them!"

A hush went through the crowd of boys that seemed to show that his words had achieved the desired effect. A silver wedding anniversary was apparently regarded with deepest respect, and one must assume that its importance was believed to outrank the defense needs of the nation's capital. According to the prevailing standards, it must have been perfectly reasonable for my parents to make their request, and for the Youth leader to grant it, as well as for the adolescent boys to feel severely punished by his rescinding my leave.

Even decades later, I at times wondered about this tragicomic episode, and what it says about the sturdiness of the laws and value systems of human society, and about the unshakable sentimentality of the human soul. Even more, one wonders how naive and blissfully ignorant we all were in those August days of 1944, being, by train, no more than three hours away from Auschwitz, and perhaps four hours from the Eastern Front where one of the most perilous battles of the war was raging on.

Not to be overly harsh, a couple of days later the leader

granted my leave after all. I have no memory at all of that anniversary, but I do recall how I was carving chess pieces on the train all the way to Berlin, carefully collecting the shavings on my lap. Indeed, some tenant in our apartment building still had a chess set around that allowed me to make an exact copy of the knight.

FIRMLY CONVINCED

Latvia, August 29, 1944
Dear Mom, dear Dad,

Today, on the day of your Silver Wedding Anniversary, my thoughts have been with you at home a whole lot. What a darn shame that I couldn't be with you and do anything to bring you joy... I wonder whether you might all be in Berlin on leave. But maybe those plans fell victim to the War Service. I hope from my heart that in these hard times it was possible for you...to have a little celebration. I also hope that, for once, you were able to forget the everyday concerns. Anyway, it serves no purpose to worry too terribly much. We just simply have to make it (through this crisis) and it is, I'm firmly convinced of that, entirely possible that we will; if we only remain united and brave and death defying, as millions of German soldiers have been, who in this war for liberty have given their lives. No matter how serious the wounds are that this war has inflicted upon us, they will heal; our cities will rise again, new and more beautiful, and all the blood that has been spilled will be replaced. Everything we will be able to replace, only freedom is an irreplaceable gift... On August 26, I was promoted captain... Was about time, too.

Now I'm sending you all my heart-felt greetings, my dear, good parents, my Gila, and you, little squirt
                    ...Friedrich, who loves you all very much

Crest-Fallen

We were tramping single file, along an east-west railroad track to the location of our next trench digging. I kept looking up, as there was a distant hum or drone in the sky, that waxed and waned as it was moving eastward, toward our backs. No sooner did the sound fade in the east than a new one appeared in the west, softly at first, then crescendoing until it was directly overhead, then fading away again on its way into the rising sun.

Suddenly a wonderful realization struck me: the new weapons! The V-1 rockets!

Finally. The great moment had arrived, and I was out here to witness it. The turning point of the war. Hitler was right, we could win! It was about time though, now that my parents and how many other people were just about to lose their nerve. Well, there they were, one about every one or two minutes, that was more like it. That silly one-per-hour bombardment of London must have only been a test, a trial series, and in the wrong direction at that. In the east, that's where we needed them.

Oh, this great day! Too bad, we couldn't listen to radios out here in the fields; I would have liked to hear that bulletin! "Since the early morning hours a new weapons system has been put into action. Hundreds of devastating rockets have already found their targets in the Soviet Union..." Another week, maybe, and they'll ask for peace terms. There came another one. I looked up, but couldn't see anything. They were evidently flying too high.

On the way back to camp, that night, I heard it again. But even though the light was different now, I could not see anything. Then I made a disturbing discovery: they were flying into the sun again! That was the wrong direction. I was bewildered; surely the Russians had not already developed a method to intercept them, to turn them around, and to send them back? I did not know what to make of it. Also, why did none of the other boys mention it? I finally asked a friend.

"Do you hear that sound up in the sky?"

He looked up and said, "What sound? Do you mean the hum of the telegraph poles?"

THE WARMTH OF COMRADESHIP

All our trenches completed, they moved us to a different location in the area to start on new ones. The countryside was hilly here, much of it wooded. We bivouacked in tents. At night, we often sat on the hillside singing. It was quite spontaneous; we knew so many songs, patriotic songs, humorous songs, marching songs, hiking songs, and so-called medieval ballads (they were very popular); songs about sailors and pirates and cowboys, and about being homesick; there was a great variety of songs, and it was customary for us to harmonize. It gave us a warm and carefree feeling. The gentleness of dusk and sunset, and of the balmy evening breeze mixed well with the enjoyment of harmony and the warm security blanket of comradeship. It wasn't home but not at all a bad substitute.

It was time to call it a day. The mosquitoes were getting out of hand. It was late, too; night had fallen hours ago. We rose from the grassy slope and stretched. Then, two of the boys shouted for us from the top of the hill.

"Come on up here and look!"

We climbed up to see what they had discovered.

They were facing west. Far in the distance, along the dark horizon, which was barely set off against the starry sky, there was a long, flat strip of flickering red. A blaze! The silent shifting of color and light was fitfully reflected from what must have been a low cloud ceiling.

We stood there and mutely stared in amazement. What we were seeing was an inferno huge enough to be seen from here, 150 kilometers away. Everyone knew at once what it was.

"My God," one of us said softly, breaking the silence of awe, "Berlin! They are getting it again!"

PART 7

WITHOUT MERCY

An Eye for an Eye

FROM 11 TO 16 SEPTEMBER 1944, President Roosevelt, Prime Minister Churchill, and Canadian Prime Minister Mackenzie King met in Quebec. At that conference, U.S. Treasury Secretary Henry Morgenthau, Jr. presented a plan that outlined principles of how to deal with Germany once she was defeated. While the plan was named after the treasury secretary, it was in reality an expression of Roosevelt's own decision. It was born out of intense rancor. It dispensed angry judgment and condemnation and prescribed terrible revenge. It was a plan that was meant, at once, to be punitive and curative. It was designed to protect the world forever from an evil foe.

Its punitive measures included a proposed list of German leaders who were to be shot on sight, provisions to exile former Party members to remote regions, and the rendering of forced labor in Allied countries by German prisoners-of-war. While all of this would have been unprecedented in previous wars and was in violation of the Geneva Convention of 1929, it was insignificant in comparison with the plan's major and curative provision, namely the permanent destruction of the German economy by dismantling its industries. Its intent was to turn the German people into an agricultural and pastoral society. It would have resulted in an economic, cultural, and social mutilation never attempted before, except perhaps for similar visions Hitler had in mind for the Slavic people in the east once he had imposed upon them the rule of the German master race.

The magnitude of such disaster is revealed in its implied mortality. Like Great Britain, Germany was unable to feed itself and depended on industrial exports for the purchase of food abroad. After 1945, following the vast territorial amputations in the east, Germany was only 61 percent agriculturally self-sufficient.[2] Thus, the elimination of its industrial productivity would have led to starvation of nearly 40 percent of its population, or some 28million people. Once again, the reader may recognize here how this strategy, indeed taken seriously briefly in Quebec that September, exemplifies how fervent anger generates uncensored reasoning and demonization; follows it with a forbiddingly amoral plan of action; and presents such mortal revenge as nothing more than rightful justice.

As would be expected, it was a short-lived plan. Bitter opposition to it in Roosevelt's cabinet and in the American press forced the president to renounce it. In his heart, however, he clung to it. Two months later, in November 1944, he told John Maynard Keynes that the German economy would indeed be reduced to a level not quite completely agrarian.[3]

Unfortunately, while the Morgenthau Plan died officially, its spirit survived and left unmistakable imprints on subsequent policies. One of these was the Joint Chiefs of Staff Directive 1067, which was to guide Gen. Eisenhower regarding the administration of conquered Germany. The later American Military Governor in Germany, Gen. Lucius Clay, considered JCS 1067 a means to create a Carthaginian Peace.[4] It included instructions for the dismantling of wide sectors of German industrial plants and their transfer to countries such as the Soviet Union, France, Britain, and the United States. This de-industrialization process was indeed carried out for years and was not terminated until 1950. For five years after the war, Henry Morgenthau's footprints left behind much depletion in a land already ruined. The consequences of the Morgenthau Plan, or perhaps more correctly, of the vindictive spirit from which it emanated were disastrous. They are not well known, but there is convincing evidence to indicate that they resulted in a monstrous death toll.

The wholesale annexation of East Germany by Poland and the Soviet Union deprived her of one quarter of her previous agricultural acreage. The remainder of the country could not possibly feed itself, let alone the additional twelve million expellees pouring in from the East. Furthermore, harvest yields declined because of the lack of fertilizers. Total fertilizer production fell to 37 percent of prewar levels and nitrogen fertilizer to 19 percent.[5] Food imports from abroad, on the other hand, were impeded by the policies of de-industrialization, which, late in 1945, had reduced industrial output to 25 percent of it prewar capacity.[6] Consequently, even in the absence of further deleterious influences, a massive famine was inevitable.

Regrettably, such deleterious circumstances were indeed present. International relief organizations, such as the Red Cross, UNRRA, and the Hoover Program, as well as aid programs by the churches that were widely active, were not permitted to supply aid to Germany for the initial one-and-a-half post-war years.[7] The mailing of food from private citizens and organizations abroad was prevented by the suspension of postal services to Germany.[8] Over one thousand freight cars and trucks of the Red Cross, arriving in German towns with food were sent back to Switzerland.[9] Canadian Mennonites and Quakers from Canada, Great Britain, and the United States were not admitted into Germany until one year after the war.

The grim determination of these starvation policies, however, is in contrast to an entirely different attitude that must have prevailed among ordinary people in the victorious countries. In July 1944, a nationwide poll conducted by the National Opinion Research Center of Denver University, found that 64 percent of Americans favored helping Germany back on her industrial feet after the war, even if this required continued rationing in the

United States.[10] Rumors about the Morgenthau Plan, in September of that year, caused public indignation. In a poll in early 1945, only 13 percent of Americans agreed with destruction of German industries.[11] Early in 1946, the U.S. Senate passed a resolution censuring the fact that the will of Congress and the American people had been ignored in decisions that created starvation among millions.[12] The outpouring of good will, as manifested by the flood of CARE packages distributed in Germany after relinquishment of official restrictions, is testimony to the fact that the Morgenthau spirit was not shared by average citizens but was limited, instead, to isolated groups within the civilian and military leadership. What reversed the calamitous tide in Germany was the onset of the Cold War, which brought about a fundamental reorientation in the minds of this very group of men. The Marshall Plan, enacted in 1948, was the result of, and a correct strategic response to, the militant challenge by the Soviet Union. Here, too, Germany was initially not meant to participate, but was incorporated after another year.

Yet, until then, the tragedy, which had been launched that day in September in 1944, when Henry Morgenthau presented his plan in Quebec, mercilessly marched forward year after year. There was mass starvation. The infant mortality in Berlin was 100 percent.[13] Claims to maintain a daily caloric intake of 1550 calories did not materialize, as for months it fell to 1250 and even 1000 calories, and at times is said to have locally fallen to 450 calories.[14] The worst year must have been 1947.[15]

In various communities throughout the country, the annual death rate, which in normal times is near eleven or twelve among a thousand people, increased two- and three-fold. In one survey, their mean was 27.6 per thousand with a range from 17.2 to 39.5. The excess death rate of about fifteen per thousand over the normal value, in a population of roughly 70 million citizens, indicates that about one million people succumbed to starvation per year. For the entire five-year period, the total excess mortality would then reach five million. No matter how far this computation may approach the real facts, and whether or not J. Bacque's statistical analysis is correct, according to which, during that period, 5.7 million deaths occurred in excess of what was reported by the military governments,[16] there can be little doubt that starvation during those first five years of peace was enormous.

DEFIANT IRRELEVANCE

Back in the city, the pattern of civilized life was rapidly disintegrating, and yet, people were defiantly or sentimentally clinging to its vestiges as long as they could. As was exemplified by our observing my parents' anniversary, the effect was often one of anachronism.

I remember a listing of all the major performances in the capital, all the operas, operettas, symphony concerts, stage plays, and cabarets, followed the midday newscast at 1:00 P.M. Since hardly a concert hall or opera house had escaped destruction, they were all listed with new, makeshift locations, such as high school gymnasiums. *The Taming of the Shrew*, *The Merry Widow*, *The Abduction from the Seraglio*, ...on and on the announcements went for about ten minutes, from 1:20 to 1:30 P.M., the way I remember. People didn't want to let go.

Later that year, my piano teacher took me to a piano recital in Potsdam. The hall was crowded, everyone wearing heavy winter coats and gloves because there was no heat. As an encore, I recall, the pianist played one of my favorites, Schubert's *Moment Musical No. 3 in F-minor*, and I felt humbled by him doing it so nimbly, in spite of the cold. My fingers wouldn't do it even when they were warm.

In much the same anachronism, someone in the Horseman

Hitler Youth had determined this to be a good time for us to give a horse show. If my memory is correct, this Sunday in October had been designated for public displays and demonstrations in support of the people's heroic spirit, and the nationwide efforts to win the war. To win the war? Well yes, that was still the goal if your thoughts were politically correct.

So there I was standing on Frederick-the-Great's drill grounds not far from the historic Garrison Church, a large square not exactly overcrowded with spectators. I was waiting for my turn to ride Harras, the black-brown gilding. Harras was still my favorite even though he had ripped the zipper tab off my pants pocket once in impatient pursuit of some treat I had saved up for him. He knew zippers could be pulled open but had pulled mine in the wrong direction. So he had ripped it off, the clumsy oaf, as though one could still buy zippers.

In my memory, two comments are associated with Frederick-the-Great's drill grounds that Sunday morning. One was uttered by a middle-aged man who stopped briefly, looked at the snorting horses, and, shaking his head, said something like, "They must be kidding," and then trudged on. The other came from one of the boys. He said, "What's the matter with your eyes? They are so yellow!"

Paperback French

The doctor was a kind, elderly gentleman. His office lay halfway between our Berlin home and my old Paulsen High School. He agreed that my eyes and my skin were yellow and, after poking my liver, informed Mother that I suffered from jaundice. He prescribed four weeks of bed rest and a nutritious diet.

Mother, not wanting to burden her sister with a bedridden patient, established me in the chamber at the end of the hallway that used to be Friedrich's.

I enjoyed that period. The only times I got up was for the air raids. I had a paperback edition of Toussaint-Langenscheidt's *"French in 30 Lessons"*. I made it to lesson XXIII, grammar and all.

FATHER'S SHOCKING SPEECH

He made me feel very uncomfortable. I felt a desire to get up and escape, but here I was, confined to this bed and besides, it was, of course, unthinkable for me to walk out while Dad was talking to me. It was not *how* he said it; he spoke with fatherly concern, earnest and like a friend. It was *what* he said. It not only contradicted my innermost feelings and desires, but it also violated my idealism, which had been burned and hardened in the patriotic kiln of war.

I knew I was right. In a bad storm on the high seas, all hands were needed, and everyone was to put forth his best effort to help save the ship. To say that you did not like the captain was a poor excuse for deserting the valiant crew. It would have been utterly dishonorable.

Besides, I had my own stakes in this. I had watched the rapid enemy advances on all fronts with growing concern and had done so for a very personal reason. At the rate the enemies were advancing, the war was going to end before I was old enough to join the Army and do my share. Well, not really to do my share; it was not that so much as it was the Iron Cross; I wanted it in the worst way. It was the noblest and proudest symbol that I knew. Created in the Napoleonic Wars, it embodied a sacred tradition of our fatherland's heritage. Black with a silvery rim, how manly and elegant, so simple in form, yet so strong and beautiful...

In another four months I would be sixteen. I was going to make it, now that the *Volkssturm* was being established, the Home

Guard, which was made up of those between the ages of sixteen and sixty not already serving. I could volunteer for it; maybe they would accept me even a few months early. I was on the threshold of what I had been waiting for these past five years, and now Father told me it was wrong.

Yes, that's what he said. After Dieter had given his life, and with Friedrich trapped out there in Latvia, and with the Eastern Plague having reached our doorsteps, he considered it wrong to fight for our country. There was not much room in the chamber, but he started to pace three to four steps back and forth. He was breathing more heavily than he needed and kept his voice down, although there was nobody in our building who would have denounced him.

I must have looked at him with an expression of cool reserve, the French primer still on my lap, and perhaps he sensed that his message failed to convince me. Anyhow, he finally pro-duced his most powerful argument—a piece of information, which he had kept from me ever since he had himself come upon it, some twelve or fourteen months earlier. We never talked about it later, but I surmise this very report to have eventually tipped the scales in his own mind.

"Remember, Peter," he asked, "when the Ministry of Agriculture sent me to Kiev last year? Let me tell you about that. At first I simply refused to believe it. People down there in the Ukraine were talking about 'living hills'. Do you know what that might be? Do you have any idea at all, what people might call 'living hills'? They were referring to mass graves, *mein Junge*. Mass graves," he said, "that we made, we, not the Russians. They have these people dig the hole themselves, then line them up at the rim, and then they machine-gun them down so they fall right into the hole. Exactly the way Stalin's GPU is doing it, no different. Then, Peter, then," he continued, with his voice becoming hoarser, "then they come and shovel the earth on top of them and fill the hole, regardless of whether they are dead or just wounded. Do you hear that, Peter? Regardless of whether they are dead or just wounded! Some of them were still moving, and, yet, they buried them alive. Oh, my God, is so much cruelty conceivable? And that is being done in the name of Germany, our country?

"That's what 'living hills' are, Peter. They buried them alive. We did, Germans did. And the world will find out. They have already found out. They are criminals, *mein Junge*, the Party, the SS, Hitler, Himmler, and the whole lot of them. They are an organized pack of criminals. The damage done by them, and the shame and disgrace they have brought upon Germany, we won't live down in a hundred years."

He finally cleared his throat and pushed up his wire-rimmed glasses. "Rogues, that's what they are, Peter, rogues without a conscience. And *they* are giving the orders and are telling people to fight? They've got nothing to do with us, *mein Junge*. They've got nothing, but *nothing* in common with the Germany you and I believe in. They are a sick bunch of scoundrels who need to be put against the wall.

"They've wrecked our country and Europe as well. And they have lost the war, Peter; it's finished. They are going through their final frenzy now *(sie toben sich noch mal aus)*, but it's just a matter of a few more months. If Stauffenberg's bomb had only killed that maniac! But now there is no choice but to wait out the final hours. And then, Peter, Germany will have to try somehow to get on her feet again, if there is anything left of it. Then," he raised his finger and his eyebrows in promise, "then we will need good people, gifted people, decent and honest men, to rebuild from the ruins and to represent Germany in the world. Men like you and Friedrich and our Dieterchen, *mein Junge*. We can't just let them all get killed and have nobody left but the draft dodgers and opportunists, who managed to sit the war out in safe places.

"You must understand this, my good little boy, I know it must bewilder you. You want to be brave like your brothers of whom you are so proud, but you can't let these rogues catch you with their patriotic phrases and run you into battle and get you killed. Yes, Germany needs you, but not now. It's the wrong Germany. Afterwards, mein Junge, afterwards Germany needs you. It's not the end; it can't be; there are eighty million of us—what is going to happen? They surely aren't going to kill all of us, not eighty million people. Even Stalin can't do that. It will be hard, but there'll be some kind of Germany left, you'll see."

In the living room, there hung the framed pictures of Friedrich and Dieter, the ones Dieter's girl friend had made for us. They were studio portraits, enlargements, showing both of them in a lieutenant's uniform.

That uniform, to me, was the most honorable garment in the world. Those who wore it were the men whom we were proud of, admired, prayed for, loved, and decorated. I had seen them in our home, my brothers' comrades, those young officers, those clean-cut, high-spirited, and idealistic men. Most of them had fallen in battle by now.

I wanted to wear that uniform.

Adults were funny sometimes. Now suddenly it was no longer right to wear that uniform, up there, on the pictures! Of course it was, no matter what Himmler had done, or Hitler. Dieter wore it when he gave his life for us, and Friedrich was still wearing it. Mother had pressed her tears into it, Friedrich's uniform.

Kiev, all right. But part of that story must have been missing. Those people killed there must have been partisans or saboteurs or something. There was a vicious guerrilla war being waged behind the German lines, everybody knew that, and neither side was taking prisoners. I had heard of a Soviet general, who had flown in by plane across the front line and had inspected his troops, an entire division of partisans. What were we supposed to do? Let them attack our troops from the rear and blow up our supply lines? The communist partisans were a fanatical and merciless lot. It was a dirty war, so dirty that they had to use SS troops to fight them. The regular Army wouldn't have had the stomach for it.

Of course I wasn't out to machine-gun people into mass graves. My country was in trouble. It needed me. I wanted to defend it. That was all I wanted to do. In this uniform. I knew of no uniform in the world more glorious or proud.

NEMMERSDORF: TERRIFYING SIGNAL

They showed it on the newsreel. Our troops had recaptured a German village in East Prussia. Nemmersdorf was its name. The Red Army had raped all the women, and all the men had been shot. It must have been a bestial orgy and a massacre. The camera filming from a slowly moving vehicle showed a row of dead bodies, perhaps twenty or thirty of them, the way they had been left by the roadside.

The footage fell on fertile ground. It was the first time the Russians had set foot on German soil. This was the moment that our terrified nation had been waiting for. What would they do to us? This carnage confirmed the worst fears.

Nemmersdorf. It became a blood-curdling signal for millions of Eastern Germans to leave their ancient homelands in desperate fright. It set in motion one of the greatest mass migrations in history, an exodus of unprecedented proportions. Over two million of these refugees were to perish as a consequence of exposure, starvation, massacre, or the bombing and machine-gunning of their treks and the sinking of their ships.

Kill Me, Soldier

In October of 1942, the man who eventually would explode the bomb under Hitler's map table, Claus von Stauffenberg, had said in a speech that Germany was sowing such hatred in the east that "our children will reap the reward of it some day".[17] It was proven to be a pitiful understatement, many millions of times, over and over again, starting in Nemmersdorf on October 20, 1944 and continuing for several years thereafter. The description of those events is distasteful. They display a hatred so severe and unbridled as to suggest that the gods of vengeance found our ten-step Scale of Anger utterly inadequate. But one might understand this bloody deluge if one accepts the three-stage mechanism of hatred.

The Soviet author Ilya Ehrenburg, publishing in the soldiers' paper *Red Star*, made a plea for revenge. His words and their subsequent implementation by the Red Army illustrate the same phenomenon, which weaves through the hostility of that war, that dreadful behavioral sequence from utmost indignation to ferocious denunciation, and then to barbaric violence. The notion of righteousness is almost movingly proclaimed in the words, "*your grandmother's request*" and "*your child's prayer*". He could as well have said, "*It is God's command,*" to indicate divine sanction, but he did not. *He* wrote:

> The Germans are not human beings. From now on the word German means to us the most terrible oath...We shall not speak any more. We shall not get excited. We shall kill. If you have not at least killed one German a day, you have wasted that day...If you cannot kill your German with a bullet, kill him with your bayonet...If you kill one German, kill another—there is nothing more amusing to us than a heap of German corpses... Kill the German—that is your grand-

mother's request. Kill the German—that is your child's prayer. Kill the German—that is your motherland's loud request. Do not miss... Kill.[18]

*   *   *

Stepping on German soil presumably caused the soldiers of the Red Army to go berserk. The reports rendered by German troops retaking areas previously lost to the Soviets, those rendered by the native population, by medical and forensic commissions, by journalists from neutral countries and by French, Belgian, and British prisoners-of-war held in those areas all spoke with one voice.

Often under the influence of alcohol, they pillaged, destroyed, raped, tortured, and murdered wherever they passed across German soil. They wiped the land clean of humans. Not knowing the difference, in one area they shot fifty French prisoners-of-war.[19] When they overtook treks of refugees on the road, they shot them wholesale or squashed them flat under the treads of their tanks.[20] They raped every female between the ages of eight and eighty-four.[21] Frequently they killed the women after raping them with a shot to the base of the skull. At other times, they killed with the rifle-butt by blows into the faces of men, women, and children; leaving them disfigured beyond recognition.[22] In Metgethen, a town west of Königsberg, several hundred German prisoners-of-war were discovered whose bodies were mutilated. Many people, of any age and both sexes, were killed by inflicting multiple bayonet wounds, some with evidence of prior beating.[23] One eighty-four year-old woman was found "sitting on a sofa...half of whose head had been sheared off with an axe or a spade."[24]

On entering a recaptured village, German troops encountered a ghost town with no sign of human life, except for the corpses strewn by the roadway and in the homes. Time and again, in different regions, they found women, often totally naked, nailed though their hands in a crucified manner to barn doors or carts.[25]

Outrage to women swept the land in a veritable epidemic wherever the Red Army appeared, be that in the large ethnic German settlements in Rumania, Hungary, Yugoslavia, and Czechoslovakia, or in East and West Prussia, Pomerania, Silesia, or in Berlin and its surrounding provinces. Of those who had not fled to the West, few escaped. Mass rape was common. There were female corpses with bloody genitals. In a large villa, some sixty women were discovered who were out of their senses and many of them needed psychiatric care. They had been raped sixty to seventy times a day.[26] A doctor reported about a patient of his who had suffered head injuries. She was raped, nonetheless, over and over again, without ever knowing anything about it.[27] Many women had been massacred by means of mutilatory sadism. They were found with their breasts cut off, with multiple stab wounds, and with their genitals stabbed through and disemboweled.[28]

Sadistic derangement had no limits. In that East Prussian town of Metgethen, two twenty year-old women were found who had been ripped apart. To each of them, the Red Army soldiers had tied one leg to the wheel of one car, and the other leg to the wheel of another car. The two cars were then driven away from each other, thus splitting each woman apart.[29]

In a village named Gross-Heydekrug, the soldiers crucified a girl on the altar cross in the church. On each side of her, they hanged a German prisoner-of-war.[30] In the same village, there stood a Soviet tank. To its back were tied the bodies of four naked women whom it had apparently dragged to death.[31]

In Metgethen again, there were numerous piles of German corpses and two veritable mountains, each with an estimated three thousand bodies, predominantly of women, children, and only a few men. Forensic examination confirmed that many had been raped and had their breasts cut off and had otherwise been mutilated and killed by means of beating and stabbing.[32] In the same town, about twenty-five men, women, and children, and a few soldiers and policemen, had been forced into a bomb crater and then were blown asunder by an explosive charge. Their cadaver parts were thrown as far as two hundred meters away and littered surrounding trees and a high tennis court fence.[33]

At the railway station, there stood a train that was surprised by the Red Army, while it was taking refugees to the Baltic port of Pillau from where tens of thousands escaped by the sea to the West. In each of its coaches, seven to nine bestially mutilated cadavers were found, of all ages and both sexes, some of the women with evidence of rape again .[34]

In the opinion of the historian and diplomat George F. Kennan, "The Russians... swept the native population clean in a manner that had no parallel since the days of the Asiatic hordes".[35]

*   *   *

Alexander Solzhenitsyn was a young officer then and witnessed the conquest of East Prussia. In his book "Gulag Archipelago" he wrote: "For three weeks the war had been going on inside Germany, and all of us knew very well that if the girls were German, they could be raped and then shot. This was almost a combat distinction." He also wrote a poem entitled "Prussian Nights" of which an excerpt reads:

> Twenty-two Höringstrasse.
> It's not been burned, just looted, rifled.
> A moaning, by the walls half muffled.
> The mother's wounded, still alive.
> The little daughter's on the mattress,
> Dead. How many have been on it?
> A platoon, a company perhaps?
> A girl's been turned into a woman,
> A woman turned into a corpse.
> It's all come down to simple phrases:
> *Do not forget! Do not forgive!*
> *Blood for blood! A tooth for a tooth!*
> The mother begs me, "*Töte mich, Soldat!*"
> Her eyes are hazy...[36]

In the Russian original, Solzhenitsyn wrote her request in German. Her three words mean, "Kill me, soldier".

* * *

The desperate exodus of the greater part of the East German population prompted by these events involved millions, predominantly
women, children and elderly people. Naval and merchant ships
evacuated 1.5 million refugees and 700,000 soldiers by sea alone.[37]
Hosts of others joined in treks to seek rescue in the west by land.
This transit over hundreds of miles through the exceptionally
severe winter of 1944/1945 caused many fatalities as a result of
exposure, the icy cold, hunger, and strafing and bombing by low
flying aircraft. The death toll of this massive exodus, extending
from the Baltic Sea to the Balkans, has been estimated at one million non-combatants.[38]

* * *

Farther south, the experiences were no less savage. Large and old
ethnic German settlements existed in Rumania, Hungary, and
Yugoslavia. There as well as in the vast areas of West Prussia, Posen,
East Pomerania, East Brandenburg, Silesia, and the Sudetenland
the sequence of events followed roughly an identical pattern.

   The fate of those in Yugoslavia can serve as an example. In
the area adjoining the Danube, north of Belgrade, bearing the
names of Banat and Bacska, there lived the so-called Danube
Swabians. They counted a little over 500,000, not a very impressive
number but, after all, it was about the same as the Jewish population of Germany in 1930. They were largely rural folks,
intermingled with Serbians, Croatians, Hungarians, and
Rumanians, and, so I am told, their prosperous and beautiful farms
were widely admired. Once Hitler's forces swept across the Balkans
in 1941, their men served in the German, Hungarian, and
Rumanian armies, and 31,000 were killed in action.[39]

   The Red Army invaded the land in October of 1944, at the
same time when they entered East Prussia. Tito's partisans followed them in due course. A wave of raping, again indiscriminate
of the victims' age, and of looting followed.[40] A mother, refusing to

reveal her daughter's hiding place, was permanently disfigured.[41] The men were rounded up next and either liquidated by mass exe-cutions[42] or deported for slave labor, either in the Urals or in other parts of the Soviet Union or in Yugoslavia.[43] Soon women were taken away in cattle cars, as well, to work in Russian coalmines.[44] In the next stage, what was left of their once peaceful society, their children, their grandparents, their elderly and their sick were evict-ed from their homes and herded into concentration camps.[45] There existed numerous concentration camps in Tito's land, the most infamous being those in Rudolfsgnad, Gakovo, Jarek, Mitrovica, Motidorf and Krushevlje. They were death camps.[46] They were sites of executions, physical abuse, starvation, rats, typhoid fever, and wagonloads of cadavers carting away the victims of hatred.[47] In Gakovo, which incarcerated 21,000 victims,[48] the daily death toll was said to be fifty to fifty-five who were disposed of in nearby mass graves. Jarek confined 25,000 starving children and old peo-ple. The report says that, a year and a half later, in April 1946, there were about 2,800 left in the camp, giving the impression that the remainder had perished.[49]

The storm of deadly passion was much the same in the German areas controlled by the Czechs and the Poles, with some minor variations. There, it subsided after two years as the Germans had either succumbed or had been expelled to the West in the summer of 1947,[50] whereas the agony in Yugoslavia apparently raged until 1949.[51] Outright massacres of several thousand Germans erupted in Prague on 5 May 1945 and in Aussig an der Elbe (Usti nad Ladem) on 31 July 1945.[52] As the Nazis had forced the Jews to display the Star of David on their coats, so the Czechs now required the Germans to wear a patch with the letter "N," the initial of the Czech word for German. The 25,000 or 30,000 Germans of Brünn (Brno), the capital of Moravia, were evicted from their homes on ten-minute notice. They were marched into a concentration camp where the daily death toll was estimated as one hundred.[53] Notorious Czech concentration camps were the previous Nazi camp at Theresienstadt and the one at Budweis. At the Polish concentration camp at Lamsdorf, in Upper Silesia, among a total of 8,064 inmates, a doctor recorded the death of

6,488 including 628 children.[54]

* * *

Expulsion transports from the amputated eastern parts of Germany and the Sudetenland were established by the new masters using sealed cattle cars, often without food or water, and lasting a week or longer. An English report in November 1945 described the arrival in Berlin of a train from the Sudetenland. It had traveled eighteen days. It had started with 2,400 expellees, but 1,050 presumably perished on the way.[55] A train from Danzig had taken seven days to Berlin. Hundreds lying in it and on the platform and the booking hall of the railroad station were described as "the dead and dying and starving flotsam left by the tide of human misery that daily reaches Berlin…".[56]

A young nurse arrived in Berlin from Stettin. Russians and Poles had robbed her three times on the trip. Whoever resisted was shot. Her father had been stabbed to death while trying to protect her from being raped, after her mother and sister had been so violated. Again, one is revolted and horrified by her report of having seen a Polish guard crush a baby's head against a post because he was bothered by its crying while he was raping his mother.[57] Another woman arrived from Upper Silesia. She wore the marks of whiplashing across her face. She had been raped thirty times during the travel. She was now pregnant.

The German Red Cross has estimated that 874,000 Germans were deported to the Soviet Union for slave labor and that 45 percent of them did not survive.

* * *

Millions after millions flooded west, first in desperate and panicky flight before the advance of the Red Army and then, upon the end of the war, being forcibly expelled chiefly by the Poles and Czechs, uprooted, freezing, starving, emaciated, destitute, and some dying. Their "transfer," as it was euphemistically called, produced an insurmountable problem for the recipient remnant of Germany and, also, for the western military authorities that were now administering their occupation zones. The millions needed food and shelter in a land where daily intake had shrunk to as low as one thousand calories and where the annihilating air raids had in some cities destroyed 80 to 90 percent of the dwellings.[58] On the twentieth of November 1945, the Allied Control Council, therefore, issued directions that were meant to replace the wild expulsions with organized transfers. As a result, the inhumanity of the forced expulsion of the remaining 6.5 million expellees was only mildly reduced in 1946 and 1947.

According to the German Ministry of Expellees, among the Germans in the vast amputated East German lands and the ethnic Germans in other east European countries, 11,730,000 refugees and expellees were successful in reaching the remaining German territories in the West. Another 2,111,000 people were listed as dead or missing.[59] They perished as a result of man-on-man and mostly man-on-woman violence, of suicide, of strafing and bombing of the refugee treks, of starvation and epidemics during the flight and in the concentration camps, of mass executions, of the sinking of refugee ships in the Baltic by submarines, and, when hundreds of thousands of them had reached Dresden in transit, in the firestorm caused by the devastating air raids on that city.

REPREHENSIONS

On 16 August 1945, Churchill said in the House of Commons, "Sparse and guarded comments of what...is happening have filtered through, but it is not impossible that tragedy on a prodigious scale is unfolding itself behind the iron curtain...".[60]

Bertrand Russell wrote in the 8 December 1945 issue of the *New Leader*:

> It was agreed at Potsdam that these expulsions should take place 'in a humane and orderly manner,' but this provision has been flouted. At a moment's notice, women and children are herded into trains, with only one suitcase each,

and they are usually robbed on the way of its contents. The journey to Berlin takes many days, during which no food is provided. Many are dead when they reach Berlin; children who die on the way are thrown out of the window. A member of the Friends' Ambulance Unit describes the Berlin station at which these trains arrive as 'Belsen over again (Nazi concentration camp liberated by British forces)—carts taking the dead from the platform, etc.' A large proportion of those ejected from their homes are not put into trains, but are left to make their way westward on foot. Exact statistics of the numbers thus expelled are not available, since only the Russians could provide them. Ernest Bevin's estimate is 9,000,000. According to a British officer now in Berlin, populations are dying, and Berlin hospitals 'make the sights of the concentration camps appear normal.'[61]

In his 1946 book, *Our Threatened Values,* Victor Gollancz said, "If the conscience of man ever again becomes sensitive, these expulsions will be remembered to the undying shame of all who committed or connived at them..."[62]

On 4 February 1946, in the New York Times, Anne O'Hare McCormick stated:

It was also agreed at Potsdam that the forced migration should be carried out 'in a humane and orderly manner.' Actually, as every one knows who has seen the awful sights at the reception centers in Berlin and Munich, the exodus takes place under nightmarish conditions, without any international supervision or any pretense of humane treatment. We share responsibility from horrors only comparable to Nazi cruelties...

In his *Memoirs* published in 1958, Field Marshall Montgomery observed:

From their behaviour it soon became clear that the Russians, though a fine fighting race, were in fact barbarous Asiatics who had never enjoyed a civilisation comparable to that of Europe. Their approach to every problem was utterly different from ours and their behaviour, especially in their treatment of women, was abhorrent to us...[63]

Today, one wonders whether the field marshal could possibly have spoken of the same Russians whom we know and read about today. One even wonders whether the acts just described could truly have been committed by them or, in fact, by anyone at all. Since there is no way of denying that indeed they did, one might forgivingly conclude that the Russians, at that time, had been seized by a terrible passion—a passion perhaps understandable and one whose barbarity was transient, and which was in no way characteristic of their otherwise respectable civilization and noble cultural achievements. That would be a judgment of which God, if all we have been told about Him is true, would probably approve.

By contrast, however, the opinion prevailing in the hearts and minds of the desperate German people during those years was not that forgiving. They were essentially ignorant of the *Einsatzgruppen* and their death toll and of the Holocaust in the gas chambers. Nor had they, of course, been informed of the deaths of one million or more Soviet prisoners-of-war in German custody. Having received only one-sided news reports during the war, as was customary in all belligerent countries, they could explain the disastrous Russian orgy in no other way than on the basis of their barbaric nature. There is no question that they would have considered Montgomery's harsh judgment stunningly correct. The tidal wave of horror, descending upon them from the East, verified to them the dreadful fears that they had had ever since Lenin's revolution, if not even before then. As popular opinion had it, there had been barbarism looming in the East, going back to the days of the Huns and the Mongolian Hordes. This very barbarism had now been unfettered to invade Europe, subjugating, enslaving, and defiling its eastern half and threatening the remainder. If there had ever been any need for proof, here, so they felt in their terrified hearts, before God and all mankind, was the deadly evidence that their dreadful fright of Stalin's empire had without question been fully justified and was bound to surmount any other conceivable fear or consideration that might exist on this earth.

The Advice of the Precinct Captain

I DECIDED I WOULD ASK THE PRECINCT CAPTAIN. Nowhere had I been able to find an announcement of where volunteers could sign up for the *Volkssturm*. I had to do it secretly, but that did not seem to present a problem in my mind. I would volunteer and then turn around and tell my parents that I was drafted.

The address was that of a small one-story home set back a bit from the street. I found it readily, in spite of the blackout; it was just a few blocks from Uncle Hans' apartment. I rang the bell. A stern, but not unfriendly looking gentleman opened, fiftyish I would say, and asked, "Yes?"

I asked him for the location of the recruiting station, and mentioned my intention to volunteer. He raised his eyebrows and inquired,

"Well, do your parents know about this?"

"No," I replied, "there is no use telling them. They wouldn't want me to go under any circumstances. But you see, sir, I do want to go."

He never changed his expression or tone of voice. I had expected him to say something like, "Good show, my boy," or "Yes indeed, the Führer needs you," maybe even pat me on my back. Instead, he remained official, with just a touch of fatherliness, as he advised me, "Well, you know, there's no point in volunteering. That doesn't get you there any sooner, and I don't think they take volunteers anyway. I think you should wait until they draft you."

I trudged home through the black streets, disappointed but

also reassured. Surely, he had to know, and if that was his advice, there was nothing else I could do.

Looking back, it seems to me, quite possibly he saved me from spending a few years in Stalin's slave labor camps. Perhaps, he had a boy my age of his own; or even lost one. Or, perhaps, in him the balance had shifted, too.

THE POLESTAR PROVED SOMETHING

It was on a weekend late in the year when, on passing through the capital, Capt. Rasmus stopped to visit with us for a few hours. In spite of his being so dear to us, it must have been a somber reunion, but I have no memories of that, nor of the visit itself. What I do remember is that, afterwards, I walked him to the train station.

It was a clear night and as we made our way through the rubble-lined streets, somehow we came to talk about the stars. I pointed in the direction of the North Pole by dropping a vertical line from the North Star, a maneuver made easier by the fact that many of the buildings no longer obstructed the view of the sky. He was curious how I knew to identify the North Star, and I explained that I had extended the rear axle of the Big Dipper six times to the right.

He then asked me, "Did you learn that in the Hitler Youth?" I said that I had.

There was a short pause before he asked me, "So, then you did learn good and useful things there?" I confirmed that, too.

While we said no more on the subject—and, in fact, I remember nothing else that happened that night—his words kept lingering in my mind and have become a lasting memory.

Still today, perhaps while walking the dog at night, when my eyes wander from the Big Dipper to the Polestar, his distant words might echo in my ear. I know that, on our walk that night, in a subtle way I had sensed that his question was about much more than the Hitler Youth. Rather, certain doubts must have crept up in his mind, and he was casting out for someone to reaffirm to him that he had been fighting for a good cause.

Perilous Encounter

Father had returned from Meseritz. The Ministry of Agriculture had less and less agricultural territory to administer. He was to assume the duties of an administrator of a large estate in the province of Mecklenburg, about 150 kilometers northwest of Berlin. Its owner was a Hamburg cigarette manufacturer, and the present administrator was needed in the Army. Father wasn't, he was fifty-four years old and had only one eye.

In the meantime, however, he received notice to register for the Berlin *Volkssturm*. I happened to spend the night in Berlin when he walked over there one evening. When he returned, he asked Mother to come out into the hallway. There was a great deal of agitated whispering, and, as it grew in intensity I knew something serious had happened. I heard Mother say "No, Daddy!" several times. The front door was being opened and there was a bit of a hustle, and I noticed an imploring element in Mother's whispers. They finally both came into the living room, but Father continued to be terribly agitated.

As I learned later, he had become involved in an argument with a young punk of a Party official who had piercingly questioned him about why he had waited until he was called up, instead of volunteering weeks ago. "The Führer," he claimed, "gave orders that all Party members have to volunteer!"

Father had bristled, I suspect. In his own mind his Party membership had lost its validity many years ago. He shot back at the man, pointing out the fact that the Führer couldn't possibly do that, because a command to volunteer was a self-contradiction. The confrontation very quickly grew physical, so that others had to separate them. This incident had punctured his pent-up anger, and, after returning home he was going to turn around and go back to really let them have it, whatever valiant rashness that would have entailed, but Mother had managed to dissuade him.

A week or so later, he received a summons to appear before a Party tribunal. That was ominous. Ever since the July 20 assassination attempt, the Party fanatics had been in an ugly mood, even though it was not for several more months before "traitors" and "deserters" were hanged from lampposts in the streets. He decided to ignore the summons, so he told me, as he was counting on the growing confusion and his impending departure for that estate in the country. He did indeed never hear from them again.

Trivial Pursuits at the Abyss

Christmas was approaching. There was, of course, nothing one could buy in the way of presents. I sat at Uncle Hans' desk and built a small case to keep stamps in. It was for Mother. I used cardboard and some printed red-and-white paper left over from Bärbel's bookbinding course. It turned out to be a very handsome little box. It had two stamp-sized bins with slanted floors, allowing the stamps to be wiped out with a finger. The lid flipped neatly open and shut, and, like the bottom, it projected beyond the sides. I showed my red-and-white masterpiece to Aunt Lotte with loving pride, and she liked it so much that she suggested I make another one for Bärbel. The little box survived. Decades later, I found it in one of Mother's desk drawers, with stamps in it.

On a Saturday night, we were sitting in our living room in Berlin. We had moved the furniture, so the chairs were crowding around the furnace. I was reading. Mother was crocheting bedroom slippers for Dad. The soles were made of felt cut in long strips from his old hats, then braided, and then rolled into a sole-shaped pad. She did not have enough brown wool for knitting the tops of both slippers, so she mixed in other leftover segments of knitting wool and thus gave it a very colorful appearance. It seems a lot of women were doing this: becoming inventive when there were no presents to buy.

Why were we still doing this? We did it for the same reason that made us go to the symphony in a bombed out concert hall. People are sentimental, and I know of no Christian country where they would not cling to Christmas, even under the most adverse circumstances and to their last breath. In addition, in many of us that brave spirit that nobody will understand, unless he has once himself been high on the adrenaline of war and patriotism, effectively subdued the sense of impending doom.

"Let me try them on for size," she interrupted my reading and took my foot. "Your feet are almost as big as Dad's now."

I do not remember that Christmas Eve at all, not even whether we spent it in Berlin or in Potsdam, not where the tree stood if we had one, or whether or not we had gone to church. But I do recall the bedroom slippers; they were for me, not Dad.

Men were not as inventive as mothers, I suppose, but they were no less sentimental. Father gave me his wristwatch. He said his pocket watch was all he needed.

MAY THE ALMIGHTY...

Courland, December 27, 1944
Dear Parents,

Thank you for your Christmas greetings and the two packages. One could actually feel the love. You created a great Christmas joy for me. And, my dear Daddy, I was really delighted about the fountain pen... The three packets for the advent season have arrived, too.

Christmas Eve in the circle of comrades was very beautiful. We had a very pretty tree inside a very nice bunker. The mood was very solemn and I thought of you a lot. Ivan was considerate enough to keep quiet. But on Christmas Day, the game resumed with customary vigor; Ivan just had to catch his breath. In the hard battles these last several days we achieved great successes. In a single day, one regiment destroyed thirty-seven enemy tanks, eight of them using close-range weapons. Therefore, today the honorable mention it in the High Command Report. Our men are very proud and are delivering a terrific fight. ...I expect Ivan will soon be exhausted. Then we will await the Fourth (Courland) Battle. You mustn't think by any means that we're going to leave from here! Here we shall remain till victory!

I doubt New Year's Day will be as beautiful and quiet as Christmas Eve... A year ago, we celebrated the New Year in a cattle wagon and it was beautiful just the same. I'm sending my heart-felt greetings to you, my dear ones, and wish you a healthy and victorious New Year!

...Friedrich

January 1, 1945
Dear Parents, Gila and Peter,

... We were lucky, we could enjoy both Christmas and New Year's Eve in complete quiet. Last night... I was thinking of you a lot. At midnight we drank a glass of red champagne to your health and to the hope that the Almighty protect our Führer for us and that He may make this year one that will bring good fortune and victory to our country...

...Don't you know a girl for me to marry...?

A Thousand Greetings
...Friedrich

Courland, January 16, 1945
Dear Parents,

Now the battle has calmed down again. Ivan really didn't achieve much. Now comes the time for all the paperwork... I'm in good shape. Presently, my telephone name is "Marital Bliss 35". How do you like that? Things in the Vistula sweep (Poland) and in Hungary really don't look very good. But I expected exactly that. Oh well, somehow it'll come out right... We've now submitted our general for the Oak-Leaf Cluster (a high decoration for valor). That was quite a job because, by Jove, a hero he is not. But it had to be done because of the men...

...Friedrich

YOUTHFUL HEROES

A fourteen year-old Silesian boy was awarded the Knight's Cross. He was said to have destroyed ten T-34 tanks using *Panzerfäuste*, armor breaking rockets fired from the hip with a range of only thirty meters.

There was a new military medal now, too, the tank plaque. It bore the image of a tank in bas-relief and was sewn to the coat sleeve below the shoulder. Occasionally one could see servicemen with tank plaques all the way down to the elbow. Initially awarded, I believe, for destroying a tank by mounting it and attaching a magnetic charge, it was now, since the introduction of the *Panzerfaust* rocket, within reach of those less athletic such as soldiers not yet fully grown.

Only one, I was wistfully thinking, if I could earn only one of these plaques before the war is over.

DRESDEN

AMONG EUROPEAN CITIES, Dresden occupied a special place. It was a treasure box of the fine arts, literature, and music. It was a baroque city famous for the splendor of its architecture. Its wealth of art, its manufacture of fine china, and its cultural distinction were cherished around the world. It bore the sobriquet of being the Florence on the Elbe River. There was no surprise that it had been exempted from aerial attacks throughout the war; after all, Rome and Paris had been too.

It was three months before the end of the war. The Red Army was approaching Silesia. A little less than four million frightened Silesians took flight to the west in one of Europe's most frigid winters. In transit, they crowded through transport junctions such as Dresden. Dresden had a prewar population of 630,000. The number of refugees present in that city that night is unknown. Some felt the populace was double its normal number; others rejected the number of 200,000 refugees as much too low an estimate.

In January 1945, the British Air Ministry designed an offensive plan by the name of Thunderclap. It was to support the Russian westward advance by causing chaos and by disrupting the flow of German refugees. Major targets were Berlin, Dresden, Chemnitz, and Magdeburg. The raid upon Berlin on February 3, by the Eighth US Air Force, caused 25,000 civilian deaths. On February 13, weather conditions were right for dealing with Dresden. The RAF sent 796 Lancaster bombers and dropped 1,479 tons of explosive bombs and 1,182 tons of incendiaries. They attacked in two waves, the first between 10:00 and 10:21 P.M. on February 13, and the second three hours later at 1:30 A.M. on February 14. The same day at 12:12 P.M., 450 US B-17s arrived for the third attack.[64] A fourth raid was carried out the next afternoon. In the two daytime assaults, low-level American aircraft machine-gunned survivors were scurrying away from the city in their escape from the inferno. Altogether, between three thousand and four thousand tons of explosive and incendiary devices were dropped.

Dresden was turned into an inferno and essentially ceased to be. None of the other assaults on German cities was as fatal and devastating as the annihilation of Dresden. A firestorm generates temperatures of one thousand and even fifteen hundred degrees Fahrenheit. The air soars above the widespread blaze and draws in air from the sides. The resulting wind intensifies the blaze, which thereby feeds upon itself to a point where the wind grows to hurricane force, where the asphalt in the streets catches fire, and where the people asphyxiate in the furnace of their air raid shelters because the oxygen is consumed in the flames.

> Burning torches. They screamed, as only people in the throes of death can scream. They collapsed. Hundreds of burning, screaming human torches collapsed and were silent. And they were followed by more, and still more. None of these survived their torment... The street was strewn with corpses, torsos hung from the twisted trees...[65]

Only six Lancaster bombers were lost.[66] Air defenses had weakened; Germany was near its end. The German death rate is unknown. Published estimates run between 70,000 and 250,000 Dresdeners and refugees.

The usefulness and moral rectitude of aerial bombing had been questioned for some time. It had long become evident that its primary purpose of breaking German morale had failed and that, in the contest with the air armada's destructiveness, "German resilience, ingenuity, and rate of repair" were gaining the upper hand.[67] It appears that despite moral criticism, Arthur Harris adhered to his policy, because he felt the defeat of Nazism was of a higher moral imperative. He is said to have responded to Churchill's questioning the need or value of the Dresden attack with the statement that he did not regard the whole of the remaining cities of Germany as worth the bones of one British grenadier.[68]

The destruction of Dresden has been the most controversial episode of the strategic bombing campaign. Ever since then, this campaign and Air Marshall Harris's role in it have been the focus of resentment and imputation, and its moral justification has been the subject of embarrassing questions on both sides of the Atlantic.

A year later, at the Nuremberg Trials in April 1946, a day after the testimony of Rudolf Höss, the commander of the Auschwitz death camp, a British reporter asked at a birthday party whether there was a moral difference between gassing people on the ground or cooking them from the air. He judged that Arthur "Bomber" Harris, the author of the level-the-cities strategy, had as much blood on his hands as a Rudolf Höss.[69]

That is grim judgment on a man who felt righteous and patriotic in his passion to protect his country and the freedom of the world and, in the carnage, did not wish to waste the life of his grenadiers. If he went wrong, where did he? He did when he fell into the treacherous trap of Righteous Anger. We all do at times.

The hostility of war, like a knee-jerk reaction, diminishes in our mind the value and size of the enemy. Mr. Lohmann had called the Poles mosquitoes. Hitler called the Jews vermin; Goebbels called them bacilli. Ilya Ehrenburg referred to the Germans as microbes. Churchill called the German soldiers locusts ("I see the dull, drilled, docile, brutish masses of the Hun soldiery plodding on like a swarm of crawling locusts").[70] The Japanese-Americans were pictured as "buck-toothed, monkey-faced sneaks" and as "Jap rats". We all do it; it is a human reflex. Arthur Harris did it too. All of the German cities, and all of the people within them, did not come up to the size of a single British grenadier. In his mind, they were very small and valueless indeed. They were a pest.

Once, on the tenth level of passionate fervor, the enemy has thus been denounced and demoted into a pest, there comes the equally instant and reflexive decision of how to deal with him. A mosquito needs to be pinched, a rat poisoned, and a swarm of crawling locust needs to be sprayed with a pesticide. It is apparently an automatic reaction that bypasses any need for deliberation. There is, so it seems, no need to observe moral or behavioral taboos. Truly, if one saw the dull, brutish masses of the Hun soldiery approaching like locusts, and if one were in command of an obedient army, would one not be tempted to use that army as a pesticide? Hitler did when confronting his vermin-like neighbors in the east. He created the *SS-Einsatzgruppen* exactly for the purpose of deploying them as a pesticide against them. Such a reflex can be activated in all of us. It erupts once we have been stirred into fiery passion and fall into the pitfall of righteous anger. But in everyday life, such verbal letting off steam is generally inconsequential. Most of us are still governed by behavioral taboos to set us straight, and even if they were disabled, no disaster ensues because, after all, we don't have an army. The problem with "Bomber" Harris was not so much his personality or conscience— yes, he must have been a brash and even more impatient and reckless man than Winston Churchill—but rather that they made him chief of Bomber Command, an obedient armada of destruction. Unlike most of us, he did indeed possess an army that could function as a pesticide. Without the appointment to that powerful position, his life would likely have taken a less controversial course.

Might he have ever had reasons to recognize that he did not kill legitimately, like a soldier, but mass-murdered the innocent without legal or moral sanction? Most likely not, because in the state of fervent patriotism, in the righteous anger aflame in the hearts of upright and moral men, the distinction between the demands of rage and the desire for justice is often not visible.

This kind of phenomenon is ubiquitous in wars, because wars create so much abhorrence and passion, because moral taboos are weakened and, of course, because then angry people have armies. He evidently saw himself as acting honorably and with proper vigor for a righteous cause. He fell into the treacherous spot in the denunciation phase of anger that could be called the trap of the wrath-of-the-just. Did Hitler not, in fact, derail at that very same place? It is forever and for all of us a deceptive and seductive pitfall, and if you or I had been in Harris's shoes, perhaps we, too, would have stumbled into it.

CALLED UP AT LAST

O N MY SIXTEENTH BIRTHDAY IN FEBRUARY 1945, I received the draft notice. It was, however, not a regular draft notice. I was ordered to report for pre-military training to the Adolf-Hitler-School in Sonthofen in the Allgäuer Alps on or near March first. This was preferential treatment, since everybody else was drafted into the *Volkssturm* to defend the capital against the Red Army, and it was related to the fact that, months earlier, I had filed my application for a career as a professional officer.

Adolf-Hitler-Schools, such as the one in Sonthofen, were institutions fashioned after traditional military schools for boys, but redone in the Fascist image and designed to train the future National-Socialist elite and leadership. At this point of the war, however, someone possessed of remarkable optimism had ordered that they be used for the purpose of providing future military officers with a little extra ideological polish and conviction.

Such unperturbed confidence was not at all uncommon. At this very time, I distinctly recall, people were consulting one another regarding the advisability of staying in Berlin or fleeing to the West. Not only did most of them choose to stay, but they did so, many of them at least, in the expectation that the turning of the tide was imminent. It goes to the credit of the incomparable Dr. Goebbels that he managed to keep morale high by fooling the gullible nation to the very end.

Even Aunt Lotte seemed unaware of the lateness of the hour. She gravely disapproved of my entering an Adolf-Hitler-School, as though I was going to be indoctrinated there for the next two years. She shook her head in deep concern and would not have done so had she not believed in some kind of military miracle that would have caused my schooling in Sonthofen to be a prolonged one.

I packed my belongings, played her piano for the last time, kissed her goodbye, and returned to Mother and Gila in Berlin. Dad had assumed his duties in Mecklenburg.

Sonthofen, near the Swiss border, was about as remote a point in our shrinking country as one could find; remote, that is, from Berlin and the dreaded Eastern Host approaching it.

EERIE DEPARTURE

The train left at night. All trains left at night in those days and stopped traveling with daybreak as enemy planes had free reign in the German skies. Mother and Gila took me to the Anhalter Railway Station. It was a dark and hostile night as the three of us traveled by streetcar through the rubble-lined streets.

The future was uncertain. No decision had been made as yet whether they would remain in Berlin or leave for Blexen. Blexen was a village behind the North Sea dike, at the estuary of the Weser River. Uncle Karl, Mother's youngest brother, was living there together with Aunt Änne and their eight children. He was employed as administrator of a three hundred acre farm and was the only member of our clan who lived in the West. The Köpkes were going to stay put; the Lohmanns were thinking of leaving for Thuringia.

I had bidden goodbye to Mr. Lohmann just a couple of days before. He was halfway up the stairway when from behind his back I said a courteous, "Hello, sir". He had turned around and looked at me somberly. He wore a captain's uniform and was due to leave for the battlefront east of Berlin. His features softened, and, forgetting his seniority, he returned down the steps toward me, where I had rung our doorbell. I had never known him so mellow, that tall regal man. "Well, Peter," he had said hesitatingly, "I suppose it's time to say goodbye. Who knows where and when we'll meet again some day." Our handshake was firm but his voice was choked almost into a whisper as he said, "Good luck to you, Peter."

We purchased my ticket. It listed the cities Leipzig, Plauen, Regensburg, Munich, Kempten, and Sonthofen. Then, in my scanty memory, I see the two women standing arm-in-arm on the station platform and four anxious eyes looking at me in the darkness. Mother advised me that she had packed the sandwiches and apples on top in the suitcase, so I would have no difficulties getting them out in the overcrowded trains. And there was something she mentioned about Blexen being the center of communications for all of us, should something happen, or if we lost track of each other.

Munich Ablaze

It was the second night when we reached Munich. The train could not enter the city. We changed trains in a suburb. As I rushed along with the crowd, switching my suitcase from arm to arm, I could see the blaze. Instead of rising straight up into the sky, the flames were leaning sideways, blown by a strong wind. Perhaps it was what everyone was talking about now, a firestorm. It was known as a mass killer.

I was lucky to find a seat. Being overtired I had difficulties keeping my head upright. I must have aroused maternal feelings in the friendly young woman sitting on my right. In her pleasant Bavarian accent she said,

"Why don't you rest your head against my shoulder? It's alright." She had addressed me with "Du," the way one speaks to children. I did and promptly fell asleep.

Scenic Travel

Up in the mountains it was still wintry, but the Iller Valley around

Sonthofen was a magnificent sight, with the majestic snow-white Alpine peaks rising to the south of us. We were quartered in the Ordensburg, a complex of impressive buildings leaning against the mountainside, the way I remember. It was done in what was then considered modern architecture, and the huge dining hall had a wall-to wall mural depicting workers, farmers, and other good citizens engaged in some sort of patriotic pursuit. We were now wearing what must have been the cadets' regular, semi-military uniforms and were very proud of it.

We did not stay long. After a few days, we boarded a train again and traveled west to the Rhine Valley. Our journey terminated in a village on the western slopes of the Black Forest called Obersasbach. There, a nuns' cloister had been converted into another Adolf-Hitler-School, which we now joined.

Why Learn English?

Classes in the mornings followed a regular high school curriculum. The teachers wore uniforms, most of them being Army officers, but one or two wore the brown uniform of the Party. The teacher in charge of our class was an Army lieutenant who lived there with his wife and small son. He was very paternal with us.

We were treated to a surprisingly tame dose of indoctrination. Why should we learn English, the language of our enemies? Well, because it was a world language, "but of course, this will change when German takes the place of English in the world," so we were informed in March of 1945.

In Geography, we were shown on the map what vast ancient Slavic territories in Eastern Europe were destined to become German in the future. Such notions were not entirely new to me. I had heard insinuations of that nature previously, but this was indeed the first time that I heard them spelled out so candidly. Then again, that kind of thinking must have been wide-spread in those days since, *vice versa*, at about the same time, the Allies were agreeing on what vast ancient territories the Germans would have to turn over to the Poles and Russians in the east. Then, after such imperialistic wisdom had been duly dispensed, we reverted to such prosaic routines as memorizing the irregular verbs, practicing the English "R," and mastering those other down-to-earth scholastic tasks exactly the way we had done in our previous schools.

I Lost a Debate

There were six of us in our bedroom. I was sitting on my cot and was rummaging through my suitcase. Someone had a radio, and the evening news was on. The announcer stated that the Allies had succeeded in establishing a bridgehead across the Rhine at Remagen.

Now this was hard to believe. We had been given to understand that victorious counter-offensives were just around the corner, in the east as well as in the west, and that the Rhine was a natural line of defense, which would buy us the time to mount them. The Rhine was the turning point, our victory chances hinged on the enemy's failure to cross it.

"Gosh," I said to no one in particular, "how are we going to still win, if they are across the Rhine? That wasn't supposed to happen."

I was harshly jarred out of my somber contemplation by a cutting voice, "Why do you want to become an officer, if you don't believe in ultimate victory?"

I looked up feeling painfully attacked. Nobody else said anything and so I assumed everyone shared his view. My defense was based on pure common sense, but as no one came to my support, it did not seem to cut any ice against the reminder that the

Führer knew best. I did not understand that then, but this is the answer one receives when living in a cult.

Suddenly I felt terribly lonesome in a hostile environment. Despondent and depressed, I turned to my suitcase again, and there I came upon an item that, at this painful moment, seemed to symbolize all the warmth and security of the home I had left behind. I held them in my hand, the brown, colorfully speckled bedroom slippers, and as I stared at them I could have cried. Never before had I tasted the bitterness of homesickness.

MORAL SUPPORT

One could recognize among our crew the accents of just about every tribe belonging to the people of the Greater German Reich. Fritz was from my neck of the woods, from a suburb of Potsdam named Bornstedt, to be exact. But while that helped, it was not the main reason for our affinity. We were both basically gentle and softhearted, yet idealistic youngsters, and so, each in need for someone to scratch his fur, we took to each other because we matched. He had a patch of lashes missing from the center of his right upper eyelid and was a trifle taller than I, even though he was only fifteen and a half years old.

RECKLESS WARRIORS

As befits a group of young warriors, we were firmly committed to display all the reckless courage and heroism that our fatherland might have need for. At the same time, I am afraid, if the enemy had had the opportunity of observing us, it would have felt more touched than intimidated.

Not far from us was an ammunition dump, which was poorly guarded. We freely roamed it in search of suitable missiles.

Depending on the specific need, we would choose from a variety of different calibers. We separated the cartridges from the bullets and emptied them. The ones used for the twenty-millimeter anti-aircraft guns were particularly useful because of their size.

On our way home from our afternoon military exercises in the fields and woods, we would collect twigs of budding greenery or even a few of the first small flowers bashfully hiding in the forests and bring them home.

In our study room, where each had his own table, there was not a single one that was not sentimentally decorated with these first signs of spring. A survey of the tables would have left no question that the anti-aircraft cartridges made the best vases.

ENEMY CATHEDRAL

I was fortunate to have been assigned the best desk of all. It was located in a small corner alcove under a window, from where I could watch the sun set in the evening behind the Vosges Mountains in Alsace. My anti-aircraft vase was mounted on the wall, across from me, at eye level. This little alcove was my niche of individuality, my "home". Our last family picture was standing there, as well as that of Dieter.

I stood up and looked out. The Allied fighter-bombers were at it again. We called them *Jagdbomber* or *Jabos*. They were attacking a train that had been standing on the tracks since morning, about five kilometers away from us. They were coming down at it, guns blazing; then they would swoop up in the air, turn around, and go after the hapless train again. Finally, the locomotive exploded and sent up a black cloud. The *Jabos* flew away.

In the distance, where I suspected the Rhine to flow, a shroud of haze was hanging low over the land. Out of the haze, there rose the spires of the Strasbourg cathedral. Strasbourg was in Allied hands.

THE TREK[71] ORDER CAME LATE

While we were spending these weeks in relative peace and safety, a heart-rending tragedy was in full progress in the East. The frightful mass exodus of the East German population, first triggered by the massacre at Nemmersdorf, was running its course throughout the winter and into spring with undiminished violence. Millions of people, only imperfectly shielded by the retreating German forces, were driven westward, before the frenzied vengeance of the Red Army.

A letter that we received, two years later, relates a small sampling of the events. In order to understand it, one must know of the end-of-the-world despair and the naked terror in the hearts of the population as the raping, torturing, killing, and pillaging Eastern Host was invading their homelands.

The events transpired in West Prussia, and the writer appears to have had a civil defense responsibility in organizing the evacuation of the civilian population.

Wirnhausen, April 12 (1947)
Dear Sir,

Many thanks for your lines dated April 6. I regret that I can give you only sad news with regard to the Rasmus family. Johannes and Margarete R. took their own lives in Rosgars two years ago, presumably on March 11. (Their) cousin in Bromberg and his wife were shot to death by the Russians. On March 8, the trek order was issued. Even though I thereupon made all the necessary arrangements, the Rosgarsers found it hard to convince themselves to leave their homeland. When at last they did leave it was already too late. No farther than eight kilometers from Rosgars, the Russians caught up with them. The Rasmus couple thereupon returned to Rosgars and at four o'clock in the morning ended their lives with a bullet. Concerning Günther's whereabouts I, too, have no idea. I have made inquiries about him but without any success. I would be much obliged to you, dear sir, if after receipt of positive information you would share it with me. Sawatzkis took refuge in our park (but) were discovered there by the Russians. Mr. S. fired a shot at his wife, which struck her in her belly. The poor woman lived another three days suffering terrible pain. The Russians surrounded her and, with the poor woman pleading for water, allowed her to receive no help. Little Uwe is also dead. I, myself, escaped from the Russians only by a narrow margin. On the ninth of March I left Jannewitz. On the tenth the Russians already took possession of our house. The trek order had, of course, been issued much too late and wouldn't have come at all if not by the chance that a commanding general had shown up (at our estate). This gentleman was surprised to find us still at Jannewitz. I held the (Rasmus) son Günther in particularly high esteem, he was a good man in every respect. I assume you know that his brother was killed in action at Stalingrad.

... Devotedly yours, Count Osten

A note attached to this letter indicates that Capt. Hans-Günther Rasmus was last heard from on March 11, 1945, at which time he was fighting in the area of the Lower Rhine in Northwest Germany. He vanished leaving behind no trace. Only recently has new evidence emerged that, at long last, might explain his fate.

BAD BLOOD

IT WOULD BE ABSURD TO DESCRIBE that war as a chivalrous one. Yet, during its early phases one could still detect, among those spirited by tradition and untouched by vicious ideologies, remnants of chivalry and of gentlemanly and honorable conduct.

At the commencement of the war, President Roosevelt made an appeal to refrain from bombing attacks upon civilians and, indeed, Britain, France, and Germany all agreed to confine air attacks to military operations.[72]

There was a brief episode of improbable knightliness that took place early in the Polish campaign. Near the seaport of Danzig, there was a small peninsula named *Westerplatte*. For several days, its small Polish garrison held out in stubborn defiance under bombardment by dive-bombers and the eleven-inch guns of an obsolete battle cruiser. At the conclusion of that battle, when the Polish commander at last surrendered, one almost feels as if taken back to the eighteenth century, for he not only was wearing a sword, but, even more surprisingly, the German commander, in a ritual of respect for his opponent's heroism, permitted him to keep that sword.[73]

The circumstances surrounding my brother's captivity in France, in 1940, also provide a telling image of civility and good will. There were the French corpsmen who, crawling on the ground, placed him on a canvas and pulled him off the battlefield. He received medical attention at the field hospital, no different from that rendered to wounded Frenchmen. Being an officer, he was assigned to a private room at the military hospital in Marseille. And, in the old city of Nimes, the medical director permitted ambulatory prisoners-of-war to visit the town and the Roman amphitheater, so long as they gave him their word of honor—that is right, their word of honor—not to try to escape. Once the armistice brought about their release, the prisoners expressed their gratitude, presented bouquets to the nurses, and voiced the hope that their two nations could once again live together in friendship.

At about the same time, a moment of silence transpired in Marshal Foch's private Pullman car, in the forest of Compiègne, the same coach where, in 1918, the defeated Germans had signed the armistice, and in which now the defeated French did the same. It was a silence reflecting a noble sentimentality, one that was considered normal and natural at the time, but of which, five years later, not a trace was left. The armistice documents had been signed by both parties. Then, before they parted, a request was made that they all rise in silence to honor the brave soldiers, of both nations, who had bled and died for their countries. That is indeed what happened in 1940: the victorious and defeated generals stood side by side in order to pay respect to the dead of friend and foe.[74]

Later that year, there came the Battle of Britain, with its host of dogfights between the Messerschmitts and Spitfires. The German airmen reportedly held their opponents in high respect. One British pilot, in particular, had caught their fancy because of his boldness and skill, and the cigarette that unfailingly dangled from his lips. His popularity among the Germans, in a spirit of good sportsmanship, had reached the point of a conspiracy among them, which, had he been downed over German-held territory, would have them secure him secretly so as to spare him the indignity of being a prisoner-of-war.[75]

In the eastern campaign, of course, Hitler had spoken against chivalry and against observing the Geneva Convention from the start. It was indeed an unforgiving war that allowed no room for sportsmanship. In that setting, my brother Dieter's wistful image of fighting in Africa, and perhaps of meeting an Englishman there with whom to exchange addresses, was only a fading hope for a residue of humaneness.

But now, several more years of escalating violence, mounting mutual vilifications, and Nazism's deranged frenzy had put an end to all such moderation. In 1945, at the end of a nearly six-year war, man's spirit was poisoned and permeated with bad blood and bitterness.

* * *

When the German armies surrendered in May of 1945, the western Allies gathered a total of nine million Germans in prison camps.[76] It was obvious beforehand that their number and sudden accumulation would make it impossible for the Allies to live up to the requirements of the Geneva Convention in providing them with food and shelter at the level enjoyed by their own troops. Gen. Eisenhower, therefore, created a new category of captives designated as Disarmed Enemy Forces or DEF, into which he could, at will and with the stroke of a pen, transfer the prisoners-of-war. This terminology and bureaucratic assignment could then be interpreted as a removal from the obligations of the Geneva Convention. In addition, no public declaration of this change of status was allowed to be made, and the International Committee of the Red Cross (ICRC), which was supposed to visit the camps and report its observations to the German government, was prevented from doing so, ostensibly because the German government had been eliminated, and the ICRC had no government to whom to report.

Back in March of 1945, Gen. Eisenhower had planned to place the responsibility of feeding the POWs on the German authorities, but the dismantling of every civilian or military authority that had existed, including, in the American Zone of Occupation, even the German Red Cross, negated that concept.[77] Consequently, there was no one left on the scene to provide for these millions of incarcerated people other than the Allied armies.

If that task went beyond the bounds of possibility, the simplest solution would, of course, have been their rapid discharge to their homes. That is, in fact, what the British and Canadians did. Of their two million prisoners, there were only 68,000 left in captivity by the next spring.[78] But there existed reasons opposed to that policy. For one thing, the Allies had agreed to consign POWs to forced labor contingents for the reconstruction of war damage in previously German-occupied countries. France, the chief western beneficiary, had requested 1.75 million men, although that number was later reduced to only 860,000.[79] Thus, prisoners could not be discharged in substantial numbers until this work requirement had been satisfied.

There was also a fear of possible guerrilla warfare to develop after the official surrender. The possibility that German men, thought to be fanatical, belligerent, and indomitable, would join underground werewolf forces to continue the fight could not be excluded.

Beyond that, Germany's enemies were quaking with anger. There were voices shouting, "Treat them rough!" The victorious world wanted to give them back some of what was thought to be their own medicine. There was little patience with people, who were seen to mollycoddle the Germans. There was a yearning for revenge. The prevailing mood was ugly.

The prisoners were channeled into camps called "prisoner-of-war temporary enclosures" (PWTE), or, more simply, "cages," which were open-fields enclosed by barbed wire, watchtowers, and floodlights. Each contained tens of thousands of people and provided "no shelter or other comforts," as Gen. Eisenhower reported to Army Chief of Staff Gen. George C. Marshall.[80] That is to say, with few exceptions there were no tents or other protection from the elements, no water for drinking or washing, no facilities for cooking, no health care, and no sanitation. Earth holes, which the POWs dug by hand, were used for shelter against the wind, unless they filled with rain or caved in under the weight of rain-soaked mud. Earth holes also served as latrines. Food was issued in insufficient amounts on some days and not at all on others. Most dreadful and perilous was the withholding of water. Thirst was a harrowing torment. Dysentery and typhus developed quickly, and the lack of water was then rapidly fatal.

Over sixteen hundred camps were spread all over France and two hundred in Germany, many of them along the Rhine River. They measured miles in circumference, and some contained 100,000 captives. Particularly notorious were the enclosures of Rheinberg on the banks of the lower Rhine near the Dutch border, Sinzig near Bonn, Dietersheim near Bingen, and those in Bad Kreuznach. Some of those in France were basically death camps. The dead were piled on trucks and driven away. According to one report from Germany, the dead were stripped, exposed to quick-lime, and stacked a meter high for disposal.[81] An article published in an American medical journal contains the following description:

> Huddled close together for warmth, behind the barbed wire was a most awesome sight—nearly 100,000 haggard, apathetic, dirty, gaunt, blank-staring men ... standing ankle-deep in mud. Here and there were dirty white blurs

which, upon a closer look were seen to be men with band-aged heads or arms or standing in shirtsleeves! The German Division Commander reported that the men had not eaten for at least two days, and the provision of water was a major problem—yet only 200 yards away was the river Rhine running bank-full.[82]

A camp survivor observed that, among hundreds of thousands of German POWs, there were sick ones taken from hospitals, amputees, women auxiliaries, and civilians, one of them over eighty years old and another one, nine years.

... Nagging hunger and agonizing thirst were their companions, and they died of dysentery. A cruel heaven pelted them week after week with streams of rain... amputees slithered like amphibians through the mud, soaking and freezing. Naked to the skies...they lay desperate in the sand of Rheinberg or slept exhaustedly into eternity in their collapsing holes.[83]

There were, as mentioned, no visits by the ICRC or by members of the news media. Of this tragedy, the world knew nothing. Mail service was absent. Families were left in the dark about their men's fate or whereabouts, nor could they send food packages.

POW camps in France, on the other hand, had indeed a particularly infamous reputation. Here, too, the prisoners starved and were described by rare visitors as living skeletons, identical in appearance with those in the concentration camps of Buchenwald and Dachau.[84] Hundreds of thousands of them, however, were transferred to the French from the American Forces, and part of the French problem arose out of the condition that the prisoners were in when transferred. The French reports render a telling impression of the dimensions the catastrophe had reached in July of 1945. In the five camps they took over at Dietersheim, totaling 103,500 inmates, they found 32,640 old men, women, boys aged eight to fourteen, and even children below the age of eight, as well as people terminally sick and crippled.[85] Among all the camps, which the French took custody of in Germany in the summer of 1945, they inherited 166,000 men, women, and children who were "in the most lamentable condition".[86] In Marseille, they judged two hundred eighty-seven of one thousand men incapable of work. In another camp, there were only eighty-five people able to work, out of a total of seven hundred. In a camp near Koblenz, they received four hundred children under the age of fifteen, some less than eight years old. In yet another camp, this one in Belgium, the Americans transferred prisoners, twenty-five percent of which the French, in their search for people they could put to work, described as "garbage".[87]

The Rheinberg cages were taken over by the British in mid-June of 1945. A survivor described the difference between British and American control as "day and night."[88]

The monumental chaos prevailing in that time makes available statistics unreliable. The total death toll can, therefore, only be estimated. Using a number of assumptions to cover periods without available data, J. Bacque has concluded that somewhere around 800,000 prisoners died while under American custody. The death figure in French camps, a number even less certain, he believes to be between 167,000 and 409,000.

These numbers have been violently rejected by indignant critics composed of both American and German historians.[88] They feel, rather, that the number of German prisoners dying in American captivity in 1945 did not exceed 56,000. While they may be closer to the truth, much of their account, based on a massive volume of data and research, corroborates Bacque's descriptions, if not his figures. They speak of a punitive and vindictive mindset on the part of the victors, enraged, as they were, by the horrifying sights in the concentrations camps. They speak of the desire for revenge and of letting the Germans stew in their own juice. They, too, state that no one went out his way to make sure food got to the overflowing prisoner cages in May of 1945. They confirm that disarmed German soldiers "hardly ate at all" during the first days of their captivity and very little during the first weeks in May and June. And they concede the presence of unbearable conditions on a massive scale in a few of the large and grossly overpopulated holding camps on the Rhine River.

In subsequent decades, on the large grounds of the previous prison enclosure at Rheinberg, construction workers and gravediggers have come upon human remains with German Army dog tags lying in close proximity in common gravesites.[89] Quite possibly, those of Capt. Hans-Günther Rasmus were among them.

Not Perfect Yet

THE WEEKS WENT BY. OUR SCHEDULE CALLED FOR SCHOOL in the mornings, military training in the afternoons. It did not satisfy the criteria of a crash course; I don't think we even reached the point of taking apart and cleaning a rifle. We were, I think, shown a *Panzerfaust* once, but did not fire it.

We learned new songs, however, solemn ones and happy, go-getter types of songs, nothing particularly political. We sang one, standing up behind our chairs, before and after each meal, instead of saying grace, I suppose. There was one that was painful for me to sing. It was more of a hymn and dealt with commemorating fallen heroes. It opened the wound that Dieter's loss had left in me, and I still remember how one of the boys nudged his neighbor and pointed toward me, as we were standing there singing with fervor. My eyes were flooded; I was so embarrassed.

I had soon found the piano in the small music room of the nuns. During off-hours, I often stole away and played all the pieces I knew by heart. Once or twice, we received mail from home.

Then one day in April, we packed up and left. It was reported that French troops were approaching from the north, and, as we were not combat ready yet, we were to retreat to the town of Triberg, in the Black Forest, to perfect our military skills.

There were no more trains. We were to march at night and sleep in the daytime. Fritz and I marched together.

Nocturnal March

The night air was crisp and filled with the sappy fragrance of pine trees. The rhythmic clatter of a hundred boots hitting the asphalt reverberated from the silent, dark wall of trees on both sides of the road.

Now I knew why it was called the Black Forest. The trees were pitch black, the way their tops silhouetted against the night's sky. Rat, rat, rat, rat...left, right, left, right, on and on we marched through the sleeping night. Nobody said much, we were tired, and the monotonous rhythm of our boots had a soporific effect. I threw my head back and looked straight up. A narrow band of starry sky pointed the way. It was as though we were standing still, and the Milky Way was standing still, while the two opposing skylines of black tree tops slowly moved to the back of us. Rat, rat, rat, rat...the forest kept moving past us. It was like marching in a dream.

After the first night, Fritz and I no longer had to march but were riding on bicycles instead; the others were still marching. Fritz, I found out, was more quick-witted than the rest of us. He had recognized a need for an advance party to find and prepare quarters, such as barns, where the weary troops could retire at daybreak and must have been successful in convincing the lieutenant that we were the ones most suited for so responsible a task. It must have been the lieutenant who confiscated the two bicycles from a farmer.

CAT AND MOUSE

Standing at the Triberg railway station, one could see the railroad tracks cross the road and then head straight for the sheer, almost vertical mountainside, there to disappear in the darkness of a tunnel.

Triberg. Mother had a picture of Triberg in her album. It showed the parents and Friedrich and Dieter when they were little boys. Mother looked very young, too, with long brunette hair wound around her pretty face. Dad was leaning against a huge rock and held a walking stick in his hand. He always used one when hiking. With a crew cut and mustache, he looked so different on that picture.

Now I was in Triberg myself. It was a small, picturesque resort town, tucked away in what I remember as a narrow valley. Over the southern end of that valley, a fighter-bomber appeared. It took a gentle swing, dipped its nose, and, as though sliding down the mountainside, headed straight for the town. He was not firing yet, though, and I was wondering when he might and what he was after. As the plane approached the bottom of the valley, it began to level off. I was standing near the station on the main road, and, to this day, I remember the moment when the bloody fool was pointing his plane right at me. Then he rose up again, disappearing in the northern skies, without ever having fired a shot.

Fighter-bombers were crazy about trains, but he could not have seen this one. I saw the front of the locomotive just inside the tunnel entrance.

WRONG CHURCH

We didn't stay long in Triberg, perhaps two days. We didn't stay long anywhere these days. The enemy was hard on our heels.

Somehow we became separated from our unit—I do not recall the circumstances—and suddenly found ourselves in the unlikely position where, in spite of our bicycles, we were unable for days to catch up with our marching comrades. Perhaps they had caught a train somewhere after all.

In the town of Überlingen, on Lake Constance, we decided to inquire at the local headquarters. A violent battle was raging just on the other side of the hills, to judge from the sound of machine gun and artillery fire. Soldiers in the town said that the SS troops were delivering one hell of a good fight.

We stepped inside the office and were immediately taken aback. They weren't Army, the two noncoms behind the counter; they were SS soldiers. It was too late now to turn around, and so we smartly saluted and asked about the position of our unit. They had no idea. Instead, they looked at each other, and one of them mumbled something that sounded like, "We could use them".

"Stay here," he ordered us, and they went into the next room, presumably to talk to their superior. As soon as we were left alone, Fritz and I looked at each other and we whispered,

"Let's get out of here!"

I remember looking back as we raced away on our bikes and said,

"It didn't say SS anywhere on the outside!"

Swiss Mirage

We bicycled around the northwestern bay of the lake, and late in the day we reached the town of Constance. We found no trace of our friends there either. After nightfall we returned to the northern shore by crossing the lake on the auto ferry.

Except for the drone of the engine and the rush of the waves, the night was silent. The lake was smooth and calm. We looked back, to the south. There we saw what impressed both of us as an incredible sight, something we had not seen in nearly six years.

A peaceful string of lights of Swiss villages and towns outlined the southern shore. Electric lights, illuminating streets and promenades! We could see how peace reigned over there; they were sitting at home with their families, reading books, playing cards with friends, or returning home from the cinema. It was like a fairy tale, as though we were staring at a different, unreal world.

We were downright upset, both of us, as if this was an inappropriate mirage. Yes, it was unreal and almost unnatural, the way this fabulous vision collided with our frame of mind. How could it be that here a nation was fighting desperately for its very life, we said, and there, separated from us by no more than a few miles of water, people lived in peace and tranquility, as though this epic struggle was no concern of theirs.

My brother was trapped in Courland; Dad was on a farm in Mecklenburg; Mother and Gila were hiding in a Berlin air raid shelter, if they had not left the city and were traveling God knew where; Dieter was a nameless corpse in a Russian swamp or, perhaps, was languishing in some Communist prison camp; Fritz and I were using the shelter of night to cross the lake and to catch up with our unit, not to miss the honor of battle—and the Swiss had their lights on. Peaceful clusters and strings of lights, each producing a vertical reflection on the calm surface of the lake...

THE TEMPTATION

Our bikes were lying on the grass, together with our rifles and knapsacks. We could hear the distant rumble of heavy guns in the north, coming from the area of Kempten. We were resting behind a shallow ridge, twenty meters or so off the road, and had feasted on cold canned lard with generous chunks of greasy pork in it, and, for desert, chocolate, no less. "Schoka-kola" it read on the wrapping.

These provisions had come into our hands the day before, when we joined local folks in cleaning out a stalled flak-train. Because the tracks had been destroyed by the *Jabos*, the train could not move in either direction, but the crew was still manning their guns.

"Help yourselves," they had told the people. Their stores were sufficient to last for weeks, and they did not believe to have need for them that long. As Fritz and I were filling our knapsacks, they had suddenly interrupted us shouting,

"You'd better move away quickly!"

They were getting ready to fire at a new flock of *Jabos* zeroing in on the train. The enemy must not have recognized, from way up in the sky, that they were attacking not just an ordinary train, but a hornet's nest.

So, today, we were lying on our bellies, well fed and happy, and were looking down upon the road from which we were hidden. It was time to move on. The sound of artillery fire continued in the north. Then Fritz voiced the same idea that had just passed through my own mind.

"What do you say, we wait here for them? It may be the last chance we get to knock off a tank! We've got a perfect shot from here, too, they can't see us from the road."

There was a discussion. "When do we have another chance like this to get a tank?" We were so eager. He was right. We would have had a perfect shot at them if we had only had *Panzerfäuste*. In Triberg, I had seen a teenage kid with two tank plaques on his sleeve. Considering the foolishness of it all, our wistful conference lasted unusually long. In the end, the inadequacy of rifles, in a confrontation with a tank, proved too worrisome, and we abandoned the idea. We sadly looked down at the road but then laughed and said, "Time to move on."

Cornered

We did not catch up with our friends until we reached Altstädten, a village a few kilometers up the Iller Valley from Sonthofen. Finally, we were now issued *Panzerfäuste*.

French troops were reportedly advancing south into the valley from Kempten. In order not to become trapped, the lieutenant had us take to the road again, a back road this time, which left the Iller Valley near Immenstadt, turning east through the northern foothills of the Alps. But it was of no avail; there, our escape route was blocked by the advancing Americans.

It was the last days of April, and, in this altitude, snow was still covering the ground.

Retreat

After nightfall, we emerged from a farmhouse and advanced single file along the roadside, down into a small valley, across a short bridge, then another five hundred meters, until we reached the hamlet of Wertach. We huddled into the first house.

To be more exact, we conquered it. I must have been farther back in the column and did not witness it, but I understand that our unit took two American prisoners. One was sleeping in the bedroom, and the other one we surprised on the toilet. We also confiscated their jeep. Word later got around, however, that the boy who was to march them back soon lost them in the darkness. The two suddenly jumped into the woods, we were told, one on each side of the road, and then vanished.

It was good to warm up. Guards were placed outside. When our turn came, I found the night to be awfully cold, awfully dark, and even though Fritz was with me, awfully lonesome. Suddenly, the uncanny silence was broken by the menacing roar of a moving tank, somewhere in the center of the village. It lasted only a moment. The lion had grumbled as he turned over in his sleep.

I knew that I was to be brave and live up to the example of my brothers, but, I had to admit, the sensation I had just experienced was of no help. It had torn clear through my guts and bones, and my heart kept racing, as I stared in spineless fear in the direction of the roar. I was about as remote as one could get from earning the Iron Cross.

The lieutenant came outside and ran back up the road, "in order to get reinforcements". Soon after, the sergeant took it upon himself to have us follow the lieutenant and to rejoin the bulk of our unit in the previous village.

Single file and off the road, under the snow-laden trees, we marched back to where we had come from. After a couple of hundred meters, before we reached the small bridge, four volunteers were positioned on the south side of the road to cover the retreat. Fritz and I were among them. We were to fire our *Panzerfäuste* at the tanks, so we were instructed, and then escape through the woods and over the mountains to Altstädten. The sound of our exploding rockets would warn our unit up the road.

About an hour later, a boy's voice summoned us from the other side of the bridge across the creek. Up on the hilltop, they had found a better place for us, and that's where we took up position. There were six of us now, three pairs brandishing a total of three *Panzerfäuste* and three rifles. About twenty meters off the road, we lay down in the snow, under the tall trees, and waited for the tanks. One stayed awake, the other five were soon sound asleep.

INTELLIGENCE REPORT

We waited all next day for the American tanks but they stayed in Wertach. The second night we spent in a mountain barn, a large wooden shed, not far from our roadside position. There we crawled under the hay and found it acceptably warm. We took turns standing watch by the road every two hours.

In the morning we were surprised to see a man come trudging up the road from the Wertach Valley, pulling behind him, not a tank but a cart loaded with shoes, if I am not mistaken. We rushed down to the road and interviewed him.

Yes, indeed, the Americans had let him pass without difficulties. Then he said something about white bread; snow-white bread, he claimed, that's what the Americans were eating. We all laughed and joked about making a deal with the enemy. Wow, snow white bread!

The Mission Was Simple Enough

A day later, Fritz and I were lying in a small riverbed up near the rim. From behind the small trees and shrubs, we had a good view of the road nearby. Beneath our feet, the clear mountain water was rushing past over rocks and gravel. Our *Panzerfaust* was mounted in perfect position to cover the road. The road emerged from behind a mountain ridge, which jutted out into the flat Iller Valley. From the other side of that promontory came the din of fierce artillery fire, perhaps one or two kilometers away.

Our instructions were simple enough: once the tanks come, get them with the *Panzerfaust*, and then run up the deep, tortuous river bed and into the woods. By now, we had been lying here for hours waiting in vain.

The war was clearly coming to an end, an end of sorts, anyway. Yesterday the villagers had told us that Hitler was dead, killed in his Berlin bunker, perhaps by suicide. But that did not seem to make that much difference, for the war was about getting the Russians off our back, no matter whether Hitler was alive or dead.

We knew the war was going to go on; only, that, at long last, there would be a different alignment. "Wait, what happens when the Americans and the British meet face to face with the Red Army!" The way we thought, in the predictable cataclysm that was sure to follow, there was no question on which side we would join the battle.

We were bored. Fritz got up and stretched. The big guns were still blazing from the north side of the promontory.

"I'll go and see what the other guys are doing," he said. Our platoon had been strung out along the meandering creek, with *Panzerfaust* positions about every fifty to eighty meters.

"They're gone!" he shouted back from the next bend, and then he proceeded on to check further. Not only had they all left, but they had also left their *Panzerfäuste* behind. They were heavy to carry. Townspeople told Fritz an order had gone out to assemble at the place in the woods, where we had left our baggage.

So we moved up the creek. It was not a very proud sight, all the abandoned weapons lying about. I picked up a rifle to replace my *Panzerfaust*. Fritz still carried the light American rifle, which he had been issued back at the hospitable cloister in the Black Forest. Our two knapsacks were the only two pieces left on the mossy ground under the tall fir trees.

JUST FOLLOWING THE DRUMMER

We set out for Altstädten, a village located about eight kilometers up the valley. We passed under the Ordensburg in Sonthofen that, up a ways on the mountainside, reflected the late afternoon sun. Up there the nation's elite was to be educated in the National-Socialist spirit. Yes, by now it seemed as if we had been there ages ago. We marched on, side by side.

I do not recall any particular emotions that evening. We could have felt relieved at not having to fight anymore, or disappointed for the same reason; we could have been depressed at the sight of the unfolding defeat of our country or hopeful of yet giving it another try, but I doubt there were any such sentiments. Not even homesickness was there nor worry about what might have happened to brother Friedrich in the meantime up in Courland, fifteen hundred kilometers away, or to Dad, Mother, or Gila in Berlin. There was no sense of fear or insecurity; there had not been, basically, all these weeks since I had left Berlin on that dark and eerie night.

I suppose it has to do with the feeling of belonging. I belonged to our group. We all belonged together; we were comrades; we were "home" for one another; we had the same thoughts, the same ideals, the same emotions; we sang the same songs; and we were glued together by a strong sense of duty, loyalty, and discipline. We were now returning to Altstädten, not wondering whether this was a proud or disgraceful road to walk; not wondering about right or wrong, hope or despair; walking neither bravely nor fearfully, but, much more simply, because that's where the others had gone, and, therefore, that's where we belonged too. Our unperturbed emotional stability rested on the fact that we were so firmly anchored in our group.

We needed it too, though, this inner stability, for fate was waiting for us, in the incarnation of Bavarian villagers, to terminate our promising military career and to deal an ignominious and utterly humiliating deathblow to all our dreams of bravery, heroism, tank plaques, and iron crosses.

Transition at Dusk

Dusk was settling over the wide Alpine valley as we reached the northern entrance of Altstädten. We approached a group of men standing by the roadside to inquire whether our unit was in the village. They said "yes" and reached for our rifles.

There was a moment of protest and minor struggle, but then they quickly prevailed with a combination of superior strength and fatherly persuasiveness. Yes, so they confirmed, all of our comrades were in the village, and they had all turned over their rifles. There was no point in our trying to be different. I should add, they also prevailed because of their seniority. The way we had been raised, we had too much respect for our elders to put up a serious fight; it would have been unseemly and disrespectful, and it just wasn't done. They directed us to the schoolhouse to find our friends.

Thus, for Fritz and me, the transition from war to peace, from one era in history to the next, was consummated within approximately forty-five seconds.

Discharge

The schoolhouse was the site of a great deal of activity. Our suitcases that had been transported here from the Black Forest had disappeared. So we were left with our knapsacks and what we wore. Some of us traded their uniforms for civilian clothes; others had them dyed by the helpful townspeople. Fritz and I, we kept ours the way they were.

A slightly graying gentleman was sitting at the typewriter. Perhaps he was the mayor of the village or the teacher, I don't know. He was the fatherly, yet resolute and organizing type, the way gym teachers and scout leaders are. He had assumed the responsibility of taking care of us boys.

He was typing up my discharge paper. Fritz showed me his. It read:

CERTIFICATE OF DISCHARGE

This is to certify that Friedrich König was duly discharged from the Farming Service on May 1, 1945.

Altstädten, May 1, 1945
Signature
Seal

Well, now. Farming Service, that designated harvesting time in autumn, while a few nights before we had still slept in the snow. But he said that would be all right. Our mothers were waiting, and there was no need for us to become prisoners-of-war. I folded mine and tucked it into my breast pocket.

The next morning we left. Everybody shook hands and said goodbye. Off to new adventures, we were in high spirits. It was a long way back for most of us. Back to Mother, yes perhaps, but we weren't too certain of that. The war had a long way to go. There was no question in anybody's mind that the German Army was going to join the Western Allies in the fight against the Red Army.

There were handshakes and laughter. "Good luck!"

"Right, good luck to you too!"

"See you all, guys," shouted that swashbuckling fellow from Berlin, "see you all on the Eastern Front!"

PART 8

THE GODS KEPT SLEEPING

PRISONER-OF-WAR

EVEN THOUGH WE TOOK THE BACK ROADS, we saw enemy troops everywhere. Across a field, we saw our first Allied vehicles—a truck and a funny looking squared-off four-seater. We ducked.

Soon enough, however, we found ourselves taken prisoner by the French, together with quite a motley group of farmers and others trying to look like ones, all rounded up in the fields. The troops were Algerian. We were standing at the back end of an armored personnel carrier as they frisked us. Our watches disappeared in their pockets. Fritz wore a brand-new *Luftwaffe* windbreaker that wound up on their pile, too. They found a rifle bullet in my pocket. Then, they came upon a length of cord and said, "*parachute.*"

That was all we needed.

"*Non, non,*" I said in my best French, "*nix parachute!*" and stooped down to show that it was part of the windbreaker. As I came up, I struck the back of my head hard against the steel corner of the armored vehicle. The soldier, who a moment ago had coldly confiscated my watch, the precious watch Father had worn for so long and had given to me for Christmas, the same soldier now winced painfully and smiled at me in genuine commiseration.

The first night they had us sleep in a barn, the next day we were transferred to a paper mill. There were only concrete walls and huge rolls of brown paper. We were hungry. Fritz got up from the concrete floor saying that he was going to look for something to eat.

I asked, "Here? Where are you going to find food in this place?"

After an hour or two, he returned holding something wrapped in paper. It was *Kunsthonig*, a sweet semi-solid substance called artificial honey. After that, everything we had, our pockets and the insides of our knapsacks became a little sticky. But it tasted great and was nutritious.

The next morning, we were lined up in the factory courtyard. The sun felt good after the cold night. Everyone, fifteen or younger, had to raise his hand. We promptly did, I certainly could have passed for fourteen.

The French soldier waved toward the gate and, with a grin, said in broken German, *"Ab! Zu Hause!*—Off! At home!"

TALL HOSTS

In Kempten, Fritz had an aunt. She took us in. I am not certain what we were roaming around the town for, but I suppose it was in search of food. Having lost our watches, we missed the curfew. There were announcements pasted to walls and bulletin boards, stating that everyone found in the streets after six o'clock would be shot.

We asked an American soldier what to do. His English was

hard to understand, (we soon learned that Americans did not speak King's English) but he directed us to the administrative building of a large factory. The Military Police was quartered there, and maybe they would have a vehicle to drive us home in.

It was dark by the time we knocked at the door. Out stepped two immensely tall soldiers, the first one a threatening sight indeed. With each hand, he pointed a revolver at us, or so at first it seemed. On closer inspection, one revolver was a flashlight of a kind we had never seen before. It was one where the light beam emerged at a right angle to the shaft. He had to hold its battery case upright, much the way one holds a revolver.

I explained our predicament as best I could, addressing the darkness above the flashlight, and mentioned the idea of a vehicle. I was very proud of that word; it was the first new English word in my vocabulary, "vehicle," and it was a prophetic first step on the way into the American age.

They did not have a vehicle; instead, they had us step inside. They checked us out for concealed weapons and expressed puzzlement over the substance wrapped in sticky, dirty paper, which I clutched in my hands. We explained that it was artificial honey. They took our word for it. They put us up for the night, in one of the offices.

CONTACTS

We enjoyed talking to the GIs. It was exciting to meet these people from that distant, legendary land across the ocean, the home of skyscrapers, Indians, Shirley Temple, Joe Louis, and yuts. Even more so, it was fun practicing our English.

By the tall wire fence enclosing the factory grounds, we were chatting with a couple of soldiers. One of them mentioned girls and then said something, which exceeded my English comprehension.

"Look," he said, setting out for a step-by-step explanation, "a grrrl - an'a boy." He held up each hand signifying two opposing entities. "Okay? Now..."

We laughed and, pretending to be old pros, said we understood. Fritz had an idea. We agreed to meet again, "Same time, same place, tomorrow."

His aunt had a young woman living with her, a maid or something. We reported to them about our contacts. She was willing.

Making Friends and Getting Even

About thirty-five kilometers northeast of Kempten, there was the beautiful town of Kaufbeuren. Fritz had an aunt there, too. With her children, she lived in one of the better homes on the hillside. Her husband was chief of the nearby military airport, or he used to be. He wasn't there now.

We roamed around Kaufbeuren, too, and befriended a group of GIs who were billeted into a large farm. They, too, were apparently intrigued meeting the former enemy and asked us up to their second-floor room. In a jovial mood, they tried a U.S. Army helmet out on me, and Fritz was cavorting around in an Army jacket. We admired our new look in the mirror, and, with all the merriment, we must have resembled children at a costume party.

At one point, one of them asked me to give him a shave. It was a strange request, I thought; I had never known anyone so extravagant to have someone else shave him. My real objection, however, was that I felt it to be unbecoming to a German patriot to render such a menial service to a foreign conqueror and was certain of my brother's disapproval. The defeated should show more pride than that. Nonetheless, they were such congenial men, these soldiers, and it would have spoiled the spirit of fraternization to turn them down, and so I obliged. One of the hardest things for me to do was to hurt somebody's feelings. I would rather swallow my pride and, in this case, learn how to use a razor. I had never used one before.

Later, we shook hands with our new friends and said goodbye. On the way back to his aunt, Fritz handed me a wrist-watch. He had one, too. He had found them by simply reaching into the coat pocket of the Army jacket. A whole pile of them was in there, and he had grabbed a couple. Now we were even with the conquerors.

WALKING HOME

After Kaufbeuren, Fritz ran out of aunts. What followed now might be called our own small version of The Long March. Being some-what shorter for him, it lasted until the end of June for me, covering the distance of approximately twelve hundred kilometers, and I estimate that I traveled nine hundred of these on foot.

Much of the memories have since faded, or have blended into a blur, with no precise fixation to calendar or map. There are, of course, brief glimpses and mental images that have remained unforgettable, such as the notice we read on a bulletin board of the surrender of the Wehrmacht. That must have been the day after we left Kaufbeuren.

There is the memory of the newly elected mayor of a small town, whose voice was as harsh as his eyes were soft. Townspeople had told us that he was a social democrat, "but" a very honest and good man.

"Sure," he snarled at us, "sure you can walk around in these uniforms. The Americans will immediately know you were just milking cows. For heavens sakes, why don't you at least remove those swastikas off your belt buckles!"

He had his secretary bring us a file. He also had her type up new papers for us in English. In them, it was stated, "We have shecked his papers and found them in order." Another new word: shecked. She explained that meant, "Examined."

And there was the farmer's wife, who let us into her living room and left us alone with a huge loaf of peasant bread and cheese and milk, so we could eat to our hearts' desire, unobserved. There were women like her everywhere we went. They were all hoping that their own men and sons would receive the same treatment, wherever they were. It was the first women's movement that I have ever seen in action; a tacit agreement, spontaneous, unanimous, and universal, which pledged: let's look after our men and help them get home.

I remember the valley near Eichstädt. The large expanse of mountainside was covered with a rolling, velvety carpet of pasture stained golden-yellow by the late afternoon sun, and on it there was a flock of sheep casting very long shadows. We stopped, Fritz and I, and watched in silence, not to disturb the peaceful panorama. It was like a vision from another world, perhaps resembling one of those eighteenth century pastoral paintings.

Then, of course, there was the American soldier on the *Autobahn*. We were trying to hitch a ride, but the only vehicles were U.S. Army trucks, and they would not stop. He had some business there, too, and so we chatted for a while. He was terribly naive, we thought.

"You ever been to Amerrrca?" he asked us in all seriousness.

"No," we admitted amiably, not quite certain how to take so innocent a soul.

"Think you'll ever go there?"

"Where?"

"Amerrrca."

Now we almost laughed. We had never even been to Luxembourg. Next he might ask us if we had plans to go to the moon or become millionaires. It would have been rude to say no, so we answered with a polite, "Perhaps." We then wished him a good day and went our way. Who had ever been to America?

Bamberg was an unbelievable sight of wholesale devastation. I do not think I saw a single house that had been spared. Endless rows and city blocks of burned out ruins and macabre compilations of rubble. And amongst the destruction, an undamaged banner was left behind, still stretched across a street from facade to facade, fluttering gaily in the wind with the message: *VICTORY OR BOLSHEVIK CHAOS!*

THE WOMEN OF EISENBERG

After we left Bamberg, Fritz and I separated. He had to stop at a place called Bad Elster where he had another aunt, whereas I wanted to check with friends of my father's in the town of Jena. Dad had given me their address as an alternate point of family communication. After these stopovers, Fritz and I had agreed to reunite at the *Autobahn* entrance of Eisenberg in Thuringia.

When I entered Eisenberg, the town was engaged in the dismantling of symbols that had outlived their usefulness, such as the massive, sculptured eagle resting on a swastika, which had adorned the portal of the party building. I stepped into a store and inquired about a youth hostel, I believe. I might as well have asked for the Hilton.

No harm done, however. The women were all over me, and I explained my need of shelter for two or three nights, while waiting for my friend. One of them took me home with her, and I slept in the bed of her son.

"I just hope," she said, "somebody else will do the same for him."

As it turned out, Fritz and I missed each other, and I waited in vain for several days.

One day, the lady upstairs asked us to come up. She wanted to do her share in feeding me. She had a piano. The small living room was quite crowded with the several women and neighbors and even one or two children as they devoutly listened to my impromptu recital. From time to time they requested me not to stop and to play some more.

Despite my suspicion of their preferring popular music, my classical pieces seemed to affect them pleasantly. Perhaps, the carefree sounds of Mozart, the happy waltz of Brahms, and the sentimental tunes of Grieg provided them with a temporary illusion of warmth and non-violence at a time when reality was cold and frightening.

CHECKPOINT

"Ausweis!" said the American officer. We were the lucky passengers of a truck taking us toward the Soviet Zone of Occupation. I was the first one on his right, and he held his hand out for my identification. I had little confidence in the credibility of my papers and stalled by fumbling in my breast pocket. He went on to the others, but my trick did not work. When he had checked them all, he returned to me.

I handed him my English language certificate and looked at him apprehensively. He took it, but then, without inspecting it, gave me a surprised second look. He passed it back to me unread, waved his hand, and, causing laughter among my companions, exclaimed, *"Ach, Kinder!"*

TO FIND HIS WIFE

Near Weissenfels, I walked the last few kilometers to the Saale

River. Crossing into the Eastern Zone was officially forbidden, but it was done every day. In fact, Russian soldiers supervised the river crossing, but it would cost me my watch, I was told.

I had acquired a new companion, a young man in his twenties, obviously a former officer. From him I heard the first reports about the Russians. They were raping just about every woman "between the ages of fourteen and seventy," he told me. He was on his way to find his wife over there.

"She is very pretty," he said. "You can imagine how I feel."

Crossing Over

We were the first ones to arrive at the designated location by the river but had to wait all day for our turn to cross. Gradually, as the morning mist gave in to the sun, others joined us. By mid-morning, there must have been a crowd of a hundred.

In the meantime, across from us a man launched an open kayak and two Red Army soldiers appeared and, wildly gesticulating, shouted across the water in Russian. The only thing I understood was the oft-repeated word "Uri, Uri!" One of us shouted back in Russian waving his wristwatch. He received permission to cross. Just as they were pushing off, someone else threw his duffel bag into the bow of the boat.

The advantage of speaking the lingo quickly caught on as we were all shouting "Uri, Uri!" and waving our watches. Permission to cross was generously granted, and so it was only a matter of waiting one's turn. The man with the duffel bag had to be next; everyone could see that. Somebody threw in his satchel. It was his turn, the next trip. A small child was added this time, and it was obviously the mother's turn after that.

We were reasonable people and readily controlled our impatience, as it would have been unfair to separate mother from child, or a man from his few precious belongings. There were those who were sick, those who were crippled, those who were old, and those unfortunately separated from their suitcases and duffel bags. They pushed and announced their disabilities and predicaments and were quickly granted priority by a crowd that was pushy and fair at the same time. We had neither duffel bags, nor children, nor infirmities, and so it fell upon us to wait.

The sun was far in the west when my friend finally spoke up.

"Now listen, this boy here and I have been here since six o'clock this morning. We were here before anyone else arrived."

Now we became the belated beneficiaries of the unwritten law of fairness. We both scrambled into the boat together. I was light.

The Russian soldier collected my companion's watch but somehow overlooked me, and so I walked away still with mine.

EASTERN CONQUERORS

In the Soviet Zone of Occupation some of the trains were rolling already, so that I traveled the remaining distance to Berlin—some two hundred kilometers—in only two days.

Conversations were rife with stories of the Russians. They had created quite a spectacle on the market square of a small town when they exhibited their first attempts of riding a bicycle by screaming and roaring with laughter and merriment as they fell off, picked themselves up, and tried it again.

A soldier was said to have stared in utter amazement at the lights as they went off and on every time he turned the wall switch. So fascinated was he by the sight of this phenomenon that he kept turning it on and off, on and off.

There was also the story of the husband and wife. A Russian

entered their room and looked at the woman. The husband got up and placed himself in front of her, facing the intruder defiantly. The soldier called his bluff. He gunned him down and raped her.

I harmlessly knocked at the door of a farmhouse, the way I had done a hundred times before. The door, to my surprise, was opened only a slit. The bitter face of a woman listened to me and then I heard the word "wait" before she bolted the door again. When she returned, she passed a sandwich through the barely opened door, and then quickly drew it shut and locked it.

NEW OCCUPANTS

I walked across the cobblestones under the tall chestnut trees, climbed up the steps, leaned against the oaken door to push it open, jumped up the eight marble stair steps, and rang our door-bell.

An unusually ugly woman opened. She was middle-aged, fat, and wore a soiled, shapeless gown. She had a severe squint on one eye and as she opened her mouth to inquire about my busi-ness, I saw that she had several teeth missing. I explained who I was, and she let me in.

We went into our living room, which was now their bed-room, hers and her mother's. The old woman must have been seventy and looked a little more respectable.

Mother and Gila were no longer there, they had left for some place in the West, I was told. I knew, Blexen. My father? No, he had not shown up either.

They had lost their dwelling, which must have been in the poorest section of the large city, and had been assigned to our apartment. As old as they were, they treated me with almost child-like respect. They entrusted me with the horrid tale of their experiences as though my knowledge of it, and perhaps my sympathy and reassuring word, would make everything a little easier to bear.

Two soldiers had come and raped her, the younger one lamented. It had no doubt been a most terrifying experience; but, while listening to her tale with compassion, I somehow found it difficult to believe that a man, no matter how wretched, would forget himself and choose her, of all women. An officer, she continued, then had appeared in the doorway, summoned by her screams. He had expelled the undiscriminating rapists, calmed down the hysterical women, and then had kept watch for the remainder of the night. All night, she reported with a grateful glow in her crossed eyes, they had heard the regular rhythm of his boots as he walked up and down the long hallway.

That stung. I know it shouldn't have, for is it not gratifying to learn of this upright Russian officer's actions and of the selfless vigil that he kept for hours in the night? To see that, in this hour of cataclysm, there were those among the victors who remained untouched by the tide of vileness? Why certainly, but that was not what I saw or felt at that moment. I saw a foreign officer, an enemy officer, pacing up and down the corridor, my corridor, our corridor! He had, so I felt, desecrated the territory of my childhood by his mere temporary presence, no matter how noble his purpose. That was the hallway to the kitchen, to the children's room, to the parents' bedroom, to my chamber, to the bathroom; it was ours! If any officer walked here with his heavy boots, it was my brothers. To me, it was a repulsive notion to think of the sound of Russian boots, all night, in my home.

ANOTHER HORRID TALE

I had used the bathroom and, in old habit, squeezed past the bathtub to open the narrow window. Across the courtyard on the second floor, Mrs. Köpke had also just used the bathroom and she, too, was at this moment opening the window.

"Peter!" she shouted across in joyous disbelief. "Heavens, Peter, you are home!" The emotion permeating her voice and expression was indescribable. It was as though I was her own son and had risen from the dead. The depth and forcefulness of her discomposure reflected the magnitude of their recent nightmare.

"Peter, oh my God, come up right away and let me take you in my arms!"

She told me of the last days of the battle of Berlin, while Mr. Köpke and Maria listened and occasionally nodded in confirmation. She recalled their fright, as they listened to the din of exploding shells and bombs from the basement, and how for weeks they had spent day and night in the bomb shelter and only rarely had ventured upstairs. And she recalled their worries about the future and their fear of the Russians. Then, her strained expression softened as she smiled at me and related how they had, at times, looked through Mrs. Karg's living room to catch a glimpse of daylight outside her basement window. That had always made them think of me, she continued, because the red tulips that I had planted outside were in full bloom, and their cheerful beauty was such an implausible sight in their woeful misery. "It almost made us cry," she said, "to see them out there in the sun of springtime..."

Then suddenly, so she went on, a Russian soldier had appeared in the doorway of the shelter. He had surveyed the people and even though Maria had been made up to look like an old woman, he had gone straight up to her, removed her glasses and scarf, and with the words "Frau, komm!" he had dragged her with him. With the exception of the very old, all the women in the building had been raped, Mrs. Köpke reported. She herself was, too, and I learned later of her suffering from venereal disease.

In the neighboring apartment building, there used to live a

very comely young woman, about eighteen years old, who had attracted even my attention with her very short skirts and perfect legs. The Russians had been standing in line for her, nine of them, I was told, and raped her one after the other.

KIND AND BENIGN

I did not quite understand how to put this together. I had never met this family that had been bombed out elsewhere and now was occupying two rooms in the third floor apartment, right above the Köpkes; and yet they treated me with unbelievable warmth and hospitality. Berliners had always been known as being people with a "big heart," but this was so unexpected.

They had heard about my arrival and had sent word that they would like to have me come upstairs for a good meal. They, too, treated me like a young gentlemen, even though I looked only fourteen, and respectfully addressed me with "Sie" and "Mr. Nennhaus". They served me rye bread covered with applesauce as though there was no tomorrow. Their faces smiling and their eyes full of good will, they sat around me and watched as I was putting it all away, only to urge me on to further helpings.

"*Nimm' Se nur, nimm' Se nur, Herr Nennhaus, sind Se nich' blöde!*" they said, here, once again, the charm of their dialect defying translation. "Help yourself, sir, don't be stupid."

I later learned the reason of their warm-hearted hospitality. In the face of the imminent arrival of the-end-of-the-world-as-we-know-it and with our family having left, they had helped themselves to the numerous preserving jars of applesauce that Mother had left behind. Now that I had returned, they obtained a measure of moral absolution by giving me generous helpings of it.

It must have been the middle of June, just over a month since the end of the war. The city in a moonscape of dust and rubble, the country in shambles and prostrate, the people uprooted and destitute, and our world in limbo: there we were, complete strangers to one another, standing helplessly between a shattered past and a forbidding future, just barely on the other side of Doomsday. Yet we were following the script of social propriety and civility to the letter. The social fabric had survived the war and final crash totally intact and, unbelievably, the facial features of human society in this big city were still benign and kind.

What I experienced was apparently not unique. A foreign visitor made a similar observation when describing the demeanor of the Berlin "*Trümmerfrauen*," the "rubble women," who had been recruited by the occupying authorities to clear the rubble from the streets. In bucket brigade fashion, they formed lines and passed bricks along, from one to the next. As they did, so the observer noted with curious amusement and probably with some exaggeration, with every brick they kept saying to each other,

"*Bitteschön!*"—"*Dankeschön!*"—"*Bitteschön!*"— "*Dankeschön!*" There you go!—Thanks!—There you go!—Thanks!

ESCAPE OF THE TARDY

Potsdam, our sanctuary for so long, was barely recognizable. One or two air raids, to pave the way for the Russians, were more than enough to demolish this charming little town.

Aunt Lotte was no longer there. Only at the last minute, I was told, had she left on bicycle. It was hard to believe that this intelligent woman, with her quick grasp of the needs and practicalities of life, had missed the last train out. In spite of her distrust of everything Nazi, she, too, had held out hope for the promised turning of the tide.

She did not bicycle alone, but rather in the company of Bärbel and Hermann. Hermann had enjoyed the dubious fortune of having been repatriated from Scotland, in a prisoner exchange, just in time for the devastating raid on Potsdam and for the Soviet offensive. With his knee shattered, infected, and stiff, he had left the smoldering town together with the two women, pedaling only with one leg. To Blexen, it was about 450 kilometers.

As I learned years later, however, once they were struck by reality and realized that disaster was upon them, they proved equal to the challenge. There was a shed in the back yard of their apartment building. Before they left, in the middle of the night, the two women undid its floor, dug a hole, and then buried the silverware as well as the sewing machine. Years later, they were able to return and to recover the treasure and to take it back to West Germany.

Also, as the three were bicycling westward, barely crossing rivers before the German Army exploded the bridges, they made an attempt to rescue their brother Achim. His anti-aircraft unit was stationed near the town of Brandenburg, and, as they passed through, they looked him up and encouraged him to desert and come along with them. Achim stayed were he was. He told them that he would not become a deserter.

BOOTY BIKE

Fritz had arrived at his home in Bornstedt a few days earlier. His mother was a school teacher, a gentle and brave woman, who alone had raised her two sons after her husband, a member of a right-wing political party, had been killed by communist militants. Fritz was born three weeks after his father's murder.

I stayed overnight. He was truly a helpful friend. Our long journey had taught him to appreciate the difference between wheel and foot. In his enterprising way, he not only advised me to acquire a bicycle, but he also knew exactly where bikes were available.

The schoolhouse in Bornstedt was a long building divided

into two wings by a central entrance hall or lobby. In the rear, this hall led out on the schoolyard. The school was not used at this time for its original purpose but rather was occupied by the Red Army. I am not certain whether they used the class rooms for housing their soldiers or as administrative offices; but the lobby, that I do know, had been designated as the storage space for all the liberated bicycles of Bornstedt.

Soldiers in their tunic-like, medal-bedecked uniforms were present in moderate abundance outside the building when we arrived. We walked briskly toward the entrance, the way one walks when late for an appointment with the commandant. Inside, we found the bikes stacked against the walls, I would estimate between fifty and sixty of them. A moment later, we emerged in the rear on the school yard pushing a bicycle between us and heading for a back road, neither displaying any haste nor wasting any time.

Safely back at Fritz's home, we proceeded, greatly overestimating the sophistication of Soviet justice, to change the evidence. Handlebars, fenders, and other removable items were exchanged between his own bike (which had so far escaped discovery) and the newly acquired one until each had lost its previous identity.

The next morning, Fritz walked me to the northern exit of Bornstedt. There we shook hands and wished each other good luck, and then I was on my way to the West.

Forty years were to elapse, before I revisited the city where I grew up.

Marshal Zhukov's Soldiers

In the town of Nauen I turned westward on the Berlin-Hamburg highway. It was a two-lane road lined by trees and a ditch on each side to collect the water running off the arched road surface. Its pavement consisted, not of asphalt, but of cobblestones. This circumstance was to assume transient relevance very soon.

I encountered a great deal of eastbound military traffic, some motorized but chiefly columns of Russian infantry interspersed with stragglers. Most of them marched wearily through the dust and heat of June, but once or twice I heard them sing. Their marching songs were melodious and beautiful, and their voices were good. Yet, it pained me to hear these typical Russian sounds in the German countryside.

Frequently I passed rows and double rows of Russian graves by the roadside, twenty to sixty in a given place. Now and then Russian trucks were speeding eastward. They were stacked with furniture. It was surprising to see that they had not failed to include the stovepipes on any of them.

Marshal Zhukov's foot-sore soldiers stared at me as I passed them on my bike.

The Attention-Getting Buzz

I had managed to travel about forty kilometers before my bicycle was reliberated. Actually, the Russian soldier who carried out this transaction was quite correct and courteous about it, and I cannot really blame him either, considering his predicament.

I heard him approach long before I saw him in the distance, as he was preceded by a harsh, rattling sound. He was on his way home to Russia on a bicycle devoid of tires, and the bare fellies, as they rolled over the small cobblestones, gave rise to a sound, which announced his arrival a mile ahead.

He stopped me, and, while I did not understand Russian, I did recognize the words "document," "commandant," and "machine". I nodded affirmatively and pulled out from my breast pocket the certificate of my discharge from the National-Socialist

Farming Service. He studied it with the same puzzled expression with which I myself had tried to decipher the Cyrillic letters of Russian inscriptions. He must have finally concluded that this document contained no authorization for me to own the machine that I was riding on; and, in handing it back, he indicated to me, being almost solicitous about it, that we were going to swap.

As I resumed my travels, I quickly recognized that the vehicle I had received in the bargain was distinguished by more than just the penetrating sound it emitted. Not only was it audible to any weary foot soldier within a mile's radius, but it also transmitted a violent whir into my hands on the handlebar, and to top it off, it lacked brakes.

My ownership of this attention-getting device was understandably brief. Only about a kilometer closer to Hamburg, I encountered another member of the Red Army whose problem was not one of riding on a defective bicycle. Rather, this unfortunate individual had no bicycle at all.

His business methods were more perfunctory and direct than those of his comrade. He shouted, "*Stoi!*"—a command for me to stop. My appraisal of the situation was entirely realistic and being more than eager to avoid any kind of trouble, I was determined to oblige, but I was unable to do so for the lack of brakes. My Russian counterpart, of course, did not know that. This explains the angry manner in which he caught his arm in mine.

As I picked myself up from the pavement, I heard a terrific buzz behind my back, which faded away in an easterly direction.

GRANDFATHER'S FARM

Conveniently, Fischershof was located merely a few miles from the highway. It was the farm of my uncle and aunt—or more correctly, it was the farm of my paternal grandfather who had bequeathed it to his seven grandchildren. Aunt Hannchen was Dad's sister. I did not know them too well, having visited only on rare and brief occasions.

My memories are shamefully scant. They spoke the local dialect and still used petroleum lamps. In the hallway, there was a picture of an ornamental design Dad had painted in his high school days. In a small room, some of our furniture had been stored for the past two years.

Foolishly, Mother had locked the drawers of her secretary and of the birch cabinet in order to prevent unauthorized entry. Now I found they had been hacked open with a hatchet.

The other farm, where Dad's bookcases had been taken for storage in a barn, I did not visit. That was no loss. As I learned later, the several hundred books soon ended up on the bottom of the nearby duck pond.

When I left Fischershof the next morning on my way to the West, one seventh of it was still my property, but not for long. In the name of socialist justice, it was soon expropriated and collectivized.

FATHER'S TALE

Conveniently also, the Berlin-Hamburg highway took me through the province of Mecklenburg where, last I knew, Dad had been administrator of a country estate. It was as if I was picking up the pieces of our family and our belongings, blown asunder by the war.

Knowing the address, I asked my way through the rural countryside, where people spoke the Low German dialect, and found the large estate without difficulty.

Dad was still there, albeit more or less in hiding in an attic room of the home of one of the farm workers. He was a sad sight —a lens was missing from his glasses and his face was covered with the stubble of a week-old beard, which scratched as he embraced me.

Fifty-five years old, he did not quite qualify for an old man; but, he was trying to look like one, so he explained, for the Russians reportedly showed more respect for old people. He certainly had reason to hope for more respect.

One day, so he told me, upon entering his room in the mansion-like farmhouse, he found several Russian soldiers looting it.

"I quickly grabbed the hand case, where I kept my papers and essentials, and turned to leave," he recalled. "But then one of them seized me, a big and strapping peasant boy, and plowed his fist in my face, you know, like he meant it, with all his strength behind it. I sailed across the room to where another one was standing. He hit me next, sending me back to the first one. It didn't look very good, Peter, they just bounced me back and forth like a ball. I didn't know what was happening to me. I had lost my glasses and couldn't see, and I remember thinking, 'This is it, they won't quit until they've finished me off.'"

He was saved by the arrival of an officer who stopped the carnage.

Yet Father had fared better than another gentleman who, I believe, had lived in the same mansion. In a defiant over-my-dead-body type of posture, he had planted himself in front of his suitcase. Life was cheap. The pillaging soldier, so I learned and was no longer surprised to hear, was not deterred. He shot him dead.

Dad had been under arrest for two or three weeks, too. His position on the estate automatically denoted him as a capitalist. Through an interpreter, the Russian commissar had asked him what kind of a doctor he was. The interpreter was a Russian woman with very limited knowledge of German. Dad had explained his degree to be one in economics, a word she did not understand, and none of his answers seemed acceptable to the commissar. Finally, doing his best to cooperate, Dad had attempted a different approach and said to her,

"Well, perhaps you understand French? In French it is called *economie politique.*"

The bloody fool! They understood the word "politique" all right and locked him up. It was during that phase, too, that they had made him clean the bathtub.

That was another story that has remained in my memory of those days. Unfamiliar with so many western facilities, they had mistaken a certain bathtub for a latrine but then were confronted with a problem when it was full. They solved it with the help of pails and several of their capitalist prisoners.

KEEN ANALYSIS

The thinker and mathematician that he was, Father had thought everything out very carefully and with a cool head at that, at a time, that is, when others acted in panic or followed their instincts. This was so, I suspect, because he lacked instinct, the instinct of opportunity and chances; the sixth sense that tells other people what to bet their money on.

He told me, "I can't go to Blexen with you. Blexen is a village; I get buried there, it has no future for me to get started again. My only chance is in the city. I must return to Berlin."

He predicted there would be a tug-of-war over Germany between the East and the West along with an economic contest, in which each side would try to prove its superiority.

"Stalin isn't going to suppress and exploit and destroy us, Peter," he said. "He'd be a fool. He wants to win over the rest of Germany. Once there are elections, he wants the Communists to win. So, whether he likes it or not, he must do everything to promote rapid recovery in his part of Germany. And where do you think the administrative center of that reconstruction is going to be located? In Berlin, Peter, where else. And they'll need good people. It's logical. You'll see how right I am."

He, like everybody else, had no idea of what was going to happen to our country. He could not imagine that, at that early stage, nobody among the victors entertained the thought promoting German economic recovery. He naively took for granted that Germany was a single country. The thought that the others wanted to carve it up into pieces and to make its people starve and suffer and pay for their sins, that thought never occurred to him. Not at all comprehending the brutal reality that descended on our country, he thought that our flight from Berlin was merely a temporary event and that we would all return there and resume our life where we had left off.

LARKS IN THE SUMMERY SKY

I left in the morning. He walked with me the first two kilometers to lead me to the road that would take me west. He was so brave. He was homesick for his family and would have liked nothing better than to come along and to join Mother and Gila with me. Without his family he felt lonesome and cold. But the harsh realities permitted no sentimentality; and thus, he had to stick it out in Berlin, under the Soviets, so he could support us again. Accordingly, it was for him to stay behind and to let his boy march off alone.

At the road crossing we stopped. He took me in his arms, just for a second but almost violently, then let go and pressed my hand and said, "Goodbye, *mein lieber Junge.*" The farewell was difficult for both of us, but we were brave and I parted quickly.

A few hundred feet down the road, I turned around and waved back at him. His unshaven face smiled sadly, only the left circle of his spectacles giving a reflection. After I had marched another few minutes we waved again. I can still see Daddy's small frame before my eyes, pitifully insignificant within the wide expanse of the fields. The future was so uncertain and the world was so hostile in the Soviet Zone. I was worried to leave him behind. Just before the road took me into a forest, I turned once more. The song of larks filled the summery air above the rural scene. In the distance, I could still see him standing at the crossing and waving his handkerchief.

Easy Passage

It was late afternoon the same day when I approached the western border of the Soviet Zone of Occupation. The British occupied the zone west from here. Local people were helpful in giving me directions and advice. There were extensive forests, which, while patrolled by the Russians, were preferred to the open fields by those trying to cross the border. I penetrated into the woods a ways, with the intention to wait for darkness before venturing any further. I met a German headed in the opposite direction who had valuable information. He directed me to a farmhouse a bit farther north. The farmer owned land on both sides of the border and was therefore permitted to cross freely in either direction.

I found the farm and, without much ado, the farmer agreed to take me across in the morning. When I entered the barn to bed down for the night, I found several more people in the hay who hoped this would be their last night in the Eastern Zone.

As it turned out, it was the easiest thing in the world. My feet dangling, I sat on the flattop horse-drawn wagon and for good measure held a pitchfork across my lap. The Russian guard standing by the side of the small forest road waved us through. We passed the British border guards with equal ease. Once out of sight around a turn, we jumped off, thanked the farmer, and went on our way. It was not even seven o'clock yet by the time I had passed my last major hurdle. From here on, I thought, it was clear sailing to Mother.

GOOD EVENING!

It was over a day's march to the Elbe River. Long before I reached it, I learned of the inexplicable decision of the British authorities to block Germans from crossing the river, which was well within their zone of occupation. At that time, nobody understood that the purpose was to stem the immense tide of millions of refugees who came from the East and for whom there was neither room nor food in the West. If there were any bridges left in Hamburg, I was told, they were barred, too. I had visions of suspending myself from underneath a freight car in order to cross a Hamburg railway bridge. Nothing was going to stop me now. But then I opted for the technique in which I was more experienced: I would try to swim across.

By mid-morning, I reached the banks of the river near the town of Boizenburg, which in my memory was probably no more than two hundred meters wide. Beyond the broad, grass-covered beach, the river was lined by a narrow strip of woods on its east side that covered the slope of a further embankment. Hiding under the trees, I could see the dike on the other side and far beyond into the flat and peaceful countryside. Above, friendly cumulus clouds stretched toward the western horizon; and, below, one could recognize scattered farms and villages, cattle on the pastures, and green fields surrounded by the dark patches of woods. So near, and yet so far! As I wistfully gazed into the sunny distance, where, somewhere, I envisioned Mother and Gila, Uncle Karl and his family, a bed and a bathtub, and food served on a cloth-covered table,

I felt as though I was seeing the Promised Land.

From time to time, two British soldiers patrolled along the dike on the far side of the river. Then two of them, who leisurely chatted with one another, passed me on my side, just twenty or thirty meters away from my shady hiding place.

The problem, though, was not merely one of crossing without being detected, but also of accomplishing this in a civilized manner. I had to have a raft to keep my clothes dry as well as the contents of my knapsack. Between patrols, I roamed the bank for suitable boards and small logs, and I also, conveniently, came across lengths of discarded military telephone cable. I was ready to start with the construction when another patrol approached, and I quickly disappeared under the trees. It was early afternoon by now, and I was growing awfully hungry, too.

The two inspected the pile of construction material and—their proper English easy for me to understand—smelled a rat. They promptly located me and confronted me with the evidence. I professed complete ignorance of these materials, their origins as well as their potential usefulness in river crossings. Nonetheless, distrustful chaps as they were, they had me dump the precious collection into the water, where it drifted away. I much preferred their English to their attitude.

In the early evening, I was ready to go. I was hiding in the reeds, down by the water, waiting for the English chatter above me to disappear. The patrol on the other side had passed ten minutes earlier. Next to me was my raft: two empty gasoline canisters tied together with telephone wire, not on top of each other but side-by-side. This flat contraption easily remained afloat with my knapsack, stuffed with my clothes and boots, strapped to its top. Its center of gravity was low enough to prevent it from tipping over. The last bit of insulated wire served to tie the raft to my wrist.

The English voices had faded away. I slipped into the water

and began to swim across with a vigorous breaststroke. With every forward thrust of my arms, the silly raft struck the back of my head, the line being too short. I anxiously scanned the bank south of me where the next patrol would be coming from, but I was the only soul around.

After I stepped ashore, I quickly untied the knapsack and found a sunny spot amongst the bushes to dry off. There were no woods on this side to hide in, just some shrubbery growing on the dike. Still half wet, I got dressed, and that was none too soon. English voices were approaching. But the soldiers just looked at me and uttered a friendly "Good evening". With equal friendliness, I returned their greeting as they continued on their way.

ARRIVAL

It was five o'clock the next evening when I stood at the ferry dock in Bremerhaven. The day had been a good one. I had traveled 130 kilometers in all, but only twenty-five of these on foot. The friendly truck driver, after listening to my story, had gone out of his way in dropping me off here at the ferry.

"Over there," he had said, "that's Blexen. Good luck!"

The cry of sea gulls and the smells of salt water, of fish, and of tar were in the air. A tugboat puttered past us. I shaded my eyes against the sun in the west and looked past the breakwater and the lighthouse. This, then, was the estuary of the Weser River. It was at least two kilometers wide if not three. On the other side I saw the flat and smooth line of a dike, and, behind it, there rose the simple, pointed steeple of a village church.

The sea gulls followed us on our twenty-minute trip across the Weser. The local people spoke Low German, but with a twang unfamiliar to me. As the dike came closer, it rose higher, while the church steeple seemed to slip off behind it.

The walk from the ferry dock to the village of Blexen was one kilometer long. Finally, I stood in front of the cemetery, which surrounded the ancient little church. People directed me to the farm. Passing through the gate and following a walk winding through a lawn and some shrubs, I was met by curious children. They were my cousins. They escorted me to the house under a big chestnut tree and shouted, "Peter is here!"

Aunt Änne came limping out of the house; she had a bad hip. Uncle Karl and Gila were just coming around the corner of the veranda, returning from the chicken coop. Uncle Karl was carrying a hatful of eggs; Gila held a few in each hand.

"Peter is here!"

Mother came running out of the house. More and more children joined the crowd, all cousins, all smiles, and a German shepherd joined in the chorus of laughter with his authoritative bark.

"*Mein Junging,* you're home!" Mother cried as we met on the steps to the veranda. I brought greetings from Dad, I said.

"Daddy? You saw him?"

I explained. A cloud of despair passed over her face, as she remonstrated, "Oh that man! Why didn't he come with you?"

Embraces, handshakes, kisses, and laughter...

Gila and I could not embrace. She was temporarily disabled, and in spite of her almost bewildered state of joy, she managed an apology to Uncle Karl. In the sudden excitement of seeing me, she had crushed the eggs in both of her hands, which were now dripping.

Life and Honor

Friedrich's last message was written on the day of the surrender of the German Armed Forces, and, incredibly, it was still delivered to some Latvian sea port and from there, across the sea, to Germany.

Courland, May 8, 1945
Dear Parents,
Dear Gila and Peter,

Now, what we have wanted to prevent in six years of fighting has happened after all: the total defeat of our Wehrmacht. We've lost the war and our freedom, loved ones have fallen and have been murdered, our homeland is devastated, and everything is being taken from us. We're only left with life and our honor. And that we must preserve under all circumstances. One must never give up, and as long as we're alive, we can fight.

Thus, there shall be no surrender (for us). We shall, as the "Volunteer Corps von Usedom" (the name of their general), hit the forests and fight our way in small groups or as a unit, depending on how the situation develops, all the way to that part of the Reich which is occupied by the Anglo-Americans. Then we shall reunite in Blexen! We have no illusions regarding the dangers, but everything has been prepared and thought-out in the best possible way; and besides, let Ivan beware in attempting to interfere with us!

So let's keep a cool head. We'll get this baby licked. I hope to find you all in good health. All of your mail has reached me. I was terribly happy about the photographs. I'll take them along...

I believe in the resurrection of our nation, so long as we don't submit to despondency.

I greet you all from my innermost heart.

Your Friedrich

A World Poisoned by Anger

THE WAR'S SAVAGE ORGY WAS COMING TO AN END. Its causes were numerous: they were geographic, strategic, historic, technologic, cultural, and religious, to name a few. Among the most seminal and ominous mechanisms in its genesis, however, was the passion of anger. Many calamitous misjudgments were made that, although easily contradicted by sober thought, prevailed because in the decision-making process anger grabbed the upper hand. The passion of anger distorts the facts, misleads common sense, and renders fervor to violent conclusions. Sadly, the clamor of anger always will overwhelm the voice of wisdom.

Early in this century, History had amassed many fearful issues, crises, and confrontations, and they were magnified and blown out of proportion by the disaster of the First World War. They were, then, too numerous and too serious for anyone to resolve dispassionately. At the Paris Peace Conference in 1919, the wisdom of Woodrow Wilson succumbed to his partners' indignant and vengeful temper. As if by special order, several of the leaders that emerged out of the universal calamity were indeed prophets of anger. Lenin was an angry revolutionary from his early days. He ended up being a harbinger of wrath. Hitler spun out of control at the time of Imperial Germany's defeat and never recovered. He demonized the Slavs and Jews and fantasized himself into a world of ideas, which again represented an ideology of anger. Similarly, it is easy to recognize the adversaries that infuriated Stalin. He hated his stubborn peasants with a vengeance; he was paranoid with regard to those whom he suspected to work to remove him from power; and he detested the capitalist countries, especially Germany. If ever there was a power-hungry and wrathful tyrant, it was Stalin.

And then, as a *coup-de-grace* for any remaining moderation, there came the Second World War, in which even sane, principled, and circumspect statesmen in the Western World finally fell victim to passion and rage. It was at that point that the European War was propelled into a disastrous World War.

Anger emanated from World War I, from its dehumanizing

trenches, from its hungry masses, and from its hate-mongering propaganda. Anger characterized the Treaty of Versailles. Anger was the central spirit of Leninism. Anger against Germany lived on in the League of Nations. Immense anger was the characteristic feature of Stalinism. Anger lay at the bottom of Hitler's racial and imperialistic ideology. Communism created an upsurge of fanatic hatred among its anti-communist opponents in our streets that led to revolution-like confrontations in many countries. Anger was no stranger to the Poles' attitude toward their minorities. Anger was a unifying principle of anti-Semitism on both sides of the Atlantic in the Depression years of the 1930s, but it was most maliciously enshrined in Nazi anti-Jewish legislation in those prewar years. Anger mounted in Germany, Poland, and Great Britain in 1939. Paranoid hatred in Britain and the United States—chiefly in their governments—prevented peace from being restored in 1940 and, instead, propelled the war into an apocalyptic escalation. An unparalleled paranoid rage created that incredible industrialized massacre that was later named the Holocaust. Merciless hatred was spelled out, likewise, in Nazi policies against the Poles and in the action of various Eastern European ethnic detachments who lent their cruel hand in the Holocaust. An explosion of vicious anger was displayed by Communist partisan fighters in Yugoslavia, in Greece, and in the Soviet Union against their non-Communist opponents and their own population. Each year, the war witnessed progressive increments of mutual animosity among the belligerent nations. Anger and the will to kill the innocent was an essential component of aerial warfare against civilian population centers. Angry brutality brought about the expulsion of fourteen million Germans from their ancient homelands. It is difficult to deny evil intent in the deaths of two million German refugees in the East, of one million or so in air raids, of mass imperilment of POWs in lethal camps, or of several millions who did not survive starvation policies after the war. If the Versailles Treaty was conceived in anger, the Potsdam Protocol of 1945 was so many times over. The Nuremberg Tribunal, likewise, was an act of anger more than a pursuit of justice. In many different ways, it was an acknowledged legal travesty. Its only legitimacy was moral rather than legal and rested solely on the discovery of the Holocaust. While that moral legitimacy has to be acknowledged even by its critics, it was a trial, nonetheless, that was conceived and carried forth in a spirit not of fairness but of revenge. That was so because the idea of such a tribunal was born months before substantial knowledge of the Holocaust was available. It was so because its original concept was not a trial, but rather it was to kill German leaders and generals, outright, without any legal preliminaries. And it was so because millions of Germans were being killed in retaliation, almost shamelessly, one might say, at the very same time as the tribunal proceeded and by the same powers who sat in judgment at Nuremberg. Had a fair pursuit of justice prevailed in those days without the interference of hatred, such a trial would have assumed a different scope and shape.

The psychology of anger is responsible for much of our various nations' moral derailment during the first part of the twentieth century. Out of a rising spate of indignation, dread, and panic there arose the Wrath-of-the-Just, and out of this wrath there grew the will to kill and destroy. Had there been a mechanism to safeguard wisdom in the midst of passion, armageddon might have been avoided. But such a safeguard to shield wisdom did not exist because it is in the nature of the Wrath-of-the-Just to wear, rightly or wrongly, that very robe of wisdom and justice. With mutual escalation of hostility, the sky was the limit and demonization created self-fulfilling prophecies. Civilization disintegrated into barbarism. This war brought about unprecedented devastation and the death of perhaps thirty million people if the twenty million victims of the Sino-Japanese War are not counted. As man had done for thousands of years before, he had once again destroyed with his savage hand what his creative hand had lovingly erected. Indeed, this was the first time ever that he knowingly was tempting the gods to destroy his own, marvelous civilization for the precise reason that he could not control his rage before it finally exhausted itself.

If there is any lesson to be learned from that war, it is the need to acquire a safeguard to shield wisdom in the midst of passion, and in particular, in the midst of the Wrath-of-the-Just. This goes beyond the time-honored principle of crime-and-punishment and beyond the religious concept of forgiveness and of turning the other cheek, all of which was, in that tragic war, totally ineffective. Instead, should we ever seek the secret of such a safeguard, our experiences suggest that they will be detected less in the realms of morality or religion or the law, than in the inner mechanism of the psychology of anger.

THE SILENCE

One lasting aftermath of that angry conflict has been the sustained public cursing and defilement of Beethoven's beautiful land. *Vox populi, vox dei*, but there should be no doubt that, rightly or wrongly, the perception the German people had of the war, at that time, differed greatly from the way it is seen today. They never doubted that they fought and suffered for a righteous cause. They waged a twenty-eight-day war against Poland, which, in their misled opinion, was unavoidable, and, in last consequence, was caused by their hateful enemies. It was as if a snowball that they had thrown had grown into the largest avalanche the world had ever known and was destined to crash down on them. Britain and France declared war on them, and it was their war, so it seemed to them, and their military movements that coerced Germany into campaigns from the Arctic to the Mediterranean. They felt that the Americans had entered the war on Britain's side long before Germany was forced to officially declare it and that they had done so even though Germany had had no quarrel with them. The only campaign that most of them believed was solely started by their own country was the one against Stalin. But that, to them, was altogether different from all that had preceded it. As in their opinion everybody in Europe knew, it was a desperately necessary and preemptive war. It was a holy war. It was a war that the churches supported and that everybody knew was morally right to wage. It was one that protected western civilization, they felt, and a war of Christianity against state-sponsored godlessness. It was a war that should have caused all civilized countries to join in on Germany's side. It was a crusade that surely God had demanded. It was a war that made the continued enmity of Great Britain and the United

THE PSYCHOLOGY OF WAR

THE GERMAN VIEW

THE ALLIED VIEW

States incomprehensible. And as that campaign began to falter, they felt they were sacrificing themselves for the benefit and safety of the rest of the world. Without any question, the Germans were convinced that, if ever a country had fought a just war, it was their struggle against Stalin's evil empire.

Those who lived through it, not only on the Allied side but in Germany as well, remember the citizen's bravery, their self-denial, their loyal submission to the demands of their country, the spirit of uplifting idealism across the whole nation, and the mutual good will uniting people of all walks of life. They rose in Germany to the emergency no less than the patriots did in France, Britain, the United States, and Russia, and they remained true comrades to one another through all the tears and suffering.

One of the enigmas of wars is the naïve goodness of men and women in the midst of violence. I have never again witnessed a society in a spirit so noble and brave, much the way the Londoners were described during the Blitz, as the Germans were, then, in their country's grimmest hour. The barbarity and fury that weave through mankind's history have pathways that somehow manage to bypass the purity of the individual soul. People are compelled to kill the enemies, to sink their ships, or to drop the atomic bomb on them without, so it appears, ever losing their personal innocence.

Few were the citizens who knew enough about the regime's criminality for them to enter or favor the resistance movement. But even the men who conspired to kill Hitler never, for a moment, questioned that it was not he, but Stalin, who menaced western civilization.

The Germans have never spoken up. They have made no attempt to present their case, the way it appeared to them during the war, in the court of world opinion. They have patiently submitted to carrying the huge cross of guilt and shame and worldwide defamation, and they have even been vigilant in muting everyone among their own citizens who speaks a word in their own favor. The reason for this surprising attitude has not been any foreign imposition or the occupation of their country by foreign armies or any cowering humility expected from a defeated country. It has also not been for the reason that one could not have presented, like a defense attorney, a remarkable set of arguments that would have evened the score somewhat, saved some of their honor, and raised embarrassing questions against their former foes. Rather, it was the depressing conviction that whatever good reasons they might voice in self-defense, they would all be too minor and insignificant when matched against that one overwhelming verdict against them for which they, inescapably, had to assume collective guilt. The burden of that verdict has buried and suffocated the feeling of righteousness that once inspired them during the war. It has been the shame and disgrace arising, like a pungent cloud, from the Holocaust that has been the major reason for their silence.

There is, yet, another reason. Underlying the change of mood that most of Europe underwent after the war was the realization that there had to be something wrong with all the righteousness and heroism and patriotism if it led to mutual destruction. Germany, if not other European countries as well, emerged from the disaster with the feeling that, somehow, the vigor of patriotism, the holiness of justice, and all the other proud virtues needed to be tuned down in favor of tolerance and reconciliation. And from this, there grew in Germany the conviction, if not in fact a dogma, that for the sake of everybody's peace and dignity, of the healing of the wounds, and of fertile cooperation in future generations, there was a need not only for atonement, made by everyone for himself, but for putting an end to attempts to settle accounts. Their silence is an expression of their unilateral decision to follow that policy. For the fifty years following the war, they have never raised their voice in self-defense. They have been silent. It has proven to be a wise and successful approach, for many people elsewhere, albeit not all, have responded in kind.

HISTORY'S THIRD BLUNDER

World War I cast a long, dark shadow across this century. Without it, the words Leninism, Hitlerism, and Germanophobia would be unknown. Yet there are reasons to believe that, one way or the other, it was bound to break out. In some way, all of Europe was apparently ready for that war. The deeper causes for it—mutual international distrust, the armament race, imperialism and nationalism, the fear of Germany's growing vitality, irredentism, the desire for freedom of captive peoples incorporated in foreign states, and the conflicts arising from industrialization, capitalism, and socialism—were not anyone's handiwork. They were the products of History. When the ominous system collapsed and war ensued, it resembled an earthquake from which nobody could escape. To have assembled such a precarious and dangerous constellation was History's first blunder of the century.

Recovery from that war was agonizingly slow, but at the end of the first postwar decade, a moderate amount of progress had been made. The world economy had improved. Hitler's early appeal to the masses had faded quickly and attracted only 2.8 percent of the electorate. The victorious powers began to become more conciliatory toward Germany. The dark clouds were beginning to dissipate. Only Leninism, now carried forth by Stalin, was in full power. It was at that time that History committed her second blunder.

The stock marked crash in 1929 struck suddenly. It, too, was a pivotal disaster. It inaugurated the worldwide Great Depression. It was, in last consequence, the sole reason for Germany's political quadriplegia and the vacuum it produced within which Hitler could maneuver to assume power. Had there been no stock market crash in 1929, there would have been no Nazi government, no Holocaust and—unless caused by Stalin, impelled by his own fanaticism—no World War II. Certainly unintended by anyone and entirely irreversible, it was ultimately the stock market collapse that had flung the gates wide open onto the unprotected road toward another world war.

Thus, one might say, the Second World War was the outgrowth of those two blunders and their consequences. At that time, two cancers, if that is a good term, namely the militant states ruled by Stalin and Hitler, threatened Europe. From the start, a war between the two was certain to occur. Whichever of the two was able to be first in assaulting the other would be the winner. If Stalin had won, he would have established Soviet hegemony over all of continental Europe. If Hitler had won, he would have similarly established Nazi hegemony over Europe and Russia. In either case, one of the two cancers would have been eliminated, but only to leave Europe stricken by the other one. In reality, though, the stage was entered by a third power, to wit, the United States of America. The entry of that country into the war resulted in the elimination of one cancer, Nazi Germany. But it also resulted in preserving the other cancer, the Soviet Union, and in salvaging, not all, but merely half of the Continent from being overrun by it. That was a remarkable benefit over the other two alternatives, and it earned America the deserved gratitude of the Free World. However, as it continued to face the Bolshevik cancer, Europe was by no means cured. The odious tragedy that befell Eastern Europe and the ensuing Cold War were the reasons why Churchill characterized the victory of 1945 as "Triumph and Tragedy". The Red Empire had come off the war with flying colors, and Communism spread to East Asia and created poisonous seedlings around the globe. The Cold War exploded into two actual and vicious wars in Korea and Vietnam, and for decades mankind lived on the brink of a nuclear exchange. Tragedy indeed, for what a blessing it would have been for all of the nations, including Russia and China, had History allowed the surgeon, the United States, to excise not merely one but both of the cancers. But this History did not permit, and that unquestionably was its third blunder.

As in the cases of the First World War and the 1929 market crash, there were again, this third time around, undeniable facts that predetermined the events. There was no way for Great Britain and the United States to have staged a campaign against the Red Army as soon as they had shaken hands with them in the center of Germany in 1945. It was out of the question, because of the unresolved war against Japan, because of public incomprehension in their own countries, and because of the dishonorable, even Machiavellian thought of plunging a knife into your erstwhile comrade-in-arms.

Nonetheless, in the eyes of the various peoples of the Continent, it was not altogether absurd to entertain that idea. A pact with the Devil emits a troublesome omen, and the people of the World became witnesses, if not in fact victims, of how troublesome it was. By 1945—and this will be a surprise to people living away from Central and Eastern Europe to hear—millions of continental Europeans had quietly hoped for such a campaign, and most of the Germans virtually expected this to happen. It was a last eleventh-hour hope in the hearts of ordinary folks all over that part of Europe giving courage to those who were in dread of Stalin's terror. In fact, disregarding for a moment the opposite sentiment among western Allies, it is tantalizing to realize how feasible it was, in purely material terms, to have cured Europe of both cancers. On their march into eastern Europe, the troops of Eisenhower and Montgomery would have been joined by the Czechs, Slovaks and Poles, the Hungarians, Rumanians and Bulgarians, and the Finns, Estonians, Latvians, and Lithuanians, and certainly the Ukrainians and even many of the Russians, all of them uniting to drive back the army of Bolshevism. With few exceptions, they would have all taken up arms and joined the great march for freedom. And the Germans? Yes, they had been hoping for such realignment for years, and every man, woman, and child would have supported Eisenhower and Montgomery from all their hearts. Of their nine million men in Allied captivity, at least eight million would have volunteered, no questions asked.

None of this happened. The callous rules of reality did not permit it. Once again, the gods did not remember us. They were still sleeping when History committed her third blunder.

LONG SHADOWS

A MONTH OR TWO AFTER MY RETURN, first Achim and then Karl-Hermann arrived having been released from British POW camps. Achim's brother Hermann had, of course, arrived after his long bicycle ride earlier and spent many months in the hospital with his infected knee. His father, Uncle Hans, nearly fifty-five years old, contracted tuberculosis in the prisoner camp and was transferred to a sanitarium where, one might suspect, he availed himself of the opportunity to play chess. Uncle Siegfried, who had been sent to fight in Italy was discharged, too, and arrived in Blexen later that fall. His wife and two daughters, Aunt Dora, Sigrid, and Ingeborg initially tried to hold on to their storkless farm but, facing Stalinist reality, fled to the West a year later.

Father doggedly stuck it out in Berlin for two years, first being recruited into rubble removing contingents, and later barely sustaining himself with other manual jobs. He eventually joined us in Blexen, painfully sobered and disheartened, and found a new job as a laborer, then, later, as an office clerk in the nearby U.S. Supply Depot that had moved into a local aircraft factory and provided welcome employment for most refugees in the area in those dismal years.

Fritz König visited us in 1946. He had joined his older brother in the West, after his mother had been taken away by the new communist authorities and had vanished. As it turned out years later, she spent years as a forced laborer in a uranium mine in a program designed to allow the Soviet Union to build an atomic bomb. Fritz and I lost track of each other, but, almost miraculously, met again twenty-eight years later, far from our homeland, and renewed our friendship.

We received the first sign of life from my brother in September of 1945. Their dare-devilish plan to fight their way from Latvia to western Germany was foiled before they got started. It would have been better for them had it succeeded.

Stalin's policies regarding his POWs changed through the years. There existed initially no organized Russian program to handle prisoners. They shot all wounded enemy soldiers on sight. For the first three years of the campaign, the mortality of their German prisoners was between 70 and 90 percent. In 1944, a policy of better treatment was instituted and as a result, until 1955 the death rate was less then one percent per year.[1] At the end of the war, over two million German POWs were in Stalin's custody. He postponed their discharge year after year, but by the end of 1949 their majority had returned home.

It is believed that the creation of the West German Federal Republic, in September 1949, was responsible for Stalin's decision to retain some of the remaining POWs as political hostages. My brother was one of them. In five-minute trials, tens of thousands were convicted as war criminals and sentenced, every one of them, to twenty-five years of forced labor. This simple stroke allowed the dictator to claim that all of his POWs had been released.

There was nobody left by that time who did not see Stalin as the man he was: imperialistic, tyrannical, aggressive, and merciless. In view of that realization, it was generally believed that for all practical purposes, after that so-called conviction, the fate of the prisoners was sealed. Most, if not all of our friends and relatives, even though they were fond of Friedrich, were writing him off. Willing to face reality, they were convinced that there was no hope for him to ever return.

During later years, the prisoners were permitted to receive packages from home, which supplemented their meager diet. As she had done through the war, and in spite of our poverty, mother then resumed sending innumerable packages to him. These were supplemented by mailings from his kindhearted friends in Belgium, whom we had never met.

Stalin died in spring of 1953. That fall, Friedrich was indeed released after all, along with fifteen thousand other prisoners. Thus, despite his unexpected salvation, life had tried him sorely: the six years he spent in the war were followed by eight years in the Gulag. Two years later, in 1955, Chancellor Adenauer traveled to Moscow and there agreed to establish diplomatic relations with the Soviet State. In exchange, the remaining fifteen thousand POWs were at last redeemed from their ten-year ordeal.

The veterans, thus repatriated, reviewed the endless lists and photographs of those still missing and unaccounted for—there were still hundreds of thousands of them. In this manner, at last, many families now learned when and where their men had perished.

No trace, however, did turn up of Dieter.

By that time, a decade had elapsed since the end of the war. Mother no longer mentioned her nocturnal receptions of his thoughts, the way she had in past times. But whenever we talked about him there was no doubt about her persistent hope of his possible return, some day, maybe even some *distant* day in the future. People were still talking about those Muted Camps, the *Schweigelager*, whose existence in popular belief was never questioned. The last time I heard Mother talk about it was in the 1980s when she hesitatingly asked me a question. "Now that the Soviet Union is becoming more humane," she said, "don't you think we should make inquiries?" That was over forty years after those terrible events. The war had cast long shadows, very long shadows indeed.

I replied in a tactful way to indicate that I did not believe such inquiry would become fruitful. She said, "yes," with a sigh of resignation, and afterwards there was silence in the room. It is my feeling that it was on that occasion that she, at long last, abandoned the last coveted shred of hope that had survived in her heart of Dieter's return.

As the years and decades passed, taking us away from that war, I still, at times, have sat down at the piano and have tried to play those tunes of the *Night Monster*, the *Little White House by the Great Blue Sea*, and *Taboo* the best way I could. But it has always been a wistful and nostalgic undertaking and, of course, it has never resurrected the laughter and cheer the way it once was when he played it so many years ago.

EPILOGUE

IF YOU WERE TO INVITE YOUR FRIENDS TO RENDER an appraisal of the story told here, you would likely find them united in expressing doubt and criticism regarding several of its commentaries. That kind of response, I fear, would be widespread anywhere in the English-speaking world and in Western Europe as well. Some readers might suspect in it residues of ancient political indoctrination. Or they might see in it a brazen attempt to vindicate the German people. Others, in a diagnostic way, might reason that the author tried to discharge old, unresolved childhood trauma by rewriting history in a manner more favorable to his native land. Surprisingly, you would have little difficulty discovering much the same reproof even in Germany.

If, however, you were to question older Germans, those who were eyewitnesses of World War II, you would be surprised to hear a starkly different opinion. Such a person is likely to look you straight in the face and declare that this account exactly corresponds to his own memories. He might even poke his finger at you and, with a sparkle in his eyes, express satisfaction that, at last, someone was politically incorrect enough to mention the unmentionable other side of the story. In fact, a variety of different sources seem to indicate that the same sturdy response could be elicited from the older generation all over Eastern Europe, from Finland to the Balkans and certainly in Russia and Ukraine. Their bitter and anguished memories of the German military occupation notwithstanding, they might express heartfelt agreement with what has been written here regarding the general consensus of the almost sacred righteousness of waging war against Stalin, their incomprehension of Churchill and Roosevelt's persistence in supporting Stalin, their utter despair at his victory, and their disbelief at the failure of the victorious Western Allies to take over the military campaign against Stalin's Red Army after the Wehrmacht had surrendered. Still today, many of the Eastern European people would agree with the dual-cancer concept in that world and with what in their view was a spurious cure when one cancer was eliminated and the other one was left behind. Such sentiments would be rare to encounter in the countries along the Atlantic Coast, but their prevalence is likely to rise the farther east one searched on the European Continent.

There existed in those war years an apprehensive anti-communist or anti-Stalinist brotherhood that encompassed large sections of the populations of almost all European countries. No doubt, it was obscured by Nazi policies, by the mounting guerrilla wars with their merciless German reprisals, and by what little was known about the Holocaust. But underneath all of that, that brotherhood was a persistent and powerful groundswell all across the continent.

Throughout the period of the Third Reich, two Germanys lived next to each other. The terrifying and malignant one, represented by the Party leadership, the Gestapo, and their genocidal annihilation camps, has been documented with due abundance ever since 1945. Its evil was of such an extreme magnitude that it escapes any attempt at defense, mitigation, or forgiveness. This is the aspect of Germany the world knows. Not many people, however, are aware of the other Germany, the one consisting of ordinary citizens and soldiers, because publications and films describing it are virtually non-existent. It is that unknown side of Germany and its people that this story portrays. It was meant to encompass the whole spectrum, ranging from their misconceptions and failures, and from their naïve gullibility and their blind faith in their leader and in the just cause of their struggle; to the idealism, bravery, and good will that were displayed by millions of their trusting people. These different facets were deliberately included for, in their entirety, they contributed to the tragic shipwreck of their country.

It is, to be sure, of no more than academic interest to wonder, at this late stage, about the merits and demerits of the ideas and illusions that dwelt in their minds in those war years. Nor should we worry much about whether today's reader accepts or rejects them, for such judgment would be of little significance either way. After all, the history books have long been written and nobody is going to revise them. But those among us who are deeply interested in the inner mechanisms of that terrible conflict would obtain only an incomplete view if they ignored the sentiments, perceptions, ideas, and reasonings the way they existed in the minds of the people at that time. No matter whether they were realistic or utopian, no matter what faults we may see in them today, they were a fundamental ingredient in the witches' cauldron of that era. They are a forgotten, but a vital part of history.

ENDNOTES

PART ONE

1 This summary is based on Richard Pipes, A Concise History of the Russian Revolution, (New York 1996).
2 Pipes, op.cit, p.260.
3 Pipes, op.cit. p.340.
4 Pipes, op.cit. p.341.
5 Pipes, op.cit. p.360.
6 Grand Duke Nicholas, quoted in Barbara T. Tuchman, The Guns of August, (New York 1962), p. 65.
7 Ibid. p. 312.
8 Ibid. p. 117.
9 Stephen McKenna, a British veteran and schoolteacher, quoted in ibid. p. 313.
10 John Toland, Adolf Hitler, (New York 1976), p. 79.
11 Paul Johnson, A History of the Jews, (New York 1988), p. 450.
12 George F. Kennan, The Decline of Bismarck's European Order. Franco-Russian Relations 1875-1890, (Princeton 1979), p. 3; quoted after Eberhard Jäckel, Das deutsche Jahrhundert, 4th ed., (Stuttgart 1998), p. 71.

PART TWO

1 Jäckel, op. cit., p.177.
2 Toland, op.cit., p. 405.

3 Ibid. p. 409.

4 Anton Gill, An Honourable Defeat, (New York 1994) p. 56-58.

5 Ibid. p. 46-50.

6 Lucy S. Davidowicz, The War Against the Jews 1933-1945, (New York 1975), p. 171.

7 William F. Buckley Jr., In Search of Anti-Semitism, (New York 1992), p. 125.

8 Dawidowicz, op. cit., p. 171.

9 Ibid., p. 195.

10 The following summary of the Great Purges is based on the account by Robert Conquest, The Great Terror, A Reassessment, (New York 1990).

11 Stephen G. Fritz, Frontsoldaten, (University Press of Kentucky 1995), p. 238.

12 Walter Laqueur, The Dream That Failed, (Oxford 1994), p. 20.

13 Conquest, op.cit., p. 472.

14 Laqueur, op.cit., p. 20.

15 Conquest, op.cit., p. 466.

16 Peter Hoffmann, German Resistance to Hitler, (Cambridge MA 1988), p. 27.

17 Toland, op.cit., p.346.

18 Laqueur, op.cit., p. 184.

19 Toland, op.cit., p. 452.

20 Ibid. p. 451.

21 Ibid. p. 452.

22 Ibid. p. 453.

23 William L. Shirer, Berlin Diary, (Boston 1940), p. 107.

24 This summary is based on Hermann Schreiber, Teuton and Slav, (Worcester 1965).

25 Lord Runciman, quoted in Alfred de Zayas, Nemesis at Potsdam, The Expulsion of the Germans from the East, 3rd ed. (Lincoln & London 1988), pp. 29-30.

26 Toland op.cit., p. 469.

27 Winston S. Churchill, The Second World War, The Gathering Storm, (Boston 1950), p.319.

28 Toland, op.cit., p. 231.

29 Dawidowicz, op cit., p. 92.

30 Ibid. p. 111.

31 Toland, op.cit., p. 517.

32 Schreiber, op.cit., p. 301.

33 Christian Jansen and Arno Weckbecker, Der "Volksdeutsche Selbstschutz in Polen 1939/40", (Munich 1992) p.20.

34 Schreiber, op.cit.

35 Much of the following summary is based on the account by C. Jansen, A. Weckbecker, op.cit., p. 12-28.

36 De Zayas, op.cit., p. 5.

37 Alfred-Maurice de Zayas, A Terrible Revenge, (New York 1986), pp.21-27.

38 Toland, op.cit., p. 531.

39 This description is based on the account given by Toland , op.cit., pp. 555-569.

PART THREE

1 Toland, op.cit. p. 799.
2 Franz Halder, Kriegstagebuch 1939-1942, ed. by Hans-Adolf Jakobson, (Stuttgart 1962-1964), 1:79, quoted in. Dawidowicz, op.cit., p. 115.
3 Toland, op.cit. p. 799.
4 Dawidowicz, op.cit., p. 200.
5 Ibid. pp. 114-5.
6 Gill, op.cit., p. 140.
7 Johnson, op.cit., p. 490.
8 Gill, op.cit., p. 140.
9 Churchill, op.cit., p. 639.
10 Robert Paxton, Vichy France (New York 1972).
11 Shirer, op. cit., p. 588; see also Dawidowicz, op. cit., p. 163; and Gill, op. cit., p. 132.
12 "Germany, Armed Forces and Special Forces," The Oxford Companion to World War II, 1995, p. 468.
13 Ponting, op.cit., p. 18.
14 Paxton, op. cit., p. 12.
15 Doris K. Goodwin, No Ordinary Time, (New York 1994), p.476.
16 Decades later, a collection of letters written during these years surfaced. They cast light on the various concerns of the day, and they are of interest because of their authenticity and immediacy to the narrative.
17 Ponting, op. cit., pp. 37-8.
18 Viktor Suvorov, Der Eisbrecher, trans. Russian into German Hans Jaeger, (Stuttgart 1989).
19 S.P. Ivanov, The initial phase of the war, (Russian) p. 211, quoted in Suvorov, op. cit., p. 249.
20 Suvorov, op. cit,. p. 249.
21 S.P. Ivanov, op. cit,. p. 212, quoted in Suvorov, op. cit., p. 383.
22 Suvorov, op. cit., p. 430.
23 Goodwin, op. cit., p. 102.
24 This was a peculiar, yet apparently common attitude among people living in an old-fashioned society. The same attitude existed in the Soviet Union during Stalin's Purges. There, too, people believed in the leader of their nation, Stalin, who in reality was the sole source of the purges, and blamed the atrocities on his underlings. R. Conquest writes on Page 53: (Ilya) Ehrenburg also tells of meeting Pasternak in the Lavrushensky Lane on a snowy night. Pasternak raised his hands to the dark sky and exclaimed, "If only someone would tell Stalin about it!" Meyerhold, too, remarked, "They conceal it from Stalin."

25 Hosokawa, op.cit. p. 275.
26 Ponting, op.cit., p.219.
27 Hosokawa, op.cit.p.275.
28 Ibid.p.276.
29 Ibid.p.277.
30 Ibid.p.347.

Part Four

1 Johnson, op. cit., p. 174.
2 Buckley, op.cit., p.147.
3 Johnson, op. cit., p. 394.
4 Julian Benda, La Jeunesse d'un clerc, (Paris 1936), quoted in Johnson, op. cit., p. 382.
5 Johnson, op. cit., p. 390.
6 Johnson, op. cit., p. 394.
7 Dawidowicz, op. cit., p. 34.
8 Ibid. p. 36.
9 Johnson, op. cit., p. 573-4.
10 Jäckel, op. cit., p. 22.
11 Hoffmann, op. cit., p. 10.
12 "Armenian Massacres," Encyclopaedia Britannica, Chicago 1997, I, p.568.
13 Ponting, op. cit., p. 231.
14 Ponting, op. cit., p. 232.
15 Ibid. p. 286.
16 Bacque, Other Losses, p. 15.
17 Ponting, op. cit., p. 174.
18 Ibid. p. 194.
19 Joseph E. Persico, Nuremberg, (New York 1994), p. 50.
20 Bacque, op. cit., p. 21.
21 De Zayas, Nemesis, p. XXV.
22 Ponting, op. cit., p. 240.
23 Ibid. p. 242.
24 The Oxford Companion to World War II, p.1076.
25 G. Thomas, M. Witts, Ruin From the Air - the Enola Gay's Atomic Mission to Hiroshima, (Chelsea 1977), p. 104
26 Ponting, op. cit., p. 243.
27 Thomas and Witts, op. cit., p. 294.
28 Winston S. Churchill, The Second World War, Triumph and Tragedy, (Boston 1959), p. 639.
29 Ponting, op. cit., p. 261.
30 Dawidowicz, op. cit., pp. 384-6.
31 Johnson, op. cit., p. 494.
32 Ibid. p. 494, also see Laqueur, op. cit., p. 132.
33 Dawidowicz, op. cit., p. 289.

34 Ibid. p. 200.
35 Johnson, op. cit., p. 499.
36 Yitzok Rudashevski, The Diary of the Vilna Ghetto: June 1941-April 1943, (Ghetto Fighters' House, Israel 1972, quoted in Dawidowicz, op. cit., p. 288.
37 Johnson, op. cit., p. 494.
38 Ibid. p. 494.
39 Dawidowicz, op. cit., p. 148.
40 Ibid. p. 314.
41 Toland, op. cit., p.676.
42 Johnson, op. cit., p.509.
43 Dawidowicz, op. cit., p. 218.
44 Vrba, I cannot forgive, p.134.
45 Vrba, op.cit., p.168.
46 Gill, op. cit., p. 171.
47 Toland, op. cit., p. 677; see also Johnson, op. cit., p. 495.
48 Gill, op. cit., pp. 231, 234, 238.
49 Gill, op. cit. p. 153.
50 Toland, op. cit., p. 713.
51 Persico, op. cit., pp. 317-20.
52 Toland, op. cit., p. 766.
53 Genesis 22:1-10.
54 Dawidowicz, op. cit., p. 294.
55 Ibid. p. 295.
56 Ibid. p. 350.
57 Gill, op. cit., p. 154.
58 Dawidowicz, op. cit., p. 350.
59 Johnson, op. cit., p. 504.
60 Goodwin, op. cit., p. 454-5.
61 Johnson, op. cit., p. 504.

Part Five

1 Ferdinand Hoff, Erlebnis und Besinnung, p. 368.

Part Six

1 Based on John Ellis. World War II, A Statistical Survey, p. 233-6.
2 Oxford Companion of World War II, p.1076.

Part Seven

2 De Zayas, Nemesis, p. 135.
3 Bacque, op. cit., p. 195.
4 Ibid. p. 31.
5 James Bacque, Verschwiegene Schuld, (Berlin 1995), p. 106.
6 Ibid. p. 53.
7 Ibid. p. 55, 63, 170.
8 Ibid. p. 54.
9 Ibid. p. 173.
10 De Zayas, Nemesis, p. 217.
11 Ibid. p. 217.
12 Bacque, Schuld, p. 54.
13 Ibid. p. 59.
14 Ibid. p. 103.
15 Ibid. pp.103, 104.
16 Ibid. pp. 126-9.
17 Gill, op. cit., p. 231.
18 De Zayas, Nemesis, pp. 65-6.
19 Ibid. pp. 62, 67.
20 Ibid. p. 62; see also De Zayas, Revenge, p. 44.
21 Ibid. pp. 64, 67, 68; see also De Zayas, Revenge, pp. 38, 39, 40, 42.
22 Ibid. p. 63; see also De Zayas, Revenge, pp. 36, 41.
23 De Zayas, Revenge, pp. 40, 41.
24 De Zayas, Nemesis, p. 63.
25 Ibid. p. 62, 63; see also De Zayas, Revenge, p. 42.
26 De Zayas, Revenge, p. 40.
27 Ibid. p. 42.
28 Ibid. p. 39, 40.
29 Ibid. p. 39.
30 Ibid. p. 41.
31 Ibid. p. 41.
32 Ibid. p. 40.
33 Ibid. p. 38.
34 Ibid. p. 38.
35 De Zayas, Nemesis, p. 66.
36 De Zayas, Revenge p. 48; translation from Russian by Robert Conquest.
37 Ibid. p.72.
38 De Zayas, Nemesis, p.103.
39 De Zayas, Revenge, p.95.
40 Ibid. pp. 95, 97, 102.
41 Ibid. p. 98.
42 Ibid. p. 99.
43 Ibid. pp. 99, 100.
44 Ibid. pp. 103, 106.

45 Ibid. pp. 98, 100, 103.
46 Ibid. p. 97.
47 Ibid. p. 101.
48 Ibid. p. 104.
49 Ibid. p. 107.
50 Ibid. pp. 89, 94.
51 Ibid. p. 100.
52 Ibid. p. 87.
53 Ibid. p. 86.
54 De Zayas, Nemesis, p. 125.
55 Ibid. p. 114.
56 Ibid. p. 110.
57 Ibid. p. 114.
58 Ibid. p. 102.
59 De Zayas, Revenge, p. 152.
60 De Zayas, Nemesis, p. 108.
61 Ibid. p. 109.
62 Ibid. p. 103.
63 Ibid. p. 71.
64 Dresden, Raid on, The Oxford Companion to World War II, (Oxford 1995), p. 311.
65 Axel Rodenberger, Der Tod von Dresden, (Frankfurt a.Main, 1960), p. 51ff. Quoted in De Zayas: Terrible Revenge, p. 75.
66 Oxford Companion, p. 311.
67 Oxford Companion, p. 1072.
68 Dresden, Raid on, Oxford Companion, p. 312.
69 Persico, op. cit., p. 321.
70 Churchill, The Grand Alliance, p. 371.
71 The Afrikaner word "trek" was used to describe the columns of East German refugees.
72 Churchill, The Grand Alliance, p. 239.
73 Shirer, op. cit., p. 215.
74 Ibid. p. 427.
75 Ibid. p. 516.
76 Bacque, Other Losses, p. 153.
77 Ibid. p. 30.
78 Ibid. p. 140.
79 Ibid. p. 88.
80 Ibid. p. 32.
81 Ibid. p. 45.
82 Col. James B. Mason, MC-USA (Ret.) and Col. Charles H. Beasley, MC-USA (Ret.), The Medical Surgeon 107:437, 1950; quoted in Bacque, Other Losses, p.35.
83 H. Janssen, Kriegsgefangenen in Rheinberg, 1988; quoted in Bacque, Other Losses, p. 36.
84 Bacque. Other Losses, p. 88.

85 Ibid. p. 88.
86 Ibid. p. 88.
87 Ibid. p. 91.
88 Ibid. p. 136.
88 Bischoff, Ambrose: Eisenhower and the German POWs.
89 Ibid. p. 46.

Part Eight

1 Bacque, Schuld, p. 74.

GLOSSARY

Anschluss	German: joining or connection. A term used for the political union between Austria and Germany in 1939.
Bismarck, Otto von	The Prussian Minister President after 1862; founder of German unification creating Imperial Germany in 1871; German chancellor until 1890.
Blitzkrieg	German: lightning war, a name applied to the rapid German military campaigns early in WW II.
Bolsheviks	The Socialist Party, later named Communist, which seized power in Russia in Lenin's 1917 coup d'état.
Chamberlain, Neville	The British prime minister from 1937 until 1940.
Chancellor	The term used in Austria, Germany and Switzerland for prime minister.
Concordat	A compact between a national government and a religious group. In this case it refers to a covenant between Hitler's government

and the Vatican.

Danzig	A German seaport at the Baltic Coast. Separated from Germany in the Treaty of Versailles, it played a major role in the dispute triggering World War II. It is now a Polish city with the name of Gdansk.
East Prussia	A German province at the south-east Baltic Coast, which was, after expulsion of its population at the end of WW II, divided between Poland and Russia.
Fifth Column	A group of secret supporters of the enemy engaging in sabotage and subversive activities. The term originated in the Spanish Civil War when four military columns advanced on Madrid and sympathizers within the city were called the Fifth Column.
Final Solution	A term coined by the Hitler regime for "solving the Jewish question," namely genocide of the Jewish race in the Holocaust.
Frederick the Great	The king of Prussia from 1740 till 1786.
Gestapo	A German acronym meaning secret state police.
Göring, Hermann	The closest associate of Hitler. He occupied numerous leading political positions even before Hitler assumed power. Among other appointments he was commander-in-chief of the *Luftwaffe*.
Gulag	A Russian acronym referring to the vast system of Soviet concentration camps.
Heil Hitler	Hail to Hitler—an official greeting imposed by the Nazi regime.
Himmler, Heinrich	The leading National Socialist politician. Among other positions he headed the

	entire SS organization including the Gestapo, the mass execution units (*Einsatzgruppen*), the concentration and annihilation camps, and *Waffen-SS*.
Hitler Youth	The National Socialist Youth Movement. Membership after age ten was obligatory.
Il Duce	Italian: the leader. Official designation of the Italian dictator Mussolini
Irredentism	An effort to incorporate territories in one's nation, which are believed to have been wrongfully made part of another country.
Kaiser	German: Emperor. Kaiser Wilhelm II abdicated in 1918. He was the last of three German emperors.
Lebensraum	German: living space. In the Third Reich the term referred to the amount of territory considered necessary for economic self-sufficiency of the German people. The alleged lack of such space was Hitler's justification for conquering Eastern European countries.
Luftwaffe	The name of the German air force during W.W. II.
Nazi	Byname, often derogatory, of the National Socialist Political Party and its members.
NKVD	The initials for "People's Commissariat for Internal Affairs" in the period of the Great Purges in the Soviet Union during the 1930s. It was the instrument administering Stalin's terror.
Ottoman Empire	The Turkish Empire that lasted from the 13th century till 1920.
Panzer	German: tank.
Panzerfaust	German: tank fist. An armor-breaking, handheld rocket launcher, similar to a

	bazooka. The plural is *Panzerfäuste*.
Paris Commune	An armed Marxist uprising led by the Paris Municipal Council against the new Republican Government in 1871.
Polish Corridor	A broad strip of land created in the Treaty of Versailles to give Poland access to the Baltic Sea through previously German land. It separated East Prussia from the German mainland and was part of the dispute leading to the German campaign against Poland in 1939.
Reich	German: empire, country, state, or commonwealth
Röhm, Ernst	The chief of Hitler's Storm Troops (SA), a paramilitary organization. He attempted to promote the socialist reorientation of Hitler's political movement through a "second revolution". Accusing him of advancing a putsch, Hitler had him and many others arrested and killed in 1934.
Ruhr area	Germany's major area of heavy industry.
Saar Territory	Industrial region bordering on France, which in the Treaty of Versailles was placed under a League of Nations government with attachment of its economy to that of France. After a plebiscite in 1934 it returned to Germany.
Schmeling, Max	A German boxer, who in 1938 surrendered his world championship to Joe Louis.
SS	The initials for *Sturm Staffel*, Storm Detail, a paramilitary Nazi organization. As it evolved, it developed notorious subdivisions such as the Gestapo, the concentration camp units, and mass execution teams.
Third Reich	The name assumed by the National

	Socialists for their regime in 1933. The First Reich was founded by Charlemagne in 800 A.D., the Second Reich by Bismarck in 1871.
Treaty of St. Germain	The peace treaty concluded in 1919 between the Allies and Austria
Treaty of Versailles	The peace treaty concluded in 1919 between the Allies and Germany
Vichy government	The French government, under Marshal Pétain, during the time of the German occupation from 1940 until 1944. Vichy is a town and spa in the region that was initially not occupied by German forces
Waffen-SS	A military subdivision of the SS organization. It was subject to ideological indoctrination and consisted of elite military units. In contrast to the other SS organizations, these were as a rule not involved in criminal activities.
Wehrmacht	Name for the German armed forces in W.W. II.
Zionism	The movement to establish a Jewish national and religious state in Palestine.

BIBLIOGRAPHY

1. Bacque, James. *Other Losses*. Prima Publishing, 1991.

2. Bacque, James. *Verschwiegene Schuld*. Berlin: Ullstein, 1995.

3. Bischof, G., Ambrose, S.E. *Eisenhower and the German POWs. Facts Against Falsehood*. Louisiana State University Press, 1992.

4. Buckley Jr., William F. *In Search of Anti-Semitism*. New York: Continuum, 1992.

5. Churchill, Winston S. *The Second World War, vols.: The Gathering Storm; The Grand Alliance; Triumph and Tragedy*. Boston: Houghton Mifflin Co., 1950.

6. Conquest, Robert. *The Great Terror. A Reassessment*. New York: Oxford University Press, 1990.

7. Dawidowicz, Lucy S. *The War against the Jews 1933-1945*. New York: Bantam, 1975.

8. DeZayas, Alfred. *Nemesis at Potsdam*. Lincoln, Nebraska: The University of Nebraska Press, 1988.

9. DeZayas, Alfred-Maurice. *A Terrible Revenge*. New York: St. Martin's Press, 1986.

10. Ellis, John. *World War II. A Statistical Survey.* New York: Facts on File, Inc., 1993.

11. *Encyclopaedia Britannica. Vol. I.* Chicago, 1997.

12. Fritz, Stephen *G. Frontsoldaten.* University Press of Kentucky. 1995.

13. Gill, Anton. *An Honourable Defeat.* New York: Henry Holt and Company, 1994.

14. Goodwin, Doris K. *No Ordinary Time.* New York: Touchtone, 1994.

15. Hoff, Ferdinand. *Erlebnis und Besinnung.* Frankfurt/M: Ullstein, 197.

16. Hoffmann, Peter. *German Resistance to Hitler.* Cambridge: Harvard University Press, 1988.

17. Hosokawa, Bill. *Nisei, the Quiet Americans.* New York: Wm. Morrow, 1969.

18. Jansen, C., Weckbecker, A. *Der Deutsche Selbstschutz in Polen 1939/40.* Munich: Oldenbourg, 1992.

19. Jäckel, Eberhard. *Das deutsche Jahrhundert.* Deutsche Verlags-Anstalt. Stuttgart, 1998.

20. Johnson, Paul. *A History of the Jews.* New. York: Harper, 1988.

21. Laqueur, Walter. *The Dream that Failed.* Oxford: Oxford University Press, 1994.

22. Paxton, Robert. *Vichy France* New York: Columbia University Press, 1972.

23. Persico, Joseph E. *Nuremberg.* New York: Penguin Putnam, 1994.

24. Pipes, Richard. *A Concise History of the Russian Revolution.* New York: Vintage Books, 1996.

25. Ponting, Clive. *Armageddon.* New York: Random House, 1995.

26. The Oxford *Companion to World War II.* Oxford University Press,

1995.

27. Shirer, William L. *Berlin Diary*. Boston: Little, Brown, 1940.

28. Schreiber, Hermann. *Teuton and Slav. Trans*. James Cleugh, Alfred A. Knopf, 1965.

29. Suvorov, Viktor. *Der Eisbrecher. Klett-Cotta*. Stuttgart, 1989.

30. Thomas, G., Witt, M. *Ruin from the Air - the Enola Gay's Atomic Mission to Hiroshima*. Chelsea: Scarborough House, 1977.

31. Toland, John. *Adolf Hitler*. New York: Doubleday, 1976.

32. Tuchman, Barbara T. *The Guns of August*. New York: MacMillan, 1962.

33. Vrba, R., Bestic, A. *I Cannot Forgive*. New York: Bantam Books, 1964.